DREAMS
OF CHAOS,
VISIONS
OF ORDER

8

CONTEMPORARY FILM AND TELEVISION SERIES

A complete listing of the books in this series can be found at the back of this volume.

GENERAL EDITOR

Patricia B. Erens
Rosary College

ADVISORY EDITORS

Lucy Fischer
University of Pittsburg

Peter Lehman
University of Arizona

Miriam White
Northwestern University

Caren J. Deming
University of Arizona

DREAMS
OF CHAOS,
VISIONS
OF ORDER:

Understanding the
American
Avant-Garde Cinema

JAMES PETERSON

Wayne State University Press   Detroit

Copyright   COPYRIGHT © 1994 BY WAYNE STATE UNIVERSITY PRESS, DETROIT,
MICHIGAN 48201. ALL RIGHTS ARE RESERVED. NO PART OF THIS
BOOK MAY BE REPRODUCED WITHOUT FORMAL PERMISSION.
MANUFACTURED IN THE UNITED STATES OF AMERICA.

99 98 97 96   5 4 3 2

**Library of Congress
Cataloging-in-
Publication Data**   PETERSON, JAMES, 1957–

  DREAMS OF CHAOS, VISIONS OF ORDER : UNDERSTANDING THE
AMERICAN AVANTE-GARDE CINEMA / JAMES PETERSON.

    P.   CM. — (CONTEMPORARY FILM AND TELEVISION SERIES)
INCLUDES BIBLIOGRAPHICAL REFERENCES AND INDEX.
  ISBN 0-8143-2456-8 (ALK. PAPER). — ISBN 0-8143-2457-6 (PBK. :
ALK. PAPER)

    1. EXPERIMENTAL FILMS—UNITED STATES—HISTORY AND
CRITICISM.   2. MOTION PICTURES—UNITED STATES—AESTHETICS.
I. TITLE. II. SERIES.
PN1995.9.E96P48   1994
791.43'75'0973—DC20   93-25672

Designer   MARY KRZEWINSKI

FOR MY GRANDFATHER,

JAMES H. PETERSON,

WHO TAUGHT ME

ABOUT CRAFTSMANSHIP.

CONTENTS

PREFACE

This book has two distinct but related aims.

First, a word of caution. This is not a comprehensive historical treatment of the American avant-garde cinema. I address what I believe are the major *types* of avant-garde filmmaking, but there are many important films and filmmakers that do not get much attention here. As I suggest in chapter 1, readers looking for such a survey should read P. Adams Sitney's *Visionary Film*, a book that I admire more every time I consult it. The term "vision" in my title acknowledges my debt to him. But students of the avant-garde should be forewarned that no book offers a truly comprehensive account of this fugitive and elusive cinema. To a large extent, our lists of its greatest works are projections of our own preoccupations.

My first aim is somewhat specialized: I try to explain how viewers make sense of the films of the post-World War II American avant-garde cinema. Since these films are often pretty darn confusing, this is a daunting task, and some readers are bound to be skeptical of my success. Nevertheless, a theory of spectatorship ought to be one of the central concerns of scholarship of the avant-garde film, so I have tried to offer one, however preliminary it might turn out to be.

My second aim is more general, though it grows out of my more specialized project. If I am at all successful in theorizing avant-garde film viewing, this book may serve as an introduction to the avant-garde for new viewers. In other words, this book is also meant as a how-to manual that shows viewers how to understand the often puzzling films of the American avant-garde cinema.

Occasionally, my two aims might conflict, and parts of my book might be a bit too specialized for general readers, or too general for specialists. I believe that such conflicts are few, but I beg the indulgence of both types of readers, and I hope they will come to share my conviction that both aims are worth pursuing.

ACKNOWLEDGMENTS

Many people and institutions have contributed to this book. For their friendship and assistance, I am most grateful.

The Jesse H. Jones Faculty Research Fund and the Institute for Scholarship in the Liberal Arts, College of Arts and Letters, University of Notre Dame, supported my research with summer stipends and research materials grants. The Wackman family, through the University of Wisconsin Department of Communication Arts, funded much of my earliest research on the avant-garde cinema. I remain particularly grateful to the University of Wisconsin Graduate School and to the late Mrs. Minne Riess Detling for the fellowship that supported me during the writing of my dissertation.

Many scholars and filmmakers shared their ideas, their work and their time with me: Paul Arthur, John Belton, Ed Branigan, Betzy Bromberg, Bruce Conner, Don Kirihara, Lewis Klahr, Jonas Mekas, Robert Nelson, William Rothman, Christophe Settele, Chick Strand, Greg Taylor and Kristin Thompson. Noël Carroll, Scott Nygren, Maureen Turim and William Wees were especially generous with their support and encouragement. My long-time friends Matthew Bernstein, Dave Estlund and Richard Neupert have helped me over countless intellectual and institutional hurdles through the years.

I have also benefited mightily from my friends, students and colleagues at the University of Notre Dame. In particular, I thank Bob Burke for his advice on many grant proposals; John Charron for his explanations of serial music; Ron Hogan for his skill and patience in the library; Randy Klawiter for translating to and from German; Bobbi McMahon for ordering and shipping so many films; Paul Weithman and Bill Ramsey for their invaluable guidance through the philosophical literature; Craig Adcock for his indispensable help with art historical questions and for his passion for twentieth-century art; Mark Pilkinton, chair of my department, for his unflagging and generous support; and the students in my courses in the avant-garde cinema, especially those who called their mothers after seeing *Window Water Baby Moving*. Most of all, I have to thank John Welle, model scholar, honest critic and true friend.

Wayne State University Press's support of this project has been most appreciated; thanks to Patricia Erens, Contemporary Film and Television Series editor; Arthur Evans, director; Mary Gillis, copy editor; and Lynn Trease, editor. I incurred many debts acquiring the illustrations for this book; my thanks to Leonardo Bezzola; Eugen Gomringer; Heloise Goodman, Andy Warhol Foundation for the Visual Arts; Sharyn Jensen, Visual Artists and Galleries Association; Jeff Levine, John Weber Gallery; Amy Pall, Leo Castelli Photo Archives; and Liz Weisberg, Artists Rights Society. Chris Lowe is to be commended for his careful printing of the frame enlargements.

Portions of chapter 6 appeared in "The Artful Mathematicians of the Avant-Garde," *Wide Angle* 7.3 (1985): 14–23. Portions of chapter 8 appeared in "Bruce Conner and the Compilation Narrative," *Wide Angle* 8.3/4 (1986): 53–62. I thank Johns Hopkins University Press, the publisher of *Wide Angle*, for permission to reprint this material.

I owe a special debt of gratitude to the fine teachers I had at the University of Wisconsin-Madison. It was my privilege to have Barbara Buenger, Keith Cohen and Vance Keply on my dissertation committee; their suggestions have vastly improved this work. David Bordwell and J. J. Murphy, my dissertation co-advisers and my friends, have maintained an inexhaustible fund of good advice and good humor.

Of course, I owe my most profound gratitude to my family. My parents, James D. and Patricia Peterson, have supported me in every conceivable way. My daughters, Lauren and Anna, are already discerning film viewers; they generously share their expertise and defend their views with enviable vigor. My wife, Susan Collins, is my most helpful collaborator and my most patient teacher. My deepest gratitude and love is for her.

Acquired Taste?
The Problem of the Viewer

There is a clear similarity between the young writers and film poets of today, be it Brakhage, Maas, Hugo, or Anger. Not only in their zombie-like characters but also in the superexcess of unintelligible details that they include in their works—details that are, most probably, full of significance to the makers but, unfortunately, convey no definite meaning to the viewer. It is clear that if all these analytical details lack meaning and impact, it is because they are not animated by a well-defined purpose or motivation.

—Jonas Mekas, writing in 1955

Most of us, novice and expert alike, take it for granted that the films of the American avant-garde cinema are challenging in at least two senses. Anyone who reads even a little about the avant-garde film will likely encounter the idea that it represents not just an alternative to commercial narrative films, but a *critique* of the Hollywood filmmaking tradition. But there is another, more fundamental sense in which the American avant-garde cinema is challenging. At least for a good many people, these films are difficult to understand. Thus, not only does the American avant-garde cinema challenge Hollywood, it challenges its own viewers. Even Jonas Mekas, who would later become a tireless advocate of the avant-garde cinema and an important filmmaker himself, was puzzled and irritated by his first encounters with the avant-garde film.

Anyone who teaches the avant-garde cinema, or even anyone who wants to start watching these films, must somehow come to terms with the fact that novice viewers struggle to make sense of these films. One way of addressing this problem is simply to valorize the films for their difficulty. The Hollywood film lulls its viewers into a stultifying passivity; the avant-garde demands the viewer's active participation, and ultimately offers a healthier experience.[1] We can think of this notion as a sort of Puritan ethic of film viewing: the spectator's labor, whether it leads to understanding or befuddlement, is valuable in itself. This argument is not completely without merit. I believe there *is* something especially valuable about the kind of activity the avant-garde cinema calls forth. Nevertheless, the idea that the avant-garde cinema is valuable because it takes more work to understand it does not explain *why* some viewers have a hard time of it. The fact remains that after struggling with an avant-garde film, some viewers manage to make sense of it, whereas others find it utterly impenetrable.

The inability of some viewers to comprehend avant-garde film sometimes erupts in hostility on all sides. Viewers stalk out of screenings and complain about having their time wasted, filmmakers are insulted, and critics and teachers condemn the narrow-mindedness of such viewers. Scott MacDonald tells one such story about Hollis Frampton. In 1973, after a screening of three Frampton films, during which the audience was decidedly restless, a woman asked the filmmaker if he thought his films communicated to an audience. Frampton responded:

> If you mean, do I think I communicated to those in the audience who tramped indignantly out of my films, the answer is no, but I think there is a problem with your idea of communication. You seem to work on the assumption that you have this hole and I have this thing, and you want me to put my thing in your hole and that will be ''communication.'' My idea of communication is very different. It involves my trying to say something I think is important and into which I have put all my thought and substantial labor. Necessarily, what I have to say will be difficult to apprehend, if it is original enough to be worth saying at all. That is my half of the communicative process. Yours must be to sensitize and educate yourself fully enough to be able to understand. It is only when two people—filmmaker and viewer in this case—can meet as equals that true communication can take place. (1978, 8)

Most filmmakers or critics would not use Frampton's hostile, sexual terms, but Frampton offers an important insight: the viewers who walked out on his films lacked something partisans of the avant-garde seem to have. But he does not explain how or where one might get the kind of sensitivity and education his films demand.

In another useful essay, one of the few that explicitly take up this question, MacDonald (1989) argues that *all* films pose great challenges until viewers become accustomed to their mode of operation. He concludes that avant-garde cinema, like any other kind of cinema, is an acquired taste. And, unfortunately, most people never get the chance to acquire a taste for the avant-garde. MacDonald's essay is insightful, but I would refine his guiding metaphor. The notion of ''acquired taste,'' it seems to me, suggests that the process is relatively passive. It is not merely constant exposure to avant-garde films that leads one to enjoy them. Through exposure to the films, as well as reading and talking about them, viewers learn to draw connections among the images and sounds they see and hear. They learn to relate one film to another, and they come to understand how each film fits into the history of the avant-garde cinema and the history of the arts in general. In other words, it is not so much a matter of acquiring taste as acquiring *skills*. This book is about the skills needed by viewers of the American avant-garde cinema.

The viewer's activity has not often been the explicit concern of scholars of the American avant-garde cinema. There are a few exceptions. Noël Carroll (1979, 1981) has examined the ways viewers comprehend shot-to-shot relationships in heavily edited avant-garde films. P. Adams Sitney (1979, 392–397) has identified a sub-genre of the American avant-garde cinema, what he calls "participatory film," that openly addresses viewers and asks them to do things, such as guess what might come later in the film. On the whole though, to the extent that we can find explanations of the viewer's activity, we must do so by reading between the lines of discussions of films and filmmaking. In the last decade or so, growing interest in reception theories has brought readers and viewers more and more to center stage in literary and film studies. It is no accident that reception studies have not had much of an impact on the scholarship of the avant-garde. Some of our most fundamental ideas about the nature of the avant-garde make understanding the role of the viewer a rather intractable problem.

Almost inevitably, introductions to the American avant-garde begin by defining it in negative terms, as the realm of film practice in which filmmakers are not encumbered by the conventions and restraints that inhibit the makers of other kinds of films. As Sheldon Renan put it in an early survey of what was then called "underground" film:

> Definitions are risky, for the underground film is nothing less than an *explosion* of cinematic styles, forms, and directions. If it can be called a genre, it is a genre that can be defined only by a cataloging of the individual works assigned to it. The film medium is rich with possibilities, and the underground film-maker has widely explored these possibilities, with the result that there are almost as many different kinds of underground films as there are underground filmmakers. (17)

Renan's survey is characteristic of an earlier mode of writing about the American avant-garde film that emphasized what were taken to be the limitless possibilities of working outside the commercial film industry. We find a similar celebratory tone in other early surveys, such as David Curtis's *Experimental Cinema* (1971) and especially Gene Youngblood's *Expanded Cinema* (1970). As the avant-garde film became the subject of academic study, the rhetoric of liberation was given a more explicitly political motivation: the avant-garde rejected the conventions of the commercial film, and thereby criticized an important manifestation of the dominant ideology.[2] To put it generally, what once was celebrated as independent, underground, or expanded cinema is now valorized as a critical cinema.[3] But a common thread runs through all these formulations: the avant-garde cinema has generally been defined in terms of what it does not do.

In large measure, these ideas about the avant-garde film derive from Stan Brakhage's critical and theoretical essays. Brakhage writes more about filmmaking than film viewing, but his theories of filmmaking have clear implications for the viewer. Like a number of the filmmakers associated with or covered by *Film Culture* in the early 1960s, Brakhage envisioned the avant-garde as a rejection of the commercial narrative film. But the avant-garde ideal he articulated went well beyond a rejection of Hollywood aesthetics. In a widely cited passage from his essay ''Metaphors on Vision,'' he wrote:

> Imagine an eye unruled by man-made laws of perspective, an eye unprejudiced by compositional logic, an eye which does not respond to the name of everything but which must know each object encountered in life through an adventure in perception. How many colors are there in a field of grass to the crawling baby unaware of ''Green''? (n.p.)

Brakhage's project of the ''unruled eye'' is so radical because it rejects not only the norms of commercial filmmaking but all norms of aesthetics and perception. According to Brakhage, everything we have been taught about art and the world itself separates us from a profound, true vision of the world. We are straitjacketed by myriad conventions that prevent us from really seeing our world. So it is with the filmmaker: the so-called rules of good filmmaking that are so carefully followed by commercial filmmakers prevent them from expressing all but the most trite reformulations of the same boy-meets-girl story. The film artist's only recourse is to throw off all these conventions as forcefully and as quickly as possible.

Brakhage embraces what we can call a *total liberation* theory of the avant-garde. His formulation of this theory and the films it inspired may be particularly radical examples of the American avant-garde cinema's aesthetic of liberation. Yet in *Visionary Film*, P. Adams Sitney's history of the American avant-garde cinema, Sitney argues that however radical Brakhage's film work might be, it is in part derived from a long tradition of Romanticism. In Sitney's view, the legacy of Romanticism informs most of the American avant-garde cinema. Even if Sitney's claims for the centrality of visionary Romanticism in the American avant-garde cinema are exaggerated, as some have suggested,[4] it is clear that Brakhage's view of filmic creation is an extension of a strain of Romantic thought about artistic creation. By giving free reign to imagination and inspiration, the Romantic artist rejects a tradition that has become meaningless, and manages to transcend the gray, mundane world of ordinary reason. This notion appears regularly in Romantic literature, but, with only a slight exaggeration, it also has become fundamental to our thinking about modern art. The artist as inspired genius who forcefully rejects an oppressive tradition and transcends petty rules and conventions is one of the most fundamental myths of the avant-garde.

Though this myth concerns artistic creation, it has clear implications for the viewer of the avant-garde film. According to Brakhage's liberation theory, the avant-garde film viewer needs only to be completely open-minded and open-eyed. The proper attitude is a relaxed, receptive one, and the viewer simply looks at the film without trying to impose some narrow interpretation on it—what is in the film is whatever each viewer finds in it. As poet Michael McClure said of Brakhage's *Anticipation of the Night* (1958), the film ''*takes place inside of a man's vision*, and the spectator merely has to watch'' (55; emphasis in original). For Brakhage, film aspired to the condition of unmediated, pre-cognitive experience, and his theoretical writing searched constantly for appropriate analogies for this kind of experience, his ''metaphors on vision'': the pre-linguistic vision of childhood; phosphenes, those sensations of light triggered by pressing on the eyelid; the hypnagogic imagery one experiences in the twilight between wakefulness and sleep. The viewer's job is to share the filmmaker's experience as it is rendered, or even captured, on film. Because each film is unique and unbounded by convention, no prior knowledge or experience is necessary. In fact, such knowledge and experience might even inhibit the direct and immediate experience of the film.

The liberation theory's suggestion that all the viewer needs to understand an avant-garde film is an open mind is not an adequate theory of the viewer's activity. In the first place, it just does not square with available evidence of what viewers actually do with avant-garde films. Judging from the casual reports of students and colleagues, not to mention published criticism of the avant-garde film, viewers seem eminently interested in identifying images, categorizing them, and integrating what they see in films with what they know about the history of cinema, about the history of art, and about the world in general. I do not mean to suggest that Brakhage says we should isolate the avant-garde film from any context whatsoever. Over the years, Brakhage has connected his work to a number of art traditions, including Abstract Expressionism, and the cinema tradition of ''Méliès, Griffith, Dreyer, Eisenstein, and all the other classically accepted film makers'' (1982, 179). But there is a prominent strain in Brakhage's thought, as well as in much work on the avant-garde cinema, that suggests that the viewer's prior knowledge and experience must be overcome when viewing an avant-garde film. Yet however appealing such a Romantic notion might be, an overwhelming tide of evidence suggests that perception cannot be so severed from cognition. Perception itself is always active and constructive and depends heavily on what we already know. And in practice, film viewers, even of the avant-garde cinema, generally do not view films without trying to figure out how they are structured and what they mean.

William C. Wees's *Light Moving in Time: Studies in the Visual Aesthetics of Avant-garde Film* (1992) is an updated rearticulation and defense of Brakhage's theory of total liberation. Wees draws on contemporary research on visual perception and tries to show that the kind of naive, untutored vision Brakhage sought to represent on film can indeed be achieved, *if* we are sensitive to the full range of our visual experiences. Wees shows how much of Brakhage's work can be understood as an attempt to find cinematic equivalents for the visual phenomena that go unnoticed during ''normal'' sight. Or, to put it somewhat more vividly, Wees shows how Brakhage takes up the Romantic struggle to liberate the eye from the tyranny of the mind.

The perceptual liberation advocated by Brakhage and Wees is an evocative metaphor for both artistic production and aesthetic experience, but even Wees's more cautious version of the liberation theory is not primarily a theory of viewers' activity. As Wees points out, Brakhage cannot actually "capture" the ephemeral visual phenomena that fascinated him on film; he has to find some sort of equivalent for them, such as painting or scratching the emulsion. The viewer, then, sees not innocent vision itself, but a *representation* of innocent vision, which has to be compared to his or her own visual experiences. Ultimately such films should sensitize viewers to a richer, more varied visual life, but film viewing itself still requires an eye in the service of the mind.

A second problem with the total liberation approach is that it encourages us to think of the American avant-garde cinema as part of a single, trans-historical avant-garde predicated exclusively on the rejection of an oppressive tradition. Indeed, our most fundamental ideas about the avant-garde derive from legends of artworks whose premieres were exemplary moments of rejection, such as Stravinsky's *Rite of Spring*, Duchamp's *Nude Descending a Staircase*, and Dali and Buñuel's *Un Chien Andalou*. Each of these works, as the story goes, was so radically original that it not only was difficult to comprehend but sent its audience into a riotous frenzy over the threat to the social order. But defining the avant-garde in this way practically precludes examining the experience of the viewer, because viewers can respond to the avant-garde in only one way: if art is a perpetual revolution in which traditional forms and values are continually rejected, the viewer is continually confounded and offended.

It is as a consequence of this rhetoric of liberation that scholars and filmmakers of the avant-garde have been largely disinterested in the question of the viewer. In spite of the manifest difficulty of most American avant-garde films, one can read volumes and find almost no mention of how to view these films. This study addresses precisely this question: how—and to what extent—can viewers make sense of American avant-garde films?

The American avant-garde cinema, as Dana Polan (1985, 51–53) has suggested, is not simply another manifestation of a trans-historical avant-garde defined solely by its difference from the products of mass culture. I argue that it is a distinct mode of film practice operating in specific institutions, with a set of formal conventions and implicit viewing procedures. This study lays out a theory of these viewing procedures. It shows how these viewing procedures evolved as the institutions and formal conventions of the avant-garde changed, and it examines the three main strains of filmmaking within the avant-garde: what I call the poetic strain, the minimal strain and the assemblage strain. The crux of my argument is that each of these strains challenges, without completely confounding, the skills viewers learn from experience with a wide range of other kinds of discourse, such as literature, painting and commercial films. These strains each trigger specific perceptual and cognitive responses on the part of the viewer, and by coming to terms with these responses, we can more completely account for the viewer's experience of the American avant-garde cinema.

My approach to the American avant-garde cinema is synthetic. I confess that, like most film theorists, I have borrowed widely and freely from other disciplines. I draw from a range of literary and art theories: from the linguistic and literary theory of Roman Jakobson, from the narrative theory of Gérard Genette and Tzvetan Todorov, and from E. H. Gombrich's theories of the visual arts. On the whole, though, my inquiry is most directly guided by cognitive theories of perception, language and reasoning. Of course, my study is not itself a theory of cognition—I leave that to philosophers, psychologists, linguists and anthropologists. But any theory of the viewer, indeed, any aesthetic or literary theory, at least implicitly appeals to a theory of mind. I have tried to set out my assumptions explicitly, and to base my theory of the viewer on what is becoming the most widely accepted account of human mental life.

Though cognitivism is supported by a broad range of research in experimental psychology, philosophy, linguistics, anthropology and artificial intelligence, there is no single, unified cognitive theory. The cognitive literature comprises a remarkably diverse set of research programs and theoretical positions; even cognitivism's most basic tenets are occasionally challenged (for a historical overview of cognitive theory, see Gardner [1985]; for challenges to some of its basic premises, see Stich [1983], Putnam [1988], and Searle [1992]). In general, though, cognitivism can be seen as a reaction against behaviorist theories of mind which held that human behavior could be explained in terms of stimuli and responses, without recourse to "mentalistic" concepts such as beliefs, plans and desires. These concepts are indispensable to cognitivists, who suggest that a wide range of mental activities are best explained as problem-solving activities, from complex, self-conscious tasks such as reading literature, to such seemingly automatic processes as perceiving color.

One might legitimately ask why I have turned to cognitive work in psychology, linguistics, and other disciplines when contemporary film theory already has its theories of film viewing—most of which are based on psychoanalytic semiotics. Of course, in the past few years the validity of these theories has been the subject of a productive but often acrimonious debate.[5] My reason for turning to a cognitive theory of mind is not that I think contemporary film theory is wrong, but that psychoanalytic semiotic theories are not especially well suited to answering the questions I have posed about avant-garde film. First, because of the primacy of the *un*conscious in psychoanalytic theories, these theories model film viewing on irrational behavior, such as dreams and slips of the tongue. This makes psychoanalytic theories best suited to explaining irrational, emotive aspects of film viewing. I do not deny that such irrational, unconscious forces might come into play in avant-garde film viewing, but my main concern is with a conscious process: the viewer's basic comprehension. Such conscious processes are explicitly the concern of cognitive theories, whereas they get little attention in psychoanalytic theories. Second, productive semiotic analyses (say, Christian Metz's Grande Syntagmatique and Roland Barthes's work on narrative) tend to address highly conventional, rule-affirming art, such as the Hollywood film or realist fiction. Because semiotics is concerned with the operation of conventional codes, it is most successful when it deals with, as semioticians like to say, the "always already" said. But the avant-garde puts a high premium on novelty, and viewers cannot always count on interpreting a novel element of a film by using a code they already know. I am not saying that semiotic concepts are wrong; in fact, I appeal to them quite regularly in this study. But there are aspects of avant-garde film viewing that are not easily explained in terms of codes, and that warrant an appeal to cognitive theories of problem solving.

There are also historical reasons why appeals to cognitive theories are now profitable (indeed even possible), though they might not have been when film studies made its first influential borrowing from linguistics and psychoanalysis. Before the last decade or so, studies of language comprehension generally addressed the sentence and smaller units. Now that linguists and psychologists have begun to study more systematically the comprehension of larger blocks of discourse, there is a substantial body of literature devoted to explaining how readers and viewers comprehend stories and other types of discourse. This research, it seems to me, bears more directly on the concerns of the film theorist than does the study of sentence grammar. Also, until recently studies of language comprehension focused on the syntactic and semantic aspects of sentences without much regard to the social context in which sentences are used. Recent pragmatic theories of language emphasize the effects of the context of social interaction on language. Avant-garde films are seen in a social context, and the institution of the avant-garde sees these films as a form of social action, which pragmatic theories can help explain.

In sharing parts of this study with colleagues, I have encountered two common objections to grounding a theory of the avant-garde film in a cognitive theory of mind. Both are based on misconceptions about the implications of a cognitive approach.

One objection derives from the connotations of the term "cognitive." For some it suggests a super-rational, computer-like viewer who takes in cues from the film and unproblematically spits out the correct interpretation. This objection is particularly common with respect to the avant-garde, since its films are so often confusing and open to a range of possible interpretations. Suggesting that viewing avant-garde films is a kind of problem solving strikes some as perverse. Any theory of the avant-garde that suggests that its viewers can unproblematically produce the proper interpretation of its films would certainly be wrong, but a cognitive theory implies no such thing. A cognitive approach does not commit one to the view that each film has only one "right" viewing experience, or that the experience always involves active engagement. Granted, the cognitive approach suggests that a good many mental processes might be understood as problem-solving procedures, but human problem solving rarely follows the rigorous principles of formal logic (Kahneman, Slovic and Tversky [1982]; Nisbett and Ross [1980]). Nowhere is this more true than in avant-garde film viewing; accordingly, my study emphasizes that viewers use heuristics, loose rules of thumb that can be applied quickly, rather than rule-bound algorithms that always produce the same result. A cognitive theory of the viewer not only acknowledges that some films support a broad range of experiences, it helps explain how and why.

Another objection is that cognitive theory is ahistorical and insensitive to cultural differences because it suggests that all human minds are alike. Cognitive theory maintains that there must be some innate features of the human mind (unlike much contemporary film theory, which generally holds to an extreme conventionalism: there is nothing about the mind that could not be different if the social formation were different in the right way). But these innate features do not directly determine aspects of human experience. Human subjectivity is a complex interaction between physiology, the physical environment and culturally determined choices. Rather than advocating an ahistorical, trans-cultural mind, cognitive theory seeks to theorize the mechanisms that account for cultural differences (see especially Rosch and Lloyd [1978] and Lakoff [1987] on categorization). Likewise, I try to demonstrate that film viewing is structured by its historical and social context: viewing heuristics evolve as the institution of the avant-garde changes.

Cognitive theory will likely continue to be far less influential than psychoanalysis in the study of film and literature, but there is growing interest in what it might contribute to our knowledge of the arts. E. H. Gombrich's work on the visual arts, especially *Art and Illusion* and *The Sense of Order*, has long been a model cognitive approach. More recently, cognitivism informs a growing number of literary studies (Holland; Turner; Lakoff and Turner). In film studies, David Bordwell's cognitively oriented work on the narrative film and the practice of film interpretation is both well known and controversial. Though some might attribute the controversy to Bordwell's contentiousness, cognitive theory sparks controversy wherever it encounters the study of the arts. I expect that my cognitive perspective will likewise make this a controversial study of the avant-garde cinema. By offering a cognitive theory of the avant-garde film viewer, I advocate an alternative to approaches to the avant-garde cinema that have long been dominant. Ultimately, my study's chief virtue may be that it enters and extends these controversies just when they have the broadest implications for the study of the arts.

A few words about the organization of this book. The next chapter sketches a cognitive theory of film viewing by showing how studies of perception, discourse comprehension and reasoning might answer some of the challenges posed by the avant-garde film. I suspect that readers who are keen to get on with a discussion of the films might find this a dreary prospect, so I have tried to be concise, and I hope such readers will be pleasantly surprised.

The rest of the book examines what I consider to be the three main strains of filmmaking in the American avant-garde: the poetic, the minimal, and the assemblage. I use the term ''strain'' because it suggests an open and flexible grouping of films. Each of these strains is characterized by a set of typical features, yet cannot be rigorously defined by listing necessary and sufficient properties. Each developed as a result of specific historical circumstances, yet these strains are not confined to clearly delimited historical periods. Common suggestions that the Structural film eclipsed the poetic avant-garde notwithstanding, to this day the poetic remains a vital strain of avant-garde filmmaking. Furthermore, any filmmaker's work, even any single film, might exhibit traits of more than one strain. For example, Bruce Baillie is often considered, along with Brakhage, a key exemplar of a poetic cinema. But because he often makes heavy use of found footage, he might also be considered a practitioner of the assemblage strain. Though they might be historically significant, such intermediate cases and classificatory ambiguities need not trouble us. What is important from our perspective is that viewers recognize these strains as broad tendencies within the avant-garde film, and understand that each calls for different, but not necessarily contradictory, strategies of comprehension. When a film calls for strategies associated with more than one strain, viewers must simply be prepared to use a broader range of strategies, applying them to whatever parts of the film make them relevant. As we will see, just about any avant-garde film requires multiple and overlapping strategies of comprehension, so films that critics might have trouble classifying unambiguously do not necessarily pose special problems for the viewer.

The first of these strains, the poetic avant-garde, is the subject of chapters 3 and 4. The poetic avant-garde includes, in addition to the work of Brakhage and Baillie, the work of Maya Deren, Sidney Peterson, Kenneth Anger, and Marie Menken, among many others. It includes much of what Sitney saw as the visionary tendency of the American avant-garde: what he called the trance film, the lyrical film, and the mythopoetic film. In general, I mean to identify the mode of filmmaking developed by the post-WWII American avant-garde up to the advent of Structural film in the mid-1960s. During much of this period, what we now call the avant-garde film was referred to as the ''film-poem.'' And as we shall see in chapter 3, this term suggests a range of viewing strategies. In chapter 4, I introduce the notion of *interpretive schemata*, powerful strategies viewers can use to make thematic interpretations of a film even when its basic comprehension is problematic. I argue that Brakhage, as an important critic of his own films, introduced the use of interpretive schemata that were then current in the world of the visual arts.

In chapters 5 and 6, I turn to the avant-garde's minimal strain. Andy Warhol's notorious career as a filmmaker marked the beginning of the film avant-garde's increasingly intimate association with other contemporary American visual arts. This association with the visual arts, together with the development of the minimal strain (later labelled Structural film), radically altered the set of formal devices characteristic of the American avant-garde film and deranged the avant-garde's implicit viewing procedures. Accordingly, in chapter 5, I begin by examining the interpretive schemata developed to deal with these novel films. I argue that for pragmatic reasons these interpretive schemata assumed enormous importance in how viewers derived meaning from these films. Chapter 6 concentrates on basic comprehension rather than thematic interpretation of the films, and asks a question critics have generally overlooked: how do viewers discover and make sense of the structures and patterns of the films of the minimal strain?

The assemblage strain comprises not only compilations of found footage, such as the well known films of Bruce Conner, but also what I call *collage animation* films in which actual paper collages are cut out and animated, as in the work of Stan Vanderbeek and Larry Jordan. Since neither compilation nor collage animation has been recognized as a major genre within the American avant-garde cinema,[6] there is no established body of criticism analyzing these films *as* a variety of assemblage art. Chapter 7 argues that interpretive schemata have been used to construct an image of assemblage art and film that makes it consistent with the Modernist project. My analysis of the assemblage strain in chapter 8 examines how the knowledge that these films are constructed of fragments of other texts influences how viewers make sense of these films. I suggest we consider assemblage filmmaking to be a kind of craft, and I argue that specific types of metaphor provide both a principle of construction and a viewing strategy for these films. Through the use of these kinds of metaphors, the films of the assemblage strain tend to take a critical stance toward the culture that supplies their imagery.

My examination of the activity of the viewer is meant neither as a thorough history, nor as a complete survey of the American avant-garde cinema. Readers interested in such overviews can turn to two books that are never more than an arm's length from my desk, both of which have been immensely helpful in my own study of the avant-garde film: Sitney's *Visionary Film: The American Avant-garde 1943–1978*, and David James's *Allegories of Cinema: American Film in the Sixties*. Sitney's account covers the greater historical span, but James, though covering a briefer period, situates the avant-garde cinema in broader and more varied cultural contexts.

Though my study is not meant as a complete overview, throughout I have tried to balance analytical depth and historical breadth. I draw examples from a wide range of films, and analyze a few films in depth. I have also tried for balance of another sort. It has always dismayed me, as it has many others, that the study of the avant-garde, among the most marginal of cinemas, is so dominated by a small canon of major filmmakers. I have chosen some examples from the well-known canon of avant-garde works, but I have also included many little-known films and filmmakers. My study of these filmmakers on

the margins of the margin suggests that some common notions about
the American avant-garde cinema are in need of revision. Yet the
revisions I offer are themselves provisional. For as writing this book
has taught me, the American avant-garde cinema has invariably been
more diverse than critical studies of it (including my own, I must
admit) tend to suggest.

2

Avant-garde Film Viewing
as Problem Solving

Film viewing is a staggeringly complex process. To understand even the simplest film, viewers must manage masses of details, grouping them into coherent units and integrating them with their knowledge of the world. Most often this proceeds unproblematically and we are never really aware of it. But when we encounter an avant-garde film, we struggle to integrate details into coherent wholes. We may even have trouble perceiving individual images. The process of comprehension, usually taken for granted, is suddenly laid bare.

The processes that the avant-garde film seems so ready to confront have become a central concern for cognitive theorists working in a number of fields, especially psychology, linguistics and computer science.[1] Three research programs within this cognitive paradigm are particularly relevant to our interest in the avant-garde film viewer: studies of perception, discourse processing, and the pragmatics of language use. My aim in this chapter is to use this research to advance the notion that avant-garde film viewing can be considered a kind of problem solving.

Perception

The study of perception has produced some of cognitive psychology's most dramatic successes. Particularly with regard to the physiology of vision, cognitive psychologists have been able to give practically definitive explanations of some perceptual phenomena, such as how the ocular motor system controls the movements of the eye. The work I am about to cite advocates a *Constructive cognitive theory* of perception, which holds that the mind constructs a representation of the world by synthesizing sense data and prior knowledge. This Constructivist view of the cognitive dimensions of perception is widely held, though not as universally accepted as the work on the physiology of perception.[2]

The Constructivist theory of perception begins with the almost indisputable fact that humans perceive more than the physical world gives to their senses. Descartes was aware of this by the seventeenth century when he pointed out the phenomenon psychologists now call *size constancy*. A person's hands, Descartes noted, always appear roughly the same size, even though the size of their images on the retina differs dramatically (*Dioptrics* 1637; cited in Gregory 1966, 152). Descartes's example demonstrates that perception is to a great extent a *top-down* process. That is, it is not determined solely by the flow of new information to the brain, but uses stored information to process and transform the sense data. *Bottom-up* processing occurs when the sense data alone determine perception without transformation in light of stored information.[3] Inadvertently touching a hot stove is a paradigm of bottom-up processing. Regardless of the context, regardless of one's knowledge of kitchen appliances, the nervous system would register heat and pain.[4]

But with modern research techniques, the top-down quality of perception, particularly as it relates to the comprehension of discourse, has been demonstrated in ever more dramatic ways. Consider the phenomenon known as the *phonemic restoration effect*. Researchers demonstrated that speech sounds in sample sentences could be replaced by meaningless sounds without affecting the comprehensibility of the sentence. Of course, this is not surprising since the context of the sentence provides cues for the missing phoneme. But the sentences were designed so that the contextual cues came well *after* the missing sounds. Subjects were given sets of sentences in the form "It was found that the *eel was on the _____." The "*" was replaced with the sound of a cough, and the sentences ended with words that would allow the subjects to fill in the missing sound. When the sentence ended with "orange," the subjects heard "peel"; when it ended with "axle," they heard "wheel"; when it ended with "shoe," they heard "heel"; and so on. But the subjects did not simply fill in the missing sound—the effect was so powerful that the subjects did not even perceive the replacement, even though they had to wait for the cue to complete the sentence.[5]

We should not think that such top-down processing is limited to optical illusions and laboratory experiments. At any given moment of our waking lives, our eyes encounter a complex array of values and hues; we must somehow determine which are due to the objects before us and which are due to the light and shadows falling on those objects. Most of the time the rectilinear objects that make up our world are projected obliquely on our retinas so that they are stretched into strange trapezoids; nonetheless, we see a world of regularity and right angles. When we move our eyes or our heads, the world cascades across our retinas; we see it as stable. As the Constructivists like to put it, at almost every turn the mind goes beyond the information given.

In light of data like these, Constructivist theory conceives of perception as a search for solutions to perceptual problems. According to R. L. Gregory:

> Perception is not determined simply by the stimulus patterns; rather it is a dynamic searching for the best interpretation of the available data.

. . . The senses do not give us a picture of the world directly; rather they provide evidence for checking hypotheses about what lies before us. Indeed, we may say that a perceived object *is* a hypothesis, suggested and tested by sensory data. (1978, 11–12)

This formulation may strike many as strange. The process of hypothesis generation and testing is often thought to be the paradigm of deliberate conscious thought; how could the instantaneous process of perception follow such a ponderous sequence of steps?

This is exactly the question addressed by Constructivist work on perception such as Irvin Rock's (1983). Rock's position might be termed ''hard'' cognitivism because he argues that thought-like, cognitive processes underlie all but the simplest forms of perception. He would admit that heat and cold may sometimes be directly sensed, but Rock maintains that the perception of even simple shapes can be explained only as a series of thought-like steps culminating in a description of the shape. When stimulated by more complex forms such as optical illusions and ambiguous figures, the perceptual system engages in problem-solving processes to account for the stimulus by developing a mental description of the conditions that produced it. For example, Rock explains the illusory contour effect as the hypothesis generated by the perceptual system to account for the systematic incompleteness of the circles in the figure (Fig. 2.1). The perceptual system ''explains'' the missing parts of the circles as occlusion caused by an opaque triangle approximately the color of the background covering a portion of the figure. Many viewers even perceive the faint contours of the triangle hypothesized to be causing the occlusion. And though perception is thought-like, it is not ponderous: perceivers are unaware of their perceptual problem solving, and they perform it very rapidly (though not quite instantaneously). Rock's conclusion, based on many ingenious experiments, is that only the hypothesis generation and testing explanation accounts for what we can observe about the working of the perceptual system.

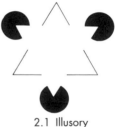

2.1 Illusory contour figure.

Work like Rock's blurs the distinction between cognition and perception: the same processes we use to solve problems consciously also regulate the recognition of shapes in the world. One important consequence of this unified view of mental activity is that it shows that the ''passive'' spectator of the Hollywood film is a myth. If the viewer of *any* film must make and test hypotheses just to understand what the images represent, comprehending the narrative of even the most formulaic Hollywood film involves very sophisticated mental processes. The question we must ask about the viewers is not whether they are active, because they always are. We must ask instead: what is the nature of their activity?

Hypothesis generation and testing is only the hollow form of the viewer's mental process. It suggests that stored knowledge interacts with the senses to generate knowledge about the world. This makes Constructivist theory a synthesis of Rationalist faith in the mind as the source of knowledge and Empiricist confidence in the observation of the physical world through the senses. Philosophically, then, Constructivist theory is the heir of Immanuel Kant, who emphasized the active role of the mind without dismissing the role of sense experience and began to theorize how the two might interact.

Kant argued that the mind comes with certain standard equipment—the "categories of thought"—that is necessary if we are to perceive the world at all, but that allows us to perceive it only in certain ways. We can never see things as they "really" are, but only as our minds are prepared to see them. For example, we cannot help but perceive objects as embedded in space, related in time and linked causally. In addition to these very general and abstract "categories" that are part of every mind, Kant postulated another set of mental constructs, the *schemata*. For Kant, the potential to develop schemata is part of the standard mental equipment, but the schemata themselves are developed only through experience with the world. The function of the schemata is to allow us to relate abstract concepts to experience. If we wish to apply a general concept to a particular instance, we must have acquired some sort of mental representation of the concept apart from our representations of all the examples we have so far encountered. If we identify a piece of furniture as a chair, for example, we must have a schema for the concept "chair."

Cognitive psychologists adapted Kant's concept of the schema to explain how the mind organizes the mass of data constantly provided by the senses.[6] Since the film viewer must routinely manage large amounts of information, the notion of the schema is one of cognitive psychology's most useful insights for the film theorist. Simply put, a *schema* is a pattern, an orderly configuration into which experience is sorted so that it might be better managed. Without recognizable patterns to guide us, a mass of sensation would overwhelm us, and our perception and memory would be erratic and unreliable.

Ulric Neisser argues that perception is a cyclic process (1976, 20–24); this is a productive model for the viewer's interaction with an artwork. Let us say the viewer of a painting tries to match the colors and values in the image to a schema for a person. The "person" schema provides a basis for hypotheses about the object's details, hypotheses that can be confirmed or disproved with further observation. The viewer looks for a head, and finds a suitably sized round shape in the painting. This prompts another hypothesis, that there should be a face within this shape, and another round of hypothesis testing and generation is under way. If the sense data do not suggest matching schemata—if the object is completely unfamiliar—the image must be broken down into units that *can* be matched to schemata.

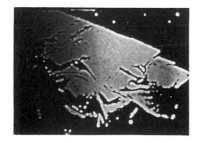

Fig. 2.2

For a demonstration of this process, consider the configuration of irregular shapes in a frame enlargement from J. J. Murphy's *Print Generation* (1973–74) (Fig. 2.2). It is not exactly the case that this configuration is imperceptible, but it is perceptible only to the extent that the viewer can match it to his or her store of schemata. In this example the best match might be a schema for a more or less random pattern. But if the viewer can match sense data to a more precise schema, the perception of the image will change accordingly. Try seeing this pattern as a picture of a woman lying on her back (Fig. 2.3).

With this schema guiding the search for new information, shapes that were previously random are now identified as the woman's face, hair and clothing. Once sense data are matched to a schema, the eyes move over the scene; attention shifts to its various details; the hypothesis is rejected or refined; another search begins. All along, the viewer's store of schemata suggests hypotheses and guides the search toward relevant features of the object. The *Print Generation* example offers a spectacular demonstration of how the avant-garde film plays with schemata in order to both disrupt and extend the viewer's engagement with the image. And, as *Print Generation* demonstrates, this schematic play is not limited to the individual image, but can be stretched across whole films.

Fig. 2.3

Schemata and Discourse Comprehension

So far we have established two basic features of human perception: it depends heavily on prior knowledge, and it is fundamentally a search for structures, what we have been calling schemata. How might these features help us explain the processing of discourse, especially avant-garde films?

Let me begin with a refinement of the concept of schema. We actually use three types of schemata as we sift through the data provided by our senses looking for familiar structures (Hastie 1981, 40–43). The simplest are *prototype schemata*, which we use to identify individual things, like the people we know, or members of a class, like birds. Prototype schemata are fundamental to the recognition of images—it was a prototype schema that came into play in the *Print Generation* example. Second, *template schemata* allow us to identify patterns, like the alphabetical pattern in a filing system, or the layout of the streets in a neighborhood, or common sequences of events, such as those involved in eating at a restaurant. Template schemata are powerful, allowing us to fill in missing pieces of patterns so that we do not have to attend to familiar objects and can direct our mental effort to more novel and complicated tasks. When searching for a phone number, for example, we do not have to read every page in the phone book, but can skip most of them, focusing our effort on the area where the number is most likely to be. Template schemata are also fundamental to our experience of films: they allow us to predict and anticipate upcoming elements, and they help us remember earlier parts. Finally, we have *procedural schemata* for skills or tasks we have mastered, such as riding a bicycle or typing, or understanding discourse. All three types of schemata figure in the viewer's comprehension of the avant-garde film, though in this section we will be especially concerned with the role of template schemata.

These three types of schemata are not only part of basic perception, they are fundamental to the comprehension of any kind of discourse, and people are quite adept at using them. Thus, making sense of avant-garde films does not require a completely unique set of comprehension skills, no matter how alien these films may at first seem. Viewers of avant-garde films rely on skills learned through exposure to normal, everyday discourse, as well as through exposure to many kinds of aesthetic discourse such as literature, painting, and fiction film.

As in just about every area of cognitive research, there is significant debate about the details of discourse comprehension. There is, nevertheless, a broad consensus about some of its basic features.[7] The most basic principle of discourse comprehension is that it is predominantly *semantic*: the reader's most fundamental goal is to make some appraisal of the text's overall meaning.[8] This semantic orientation has several important consequences.

First, structure is vital to successful comprehension. Readers who aim to construct a discourse's overall meaning face a problem: appraisals of global meaning must be derived solely from moment-by-moment contact with *local* details. Viewers integrate details into larger structures by matching these details to schemata, which provide a way of managing large groups of details. For example, imagine a shot of a person sitting and reading a menu. These details fit the schema for eating in a restaurant, and later in the film a coherent restaurant scene will be both more memorable and more useful in making sense of the story than a collection of isolated details would be. In fact, we might integrate the restaurant episode itself into an even larger schema, say, for example, a cross-country trip. From this perspective, we might even say that comprehension *is* the process of matching schemata to discourse.

A second consequence of the semantic orientation of normal discourse processing is that surface detail tends to be lost. Surface details—such as the exact wording of a sentence or the exact configuration of colors and shapes in an image—are actually all the reader or viewer has direct contact with. But once surface detail is organized and integrated into coherent, meaningful units, say an image of a character, those meaningful units are remembered and the surface details are lost. After we read a book, we do not usually recall passages word for word. In most film viewing, we concentrate on objects and events in the images, and we do not generally notice or remember such details as the grain, the framing or the exact sequences of shots. One reason for this is the limit of human memory. Because we cannot remember everything in a text, we remember what is most meaningful and useful. If we are watching a videotape to learn how to register for next semester's courses, for example, the camera angles are not going to be especially useful. And if we think that the fiction film we are watching is entertaining because of the funny predicaments in which Bill and Ted find themselves, surface detail is useful only provisionally, as a means of constructing representations of those situations. Another reason surface detail is lost is that we notice and remember what we can match to template schemata. And generally we have lots of template schemata for things like event sequences, whereas we have relatively few template schemata for patterns of surface detail.

A third consequence of the semantic orientation is that comprehension involves both bottom-up and top-down processes. Sometimes the details of a text seem to demand a particular interpretation.

When we see a picture of a face, for example, it is usually very hard for us *not* to see it as a face. In this case, we can say that comprehension is bottom-up, or data-driven, because the details are rather complete and "demand" to be comprehended in one specific way. On the other hand, sometimes comprehension requires us to fill in material that is not explicitly given. Imagine our restaurant scene again. This time, after we see our characters reading the menu, we see them paying the bill; we do not actually see them eating. If we know the restaurant schema, we can flesh out this scene and understand that they have eaten, even though the eating is not explicitly shown. We can call this kind of comprehension top-down, or hypothesis-driven, because our knowledge about the world leads us to fill in missing information. To the extent the information we have to fill in is well known and clearly specified by the text, top-down processes come into play without troubling our comprehension.

I have begun with normal discourse comprehension because the avant-garde film viewer depends heavily on many of the same processes used to comprehend other sorts of discourse. But having begun with a sketch of normal discourse comprehension, our task now is to throw into relief the difference between it and the comprehension of the avant-garde film. Our first question concerns the goal of avant-garde film viewing.

Theories of normal discourse comprehension assume that the goal of comprehension is to derive overall meaning. This might be a reasonable assumption about the simple stories that most studies of discourse comprehension use. But with more complex kinds of discourse, this assumption about the reader's goal needs some refinement. For example, the overall meaning of *The Wizard of Oz* (1939) might be paraphrased thus: though exotic places and people seem appealing, ultimately they are not as important as one's family. Or, to quote the film itself, "There's no place like home." But film viewers do more than just identify the overall theme, they also try to identify the film's structure. The structure of *The Wizard of Oz*, put somewhat sketchily, is a narrative about a girl's dream. We can call this overarching structure that establishes coherence among the film's parts the *schematic* structure.

Viewers do not simply try to find *any* schematic structure that will fit; they try to find schematic structures that establish coherence for the whole film. The dream schema does match *The Wizard of Oz*, but for most viewers, it alone will not establish sufficient coherence, and will need further elaboration. In the dream, Dorothy travels to a faraway land, encounters fantastic characters who join her search for the wizard, and so on. If I am a first-time viewer of the film, I will probably be satisfied with a schematic structure that specifies the basic elements of the story, especially the main characters' goals and the steps they take to achieve them. Of course, what counts as sufficient coherence varies to a degree. If I am writing a critical analysis of the film, I will want to embellish this schematic structure by tracking major motifs across the film, by noting contrasts between reality and fantasy, between urban and rural, and between color and black-and-white. In spite of such variations, the viewer of the classical Holly-wood cinema generally starts with a reasonably well-defined goal. According to David Bordwell (1985), viewers of classical Hollywood cinema have as their primary goal the reconstruction of the story's chain of causes and effects, based on cues supplied by the film.

Even if we grant that this is a reasonable assumption about the classical Hollywood cinema (and many would not),[9] certainly the avant-garde film viewer's goal cannot be specified with such preci-sion. The comprehension of the avant-garde film is what problem-solving theorists call an ''ill-structured'' problem. Unlike well-struc-tured problems, such as puzzles (and, to a degree, classical Hollywood narratives), ill-structured problems have no single, unequivocal so-lution, and there is no decisive way to tell when they have been solved. If the avant-garde film is an ill-structured problem, the viewer's goal must be stated in terms flexible enough to admit a wide range of solutions, yet precise enough to allow us to analyze how viewers might proceed. As a first approximation of the avant-garde film viewer's goal, let us follow theories of normal discourse comprehension and assume that the viewer of the avant-garde film begins with a general goal not unlike that of any film viewer: to make sense of the film.

Let me acknowledge straightaway that there might be excep-tions to this common-sense assumption. As with any other kind of film, an individual viewer, for idiosyncratic reasons, might simply be unable or unwilling to pay attention to the film. But a more interesting possibility is that a film might encourage, or even induce, some state of reception other than active sense-making. Such claims are some-times made about psychedelic avant-garde films, particularly the work of Jordan Belson and John and James Whitney. Perhaps the most extravagant claims of this sort have been made by Standish Lawder about his loop-printed *Raindance* (1972): ''*Raindance* plays directly on the mind through programmatic stimulation of the central nervous system. Individual frames of the film are imprinted on the retina of the eye in a rhythm, sequence, and intensity that corresponds to Alpha-Wave frequencies of the brain. . . . The film directs our mental processes, controlling how we think as well as what we see'' (*Canyon Cinema Catalog* 6, [1988] 149).

I am intrigued by the possibility of films inducing trance-like states in the viewer. But we can question, on at least three grounds, whether psychedelic films represent a significant counter-example to the proposal that viewers actively try to make sense of avant-garde films. First, we ought to wonder whether these trance-inducing films are effective. Based on my own experience of *Raindance*, if one is in the right frame of mind, viewing the film *is* the kind of soothing experience that the stimulation of alpha-waves should produce. But as far as I know, the experience of most viewers is not as dramatic as Lawder's description. Second, over and above their trance-inducing potential, psychedelic films create salient patterns that can be (and are, I would argue) consciously noted by viewers. *Raindance* is structured as a theme-and-variations on a fragment of cartoon. And the cartoon fragment depicts the shooting of a movie, so that the film has a reflexive dimension common among avant-garde films of its time. Judging by published analyses of these films, critics find much more to analyze than their trance-inducing qualities.[10] Third, the psychedelic sub-genre is relatively small, so that even if the films of that sub-genre did induce trances and nothing else, most avant-garde films would still call for the viewer's active sense-making.

Avant-garde films might also be said to stimulate something other than active sense-making with images of great power or beauty that supposedly defy interpretation.[11] I agree completely: the avant-garde cinema is filled with images whose sensuous appeal apparently outstrips what they contribute to the film's structure and meaning. Scott Nygren has suggested that this sensuous appeal is a particularly important aspect of the work of Bruce Baillie, whose color films include some of the most glorious images in the avant-garde. Nevertheless, it might still be possible to analyze such imagery along the problem-solving lines suggested by Constructivist theories of perception. Fred Lerdahl and Ray Jackendoff's study of musical cognition, *A Generative Theory of Tonal Music*, and E.H. Gombrich's study of decorative art, *The Sense of Order*, suggest one such line of attack. These studies aim to show how even the comprehension of abstract art can be explained as a search for structures that match the details of the artwork. One finds a different, but possibly compatible, approach in phenomenology.[12] But again, as with trance-inducing imagery, over and above their sensual power, visually stunning images are generally woven into structures that do call for analysis.

For these reasons, I will assume, however provisionally, that the avant-garde film viewer's goal is to make sense of the film. But what exactly counts as ''making sense'' of an avant-garde film? To use the terms we used in our discussion of normal discourse comprehension, we can define making sense as discerning the overall meaning and the overall schematic structure. Or, to put it in slightly more formal terms, we can say that viewers have made sense of a film when they have established sufficient coherence among the film's elements by matching those elements to template schemata.

Making sense of the avant-garde film is an ill-formed problem with no clear-cut solution; what constitutes sufficient coherence in the avant-garde cinema varies widely from viewer to viewer. However, problem-solving theory suggests three broad approaches to such open-ended problems.[13] *Maximizing* strategies are generally appropriate for well-formed problems for which there are clear-cut solutions. A jigsaw puzzle, for example, is not considered solved until every piece is put in place. The maximizing strategy aims to produce the best possible solution regardless of cost. On the other hand, *satisficing* strategies minimize problem-solving effort and aim to produce only ''good enough'' solutions. Theorists suggest that satisficing strategies are common approaches to real world problems, which tend to be ill-formed, and which often must be solved quickly and with incomplete information. *Optimizing* strategies produce better solutions than satisficing strategies, but at the cost of somewhat greater problem-solving effort. The optimizer weighs the cost of additional effort against the benefit of the improved solution, and, unlike the maximizer, at a certain point decides that the extra effort no longer pays enough.

Using problem-solving theory, we can speculate that viewers might take these same three approaches to the avant-garde film. I suspect that satisficing is a common enough approach for viewers of the avant-garde. Viewers might try to derive a very general notion of the film's theme, and they will try to get an idea of the film's overall structure, to the extent that it is readily apparent on a single viewing. In particular, students who are viewing an avant-garde film for some academic reason might use a satisficing strategy. For example, if I instruct my students to watch *Meshes of the Afternoon* (1943) as an example of the influence of Surrealism on the American avant-garde, they might note the film's sexual themes and its dream structure without engaging the finer points of the film's use of space or its systematic use of props.

Most viewers and critics of the avant-garde are optimizers who are not satisfied with establishing minimal coherence. The supposition in the avant-garde seems to be that one should get as much out of these films as one can, and that one should be sensitive to a wider range of effects in the avant-garde than in other modes of filmmaking. By reading about films and filmmakers, optimizing viewers collect information that will help them establish greater coherence among the elements of the film. Additional information can also be gathered through repeated viewings of the same film. Such repeated viewings are cited as an ideal by critics and filmmakers (though no one knows how often this ideal is realized for viewers who are not also teachers or critics).[14]

Maximizing strategies are generally appropriate to well-formed problems where absolute success is possible. In the avant-garde cinema it is inconceivable that a viewer could establish coherence among every last detail in a film. Yet critics and academics might be considered to pursue maximizing strategies to the extent that they are willing to continue to collect information regardless of the cost. They might read everything ever written about a particular film. They might view the film repeatedly and examine it shot-by-shot on an editing bench. Practically, though, even such dedicated critics (and I know of some) are optimizers. No one accounts for every element in a film. And even though some critics might collect an infinite amount of information, in writing they use only enough to make a persuasive analysis.

Generally, then, I assume that avant-garde film viewers are optimizers whose goal is to establish as much coherence as they can on the basis of limited viewing of the film, their knowledge of the work of the filmmaker at hand, and their knowledge of the history of the avant-garde cinema. This description of the viewer's goal is reasonably open-ended, and framing the film viewer's goal as an attempt to establish coherence highlights the similarity between avant-garde film viewing and the comprehension of normal discourse. Yet we still have to come to terms with the ways in which the avant-garde film systematically frustrates normal comprehension.

First, the avant-garde film emphasizes surface structure. In normal discourse, surface structure is remembered only provisionally, as a means of deriving meaning, but it plays a more central role in the avant-garde film. Particularly in the minimal strain, many films emphasize aspects of the film image that other films ignore. David Rimmer's *Surfacing on the Thames* (1970) (Fig. 2.4) uses optical printing to draw attention to scratches on the film image. The imagery in Ernie Gehr's *History* (1970) is simply the grain of the film stock. And with George Landow's *Film in which there appear sprocket holes, edge lettering, dirt particles, etc.* (1965–66), this shift of attention toward normally marginal surface qualities is obvious from the title. The poetic and assemblage strains emphasize surface structure, too, though not always in ways so self-conscious of the film medium. These films often juxtapose shots whose colors, shapes or movements match even though the subject matter of the shots might be very different. Thus, viewers of the avant-garde need to attend to patterns of textures, colors, shapes and movements, as they would attend to characters, settings and events in a commercial film.

Fig. 2.4

A second reason the avant-garde film can confound normal comprehension is because it is radically top-down. In our restaurant example, figuring out that our characters had eaten even though eating was not explicitly shown is not difficult, because for most of us the material we are asked to fill in is familiar and clearly specified by the text. We often make these kinds of hypotheses without even realizing it. On the other hand, sometimes the details seem to lack a single definite structure and seem to be open to a wide range of interpretation, and we are likely to be more self-conscious about comprehension. Consider this scene from Christopher Maclaine's *The End* (1953). A character has committed a murder. We see him wandering about San Francisco as a voice-over narrator explains that the character has murdered his landlady and her daughter, and does not want to spend the rest of his days in prison. We see the character pass through a turnstile at Golden Gate Park, and the segment ends. The Golden Gate Park shots could fit a number of schemata. Perhaps he has gone to the park to think things over; perhaps he is crazy and is acting irrationally. Another schema these details fit is that our character commits suicide, but this conclusion is hardly inescapable. In this kind of situation, we often speak of ''imposing'' our interpretation on the discourse, whereas we ''discover'' it in the more ''normal'' restaurant example. I am arguing that it is not so much a matter of discovering *or* imposing as it is a matter of *matching* the details of the discourse to the schema that fits best. Sometimes the details will fit only a few schemata (our restaurant example) and sometimes the details will fit many schemata (the Golden Gate Park example). Sometimes the match will be obvious, and sometimes the match will require some creative thinking and, perhaps, some specific knowledge, such as that the Golden Gate Bridge is considered a good place to commit suicide. To the extent that the details suggest matches with few schemata, and to the extent that these matches are obvious, top-down processing appears automatic. With the exception of many films of the minimal strain, making sense of the avant-garde film is rarely automatic in this way.

The comprehension of the poetic and assemblage strains of the avant-garde is so rarely automatic because their films often make use of unusual and unexpected template schemata. In this respect, these strains are typical of avant-garde art in general. (Again, within the realm of the avant-garde film, the exception to this generalization is the minimal strain, whose films often use eminently simple and identifiable global schemata.) The template schema in the restaurant example is based on a cause-and-effect chain. Most overall template schemata in narrative films are cause-and-effect chains, but there are many other patterns that can serve as global template schemata in works of art. For example, the Shakespearean sonnet has fourteen lines and a specific rhyme scheme (abab cdcd efef gg). Musical forms also have standard, and therefore predictable, patterns, such as the exposition, development and recapitulation of the sonata. Individual works might use template schemata not dictated by standard aesthetic forms. Michel Butor's *Mobile: A Project for a Representation of the United States* (1962) is a long poem that "tours" the United States through an alphabetical listing of American place names; thus its global template schema is the alphabet. John Knecht's film *The Primary Concerns of Roy G. Biv* (1978) has one section for each color of the rainbow, and the order of colors in the spectrum determines their positions in the film. A notorious example of the use of obscure template schemata is Joyce's *Ulysses*. The novel fits its basic narrative into several template schemata: the hours of the day, the journey of Ulysses, and the organs of the body. Avant-garde art, film included, tends to favor such novel and obscure template schemata, which viewers often have trouble identifying.

Nevertheless, narrative template schemata do play a prominent role in many avant-garde films. Though a wide variety of template schemata has been used to structure works of art, the cause-and-effect chains that distinguish narrative from other types of textual organization are especially powerful. As a great deal of research on story comprehension suggests (e.g. Mandler 1984), all template schemata aid perception and memory, but the causal and spatial template schemata of stories have much greater processing benefits. Discourse organized causally is both easier to understand and easier to remember than discourse organized in other ways. Given a series of events, perceivers will tend to supply causal connections even if they are not explicitly mentioned. In fact, it is well documented that perceivers impose order if they cannot discover it; research suggests that narrative is the first organizational structure perceivers try to impose. Of course, avant-garde films typically do not have the kind of narratives characteristic of the classical Hollywood cinema. Even so, narrative schemata do structure parts of many avant-garde films, especially in the poetic and assemblage strains. Thus, narrative is a factor in the viewer's experience, even of films that we may not think of as primarily stories.

I have assumed that the viewer's goal is to establish as much coherence as possible on the basis of the information at hand. But this does not imply that viewers always establish coherence in the same way or to the same degree. Parker Tyler, in surveying the American avant-garde of the early 1960s, saw "a deliberately relaxed attention to craft, in which a free-wheeling private fantasy, utterly self-indulgent, simply throws *film form* onto the cutting room floor of the mind before even a single reel is shot" (1967, 31–32; emphasis in original). A more charitable view of such works of art is articulated by Teun van Dijk (1979). Van Dijk suggests that the comprehension of certain types of aesthetic discourse might be understood as play with what he calls *free interpretation sets*, sets of potential meanings that fit some of the details, but leave many others unexplained. Faced with an apparently loosely organized discourse, readers try out these possible meanings, perhaps settling on one that seems to fit best, perhaps entertaining a number of them indefinitely.

Because the avant-garde encourages intuitive and random working methods, the play with free interpretation sets is a useful way of thinking about how viewers try to establish coherence in the avant-garde film. David Brook's *Nightspring Daystar* (1964), for example, not only takes a jazz performance as its subject, but also aspires to the improvisational structure of jazz. Improvisational procedures often produce details that viewers may not be able to match to global (or even, for that matter, local) template schema. In *Nightspring Daystar*, the viewer probably notices a loose system of contrasts—night/day, winter/spring, sound/silence—but many details of the film cannot be matched to a specific schema, except, of course, a schema for "loose improvisation." Furthermore, no single schema is likely to account for all, or even most, of a film's local detail. Though the classical narrative cinema characteristically has a dominant overall structure, avant-garde films are often not so dominated. They may be organized by multiple, overlapping structures, with the dominant structure fluctuating moment by moment. *Nightspring Daystar* is not "best" understood as a series of structured oppositions, or as play with the graphic qualities of the image, or as a representation of a musical performance, but as a mixture of all these. Any particular viewer will probably perceive only some of these structures, leaving significant parts of the film unschematized and uncomprehended. Viewers accept that their efforts are likely to produce only partial comprehension, and expect that with another viewing, they will discover patterns, structures, and pleasures they missed earlier.

The Pragmatic Perspective

So far, we have been concerned with how the viewer establishes the *intrinsic* coherence of an avant-garde film, that is, the coherence among the elements actually present in the film. But the avant-garde film is also a form of social interaction, whose coherence derives not just from the elements in the film itself, but from the context in which the film circulates.

The way in which the context of social interaction affects the meaning of language has become the topic of lively debate in linguistics. Historically, linguistic theories have been theories of semantics and, especially in Chomsky's work, of syntax. But in roughly the last two decades, pragmatics, the study of how utterances have meaning in contexts, has been rescued from the margins of linguistics. In fact, some pragmatic theorists argue that many phenomena once thought to be aspects of semantics and syntax are actually best explained as effects of the context of language use, and that pragmatics therefore ought to be accorded a more central role in linguistics.[15]

Pragmatic theories of language and communication aim to account for the difference between the linguistically encoded meaning of sentences and the meaning of utterances as they are used by speakers in context. Consider the sentence, "The door is open." Its linguistically encoded meaning is a report on the condition of a door. Semantically, however, this sentence is ambiguous. "Open" might be used either in the sense of "not closed" or in the sense of "unlocked." And, of course, the referent of "the door" is undefined. If we encountered this sentence in an actual conversation, however, the referent would be clear because we would probably be standing by a single door, and the term "open" would not be ambiguous because we could see whether the door was closed. But there is even more to determining the meaning of utterances than disambiguating them and determining their referents. Imagine that a student visits a teacher's office. When he arrives he knocks and says, "May I come in?" The teacher responds from behind her closed office door, "The door's open." The teacher's sentence is unambiguous ("open" means "unlocked" since the door is obviously closed) and refers clearly to her office door, but it does not directly answer the student's question. Pragmatically, though, the sentence is more than a report on the condition of the door. It is an invitation for the student to enter, and we would paraphrase it not as "the entrance to my office is unlocked," but as "yes, come in." Pragmatics explains how receivers derive meaning from such seemingly evasive utterances.

According to a pragmatic theory of language, participants in a communicative exchange must assume that their partner is cooperating, or communication would not be possible. As formulated by H. P. Grice, the "cooperative principle" amounts to the demand to be truthful, relevant and clear. For example, if partner A suspected that partner B was just as likely to lie as to tell the truth, nothing B could say would be communication with A, because A would be completely uncertain about the truth of B's statements. On the other hand, if A assumes the speaker's compliance with the cooperative principle, then A can infer a great deal about B's intentions.

But to make these inferences, the "cooperative principle" must be refined; we never assume that speakers always tell the simple truth. In practice, we see that "cooperation" with the listener is often mediated by the need to be polite, or the desire to be funny, or the wish to seem modest. A pragmatic theory holds that the listener knows what sorts of things might compromise the speaker's adherence to the cooperative principle, so that any apparent deviation from it can be understood as motivated by one of these competing demands. Imagine, for example, that you have asked whether my boss is a good administrator, and I reply that he is a very nice fellow. In one sense, my answer is evasive, apparently a violation of the co-operative principle. But if you assume that I am following the co-operative principle, and that I have tried to give you a relevant answer, you can make sense of my response. You understand that I might be reluctant to discuss my boss's shortcomings (basically out of politeness; I do not want to risk offending my boss), and you infer that my evasion means that I do not think my boss is a good admin-istrator. Even when speakers do not tell the literal truth, we under-stand them because we infer their motivation for not being com-pletely honest. Communication takes place, but it often takes place "between the lines."[16]

Film viewing, too, proceeds on the basis of pragmatic principles, though the exact principles of film pragmatics are bound to be dif-ferent from the principles of conversational pragmatics. To take a single but vital example of this difference, as viewers we do not assume that most films are uniformly truthful. Nor do we assume they lie. Many films are fictional, and their literal truthfulness just does not matter. On the other hand, just as in conversation, we operate under the basic assumption that the material in films will be relevant and clear. Of course, it is not the case that all films are uniformly relevant and clear, especially in the avant-garde. But just as in a conversation, the violation of these principles sets viewers on a search for the competing principles that explain the apparent violation.

Exactly what these competing principles are is the subject of later chapters. For now, let me suggest a few ideas about how prag-matic principles come into play in avant-garde film viewing.

One of the basic assumptions of pragmatic theories is that the parties to the communicative exchange both know the context. In conversational exchanges, which much pragmatic theory is designed to explain, both speakers can rely on many cues about their partner's beliefs and goals. But since the filmmaker and the viewer only oc-casionally meet face-to-face, in avant-garde film viewing this mutu-ally known context is established by the institutions of the avant-garde cinema. The world of the American avant-garde film comprises a small number of tightly interconnected institutions. Its films are shown mostly at universities, museums, and a handful of non-academic exhibition outlets in major cities. A relatively small number of jour-nals publish essays on avant-garde film, and, more than other aca-demic film journals, avant-garde film journals are especially interested in publishing interviews, statements of principle, proposals for films or descriptions of works in progress.[17] Filmmakers regularly appear at screenings of their films so that viewers might be provided with proper introductions, explanations, and answers to their questions. Critics of the avant-garde film are also generally teachers, so that many potential avant-garde film viewers get explicit training in how to view films. As a result of all these interconnections, the avant-garde's critical environment establishes and makes known the pragmatic prin-ciples viewers use to make sense of the films.

In subsequent chapters, we will have occasion to examine carefully this critical environment and the pragmatic principles it proposes. Here I will mention only the most basic of these pragmatic principles. It derives from the common idea that avant-garde art is defined by its rejection of tradition, and that such a rejection is valuable. Using this principle, what we may call the *brute avant-garde principle*, if a film is apparently incomprehensible, the viewer can establish minimal pragmatic coherence by interpreting the film as a rejection of conventional film form and style meant to shock viewers out of their complacency. Of course, this principle establishes only the most minimal coherence and is therefore the pragmatic principle of last resort. More often, the brute avant-garde principle is modified in sophisticated ways that allow the viewer to draw connections between the avant-garde film and the principles of Modernism. Nevertheless, sometimes those sophisticated versions fail to apply. Such is the case with the work of Peter Gidal, whose films not only reject the norms of commercial filmmaking, but also reject the avant-garde's manner of rejecting those norms. Unlike most American Structural films, Gidal's films have no apparent structure and offer only momentary glimpses of scarcely recognizable representation. Gidal asserts that the prominent patterns of the Structural film are yet another means of concealing the material nature of the cinema, which his own films aim to display.[18] Strictly speaking, then, it is impossible that a film would be completely incomprehensible in the avant-garde, since that incomprehensibility itself can be recuperated with the brute avant-garde principle.

To summarize this chapter, we have put the viewer on the horns of a dilemma. On one hand, we established that the viewer's goal is to integrate local detail into an appraisal of the film's overall meaning and overall schematic structure. On the other hand, we established that American avant-garde film will systematically confound the viewer's effort to do so. The rest of this book is concerned with how viewers might solve this dilemma and make the passage from the local details to the global structure and meaning of the avant-garde film.

3

The Poetic Strain of the Avant-garde

In the two decades following World War II, poetry provided not only a model but a name for the American avant-garde film, which was then called the "film poem." During this period the relationship between film and poetry was the subject of regular debate, though the terms of the analogy between film and poetry were never precisely specified. In practice, the film poem label was primarily an emblem of the avant-garde's difference from the commercial narrative film.

The film/poem analogy is nevertheless suggestive of certain practices and expectations. In the first place, as poems are generally shorter than novels, film poems are usually short compared to the standard two-hour feature film. The abbreviated form of the film poem not only betrays its tenuous financial situation, but suggests greater emotional and spiritual intensity. The novelistic cinema was concerned with action; the film poem sought to represent, or better, to recreate a realm of feeling. Like poetry, especially as it was practiced in the United States after the war, the film poem encouraged experiments with untraditional forms and techniques. Above all, the film poem is personal, and not merely in the sense that such films were the product of an artisan mode of production, in which filmmakers usually wrote, shot, and edited their own films. The film poem is also personal in the sense that the proper subject matter of the film poem was the filmmaker's own experience. As we shall see, the significance of this notion is hard to exaggerate.

By identifying the post-war American avant-garde with the film poem, I have risked some confusion that I would do well to clarify. Overviews of the American independent or experimental film in the 1950s, such as those that appeared in *Film Culture*, generally identified two genres: the film poem and the graphic cinema. As one such review saw the avant-garde of the late 1950s, there were the "cine-poets," concerned with the representation of subjectivity, and the "cine-plasts," concerned with the manipulation of the plastics of the image (Mekas 1955).

In the European avant-garde of the 1920s, the subjective cinema and the graphic cinema represented two reasonably distinct approaches to film experimentation. In *The Cubist Cinema*, Standish Lawder traces the development of a European graphic cinema that aimed to apply the formal devices of early Modernist painting to film. As their musical titles suggest, works like Hans Richter's *Rhythmus 21* (1921), Viking Eggeling's *Symphonie Diagonale* (c. 1925) and Fernand Léger's *Ballet Mécanique* (1924) tend toward abstraction in their play with film technique. On the other hand, in works like Jean Epstein's *La Glace à Trois Faces* (1927), Germaine Dulac's *La Souriante Madame Beudet* (1922) and Dimitri Kirsanov's *Ménilmontant* (1926), experimental film techniques represent the subjective states of characters.

In the American avant-garde cinema, the two approaches are not so distinct, and my talk of the poetic strain is meant to encompass them both; however, my label "poetic strain" gives pre-eminence to the cine-poets for two reasons. First, the avant-garde's own critical rhetoric, in Parker Tyler's criticism and in *Film Culture*'s coverage of the 1950s, concentrated on the film poem and relegated the graphic cinema to secondary status. Second, increasingly, even abstract films were taken to be representations of psychological states. Jordan Belson's abstract films, for example, have been inevitably understood as attempts to render states of disembodied consciousness attained through extended, intense meditation (or through hallucinogens).[1] Likewise, by the late 1950s, the influence of the graphic cinema had transformed the subjective tradition. For example, Marie Menken's abstract imagery and her means of producing it became staples of her friend Stan Brakhage's work, as shown by *Anticipation of the Night* (1958), an early example of Brakhage's mature style. As a consequence of such cross-fertilization, by the time Brakhage made *Anticipation of the Night*, the graphic and the subjective traditions had merged into a *mode* of filmmaking: a historically distinct set of norms of film construction and comprehension.[2] In the two decades after WWII, this mode was virtually synonymous with the film poem. Today this mode is more diverse; we usually call it the avant-garde cinema, and it includes not only the film poem, but all three strains of filmmaking I address in this book.

What I mean by the poetic strain, then, is something more pervasive than specific types of avant-garde film, such as Tyler's "trance" film or Sitney's "lyrical" film, though these are certainly examples of it. The poetic avant-garde includes a fairly broad spectrum of work. One end of this spectrum is marked by films we often think of as abstract, such as the work of Menken, Harry Smith and John and James Whitney. The other end is marked by experimental narratives, such as those of Maya Deren, Sidney Peterson and Kenneth Anger. And in the middle of this spectrum are the prototypically lyrical films, such as the work of Brakhage and Bruce Baillie. From our post-*Wavelength* (1966–67) vantage point, it is tempting to think of the film poem as a closed chapter in the history of the American avant-garde cinema, but works by M. M. Serra, Michael Hoolboom,

Janis Crystal Lipzin, Phil Solomon, Luther Price, Su Friedrich and Betzy Bromberg attest to its continuing vitality. Speaking generally, the poetic avant-garde is not so much a specific kind of film as it is an approach to cinema, with a set of principles of film construction and implicit viewing procedures modelled roughly on those of modern poetry.

It would be impossible to specify precisely, step by step, how the viewer of the poetic avant-garde goes about making sense of one of these films. The poetic avant-garde encourages experimentation and places a premium on novelty; its films are remarkably varied. But viewers familiar with the general contours of the poetic avant-garde can apply a few rules of thumb to help them integrate the film's details into a coherent, though not necessarily highly unified, whole. To put it in the terms laid out in the last chapter, these rules of thumb, what problem-solving theorists call heuristics, help viewers match local detail with more global schemata. My aim in this chapter is to spell out some of these heuristics.

A Mode of Subjectivity

More than any other filmmaking tradition, with the possible exception of the home movie, the American avant-garde is thought to be a personal cinema. Avant-garde filmmakers generally shoot and edit their own films; quite often they perform in them as well. And historically at least, avant-garde filmmakers have financed their films out of their own pockets. With rare exceptions, grant money and academic positions became available to a select group of avant-garde filmmakers only since the 1970s.[3] The avant-garde as a whole, then, is personal in the sense that the filmmaker has personal responsibility for, and control over, most aspects of production. But particularly in the poetic strain of the avant-garde, the notion that these are personal films has important implications for how viewers make sense of them.

One implication of the assumption that the filmmaker has personal control over the film is that viewers tend to see the poetic avant-garde film as autonomous, standing apart from traditions and genres. Of course, this plays nicely into the assumption that the avant-garde is a systematic rejection of tradition. But it also makes the film poem an open, unpredictable experience, at least relative to other modes of cinema. Our response to the commercial film is shaped not only intrinsically, by the structure of the film itself, but extrinsically, by a set of reasonably specific expectations derived from our knowledge of narrative cinema. We expect to see a protagonist clearly identified, and we expect the protagonist's pursuit of his or her goals to map the overall trajectory of the film. And in the Hollywood tradition, we will, of course, expect this pursuit to end happily. In genre films these expectations are even more specific. But the institutional factors that shape the commercial narrative film do not pertain to the poetic avant-garde, in which the viewer's cycles of anticipation and satisfaction derive primarily from the film's intrinsic structure. I am not suggesting that the avant-garde is not shaped by institutions, nor am I suggesting that we have no extrinsic expectations when we view a poetic avant-garde film.[4] But our confidence in the filmmaker's autonomy and personal control over the film makes the experience of the poetic film relatively unpredictable, and the strategies viewers use for coping with such films must be relatively open-ended.

The poetic avant-garde film is personal not only in the sense that it is personally controlled by the filmmaker, but also in that it addresses the *private* concerns of the filmmaker. Many film poems document intimate moments of the filmmaker's life. The diary film, whose most notable practitioner is Jonas Mekas, is founded on the impulse to collect images of private moments. In the work of David Brooks, we see such images not only in his diary films, but in epistolary form in *Letter to D. H. in Paris* (1967). And many of Brakhage's films are about extremely private events: masturbation (*Flesh of Morning* [1956]), quarrelling and lovemaking (*Wedlock House: An Intercourse* [1959]), childbirth (*Window Water Baby Moving* [1959] and *Thigh Line Lyre Triangular* [1961]). The link between the autonomy of the poetic avant-garde and its private subject matter in Brakhage's work is nicely summed up by David James: "In the blankest rejection of the history of the medium, he made home movies the essential practice of film" (35).

The poetic film does not concern itself exclusively with moments of personal intimacy. Even in Brakhage's work there are films addressing popular culture (*Aftermath* [1981]), the Vietnam War (*23rd Psalm Branch* [1966/78]) and violence (*Murder Psalm* [1981]). His Pittsburgh trilogy (1971) is a set of documentaries about public institutions: a hospital (*Deus Ex*), the police force (*eyes*), and a morgue (*The Act of Seeing with One's Own Eyes*).[5] However, the Pittsburgh trilogy is somewhat anomalous in Brakhage's films; engagement with the contradictions and traumas of twentieth-century life is more central to Bruce Baillie's work. Baillie's *Mass for the Dakota Sioux* (1963–64) views the American landscape and culture as a wasteland founded on the destruction of a native culture. In Baillie's *Quixote* (1964–65), the settlement of the western United States is seen as an imperialist conquest and is linked to the civil rights struggle of the 1950s and 1960s and the Vietnam War. Nevertheless, in the poetic avant-garde such public places and events are inevitably personalized: even at the highest level of their political engagement, these films ultimately are about the filmmaker's way of seeing these places and events.

The heightened and pervasive subjectivity of the film poem made it easy for early critics to legitimize the avant-garde cinema by connecting it to the concerns of modern art. In a 1960 essay titled "Dream Structure: The Basis of Experimental Film," Parker Tyler defended the film poem against charges that it was decadent, obscure and incomprehensible by comparing it to modern poetry: "Modern poetry is especially complex and 'irregular'; its basic order, like that of dreams, is the psychic order of association and suggestibleness. A 'poem,' one might remark, is what a cine-poem normally sets out to be" (61). Tyler went on to argue that true art must engage an expanded notion of reality that includes not just the external world but the imagination:

> Among the greatest works of drama, poetry, and painting, nature and "normal" reality are indeed usually present but sometimes, notably, in symbolic forms of all kinds. The imagination uses facts only as starting points, as elements of composition, for a total form *expressing* if not always *identical with* a complete human experience.
>
> As a human motive, art has its genesis within man, and without this basic innerness, man is not a living soul but a living thing. (62–63)

Tyler's essay is not just a description of a common preoccupation of poetic filmmakers. Neither is it merely an effort to legitimize the avant-garde cinema. Tyler's appeal to the film poem's "basic innerness" is an early attempt to lay out a strategy for making sense of the poetic strain of the American avant-garde cinema. Against charges that the film poem was obscure and incomprehensible, Tyler argued that the film poem should be seen as analogous to the dream or the hallucination. Viewers could understand these films, Tyler suggested, by personifying the camera as a stand-in for the filmmaker's consciousness, "for the camera is capable of imitating all mental impulses, whether as simple as shifting gaze or as complex as a sudden hallucination" (63).

The kind of personification strategies that Tyler introduced to the avant-garde cinema are more systematically laid out in David Bordwell's study of film interpretation (1989). Bordwell argues that some kinds of personification are fundamental to the comprehension of all types of film. Since "humans are predisposed, biologically and culturally, to attend to humanlike agents in representations" (153), critics and viewers try to organize elements of films around such humanlike entities. The most available humanlike entities, of course, are characters. When we see a body (usually human, but not always) represented in a film, we personify it by attributing to it traits, thoughts, feelings or goals. This much is just an inescapable part of basic comprehension. Bordwell goes on to argue that critics can extend this strategy of personification to produce what the institution of film criticism sanctions as novel and persuasive interpretations. One basic way a critic might use the personification strategy to advance a novel interpretation of a film is by making characters "stand for" various positions, ideas, and ways of life, and by interpreting conflicts between characters as clashes between these positions, ideas or ways of life.

Bordwell goes on to suggest two personification strategies that bear directly on the comprehension of the poetic avant-garde. Using the first of these strategies, critics—of all kinds of films—commonly attribute humanlike qualities not only to a film's characters, but to the filmmaker. This personification is made easier if the filmmaker is embodied in the film (through a voice-over, for example), though such embodiment is not necessary. Once the filmmaker is personified, critics can interpret the elements of the film as evidence of the filmmaker's interests, thoughts, feelings, or goals.

As Bordwell points out, the personification-of-the-filmmaker strategy is widely used by interpreters of the avant-garde cinema. Bordwell is primarily concerned with the task of film critics, whose aim is to produce novel interpretations of films. But in the poetic avant-garde, personifying the filmmaker is not the prerogative solely of critics; viewers do it, too, as part of their basic comprehension of the film. In fact, the personification of the filmmaker is a basic condition of intelligibility of the poetic strain of the avant-garde. To make sense of *Psycho* (1960), a viewer need not personify the filmmaker as voyeuristic or misogynistic, traits we associate with Hitchcock; one can make sense of *Psycho* without thinking of Hitchcock at all. But one cannot make sense of *Scenes from Under Childhood* (four parts, 1967–70) without thinking of Brakhage and attributing a personality to the film's source. Likewise, without considering a film like Jonas Mekas's *Reminiscences of a Journey to Lithuania* (1971–72) to be a personal diary, one cannot make any sense of it whatsoever. We assume that images and sounds in a film poem have as their source an individual filmmaker who has (almost) complete control over the film. Without such an assumption, many elements of these films, and sometimes whole films, would be unintelligible.

The general strategy of personifying the filmmaker suggests specific heuristics viewers can use to make sense of the poetic strain of the avant-garde film. The most basic of these is: make sense of the film by relating it to the concerns of the filmmaker. For example, Peter Hutton's *New York Near Sleep for Saskia* (1972) consists of a series of beautifully photographed, deserted, mostly urban spaces (Fig. 3.1). The film is black-and-white, and silent. The most remarkable feature of these images, other than their beauty, is their lack of movement. So still are these images that we might mistake some of them for photographs. If we know nothing about the filmmaker, this heuristic suggests only that we understand the film as an expression of the filmmaker's interest in what is shown. Since Hutton's film is filled with images of deserted New York streets, we understand that Hutton thinks deserted New York streets are worth filming, and that images of them are worth looking at. Of course, we will probably try to figure out *why* he would be interested in such things, using any available cues to determine his attitude toward these scenes. In *New York Near Sleep for Saskia* such cues are few, but we can speculate: perhaps he is fascinated with the beauty of these spaces; the emptiness of these spaces gives the film a melancholy mood—perhaps he wishes to express the sadness these spaces evoke for him. If we have some independent knowledge of Hutton and his work (as we might if he were present at the screening to discuss his films), this heuristic suggests that we make sense of the film by relating it to the filmmaker's life and work. With *New York Near Sleep for Saskia*, we would understand that such evocative, nearly still black-and-white images are Hutton's stylistic trademark. We might know that Hutton lives in New York and that he sees his films as a kind of journal in which he records the spaces in which he lives. And we might know that Hutton sees his work as an exploration of the boundary between

Fig. 3.1

film and photography, and as an exploration of the experience of time. If the filmmaker's work is unified around such a "project," knowledge of this project can help the viewer make sense of otherwise puzzling images.

Another heuristic derived from the personification of the filmmaker suggests that we try to understand the characters of the film poem as stand-ins for the filmmaker. Call this the character-as-filmmaker heuristic. This heuristic is easiest to apply when the filmmaker actually appears in the film, which is common in diary films and in the work of Brakhage, Baillie, Maya Deren and Jack Smith, among others. When the filmmaker appears in the film, we can sometimes make sense of the film as a straightforward autobiography, in which we assume that the body in the film actually *is* the filmmaker. This is a basic assumption about diary films. And many of the films in which Brakhage appears can be understood as documentaries of the everyday lives of the Brakhage family. Granted, the style of his films may be a bit obscure, but when we see Brakhage's grinning face at the end of *Window Water Baby Moving* we have no trouble understanding that that persona is identical with the Brakhage who held the camera and later edited the film.

Filmmakers often appear in poetic avant-garde films in roles that we cannot simply assume are identical with the filmmaker. But even then, this character-as-filmmaker heuristic suggests that we try to understand the character played by the filmmaker as equivalent to the filmmaker him- or herself in some respects. We might, for example, be able to make sense of the film as a kind of fictionalized autobiography, in which the events shown, although staged, nevertheless represent some aspect of the filmmaker's life. Consider, for instance, Maya Deren's *Meshes of the Afternoon* (1943). We might try to understand the ambivalent relationship between Deren's character and her lover (played by Deren's husband, Alexander Hammid) as a working through of tensions in their real-life marriage. I do not know what evidence actually supports such interpretations; Deren herself discouraged them in the program notes written for a screening of her work in 1960 (cited in Sitney 1979, 13). But the urge to interpret as a kind of autobiography a poetic avant-garde film in which the filmmaker appears is practically irresistible. Parker Tyler asserts that Deren's film is about the "death of her narcissistic youth" (cited in Sitney 1979, 10); for Sitney the film is also Hammid's portrait of his young wife (1979, 10).

If we can't link the elements of the film to the details of the filmmaker's biography, another variant of the character-as-filmmaker heuristic may be useful: make sense of the character's activities as somehow analogous to the activity of filmmaking. Even if we do not know anything about the filmmaker, even if the filmmaker does not appear in the film, we can still interpret the film as a weak form of autobiography. Of course, if the filmmaker does appear, that provides a strong cue about which character to try to analogize to the filmmaker. We find such stand-ins for the film artist throughout the poetic avant-garde cinema: in the blind man in Brakhage's *Reflections on Black*

Fig. 3.2

Fig. 3.3

(1955) (Fig. 3.2), in the young man (poet Michael McClure) exploring the sights of San Francisco in Larry Jordan's *Visions of a City* (shot 1957, edited 1978), even in the wandering, disembodied eye of the mad artist in Sidney Peterson's *The Cage* (1947) (Fig. 3.3).

The work of Kenneth Anger demonstrates the usefulness of this heuristic. Consider *Lucifer Rising* (1980), Anger's film about the invocation of the spirit of Lucifer. For Anger, Lucifer represents not Satan but the Light God, whose motto is, according to Anger, "The Key of Joy is Disobedience" (cited in Haller 1980, 8). In *Lucifer Rising*, Anger plays a magus whose rituals put into play the forces of nature, personified by the mythical figures of Isis, Osiris, Lilith, and Chaos. These mythical figures, in turn, bring Lucifer forth. It is quite easy to see Anger the filmmaker as parallel to the magus in *Lucifer Rising*. In a literal sense, Anger has orchestrated the appearances of these mythical figures by staging and shooting the film, just as the magus makes them appear through ritual. Metaphorically, we might view Anger-the-filmmaker as the magus-like orchestrator of cinematic effects: he has mobilized these forces (that is to say, these images and sounds) to awe and amaze the viewer. We might even take this one step further, and suggest that Anger actually *is* a magus who invokes Lucifer through the film. Anger himself proposes such an interpretation:

> I'm showing actual ceremonies in the film; what is performed in front of the camera won't be a re-enactment and the purpose will be to make Lucifer rise. . . . It's the birthday party for the Aquarian age . . . Everything I've been saying so far has been leading up to this. I've been exploring myself and now I've got to communicate it. Lucifer is the Rebel Angel behind what's happening in the world today. (cited in Haller 1980, 8)

Critics have been eager to apply the character-as-filmmaker heuristic to Anger's work by seeing Anger as such a magus and by interpreting his films as invocations of supernatural forces. For example, in his appraisal of Anger's oeuvre, David James uses the character-as-filmmaker heuristic to link Anger to the magi that appear throughout Anger's films: "Thus Lucifer inhabits Anger's cinema as both the figure of its mythology and its basis as formal practice and material event. As an agent of Lucifer, Anger documents magic, and his practice is itself magic; his lifework is MAGICK, the cinematograph is his Magical Weapon, and his films are a Magick Lantern Cycle, all illuminating Lucifer and illuminated by him" (150–51). In fact, according to James, Anger is akin to a Lucifer-invoking magus even when his films do not explicitly show a magus character, as in *Scorpio Rising* (1963). In James's view, just as Lucifer is poised between the forces of light and the forces of darkness, Anger is poised between two analogous forces: the independent cinema and the Hollywood cinema his work so often cites. James's analysis points up the reason critics are so ready to see Anger's work as a "Luciferian" cinema. Given the motto Anger attributes to him, "The Key of Joy is Disobedience," Lucifer emblematizes the "disobedience" of the avant-garde cinema as a whole.

Bordwell identifies a second personification strategy: personification of the film's *style*, especially the cinematography, as a representation of the filmmaker's consciousness. This is the strategy Tyler had proposed for the poetic avant-garde. Bordwell finds this strategy used by critics of all kinds of film. As he puts it:

> The camera construct allows the critic to posit the image as a perceptual activity (that is, as a framed vision), as a trace of mental or emotional processes (something is shown because it is significant, or shocking), and as a bearer of decisions or traits (the camera deliberately shows us this, is obsessed with that). Once such properties are ascribed to the camera, the critic is free to map them onto the filmmaker, the narrator, or other personified agents. (163)

Once again, in the poetic avant-garde, this strategy is not limited to critics who aim to produce novel interpretations of films, but is used by viewers in the course of their basic comprehension.

This notion that a film's style can be seen as a representation of consciousness suggests heuristics that are particularly useful for making sense of the strange stylistic devices one finds in the poetic avant-garde film. As I have suggested, the poetic avant-garde places a premium on novelty, and it encourages filmmakers to experiment with novel means of producing and manipulating images. But if these novel images are not to be dismissed as mere experiments, they must be placed in contexts that make them meaningful. Thus, the task for filmmakers and viewers is to find ways of making sense of the anomalous imagery characteristic of the poetic strain of the avant-garde. We might phrase this style-as-consciousness heuristic as: interpret overt manipulations of film style, especially camerawork and editing, as evidence of the filmmaker's response to what is shown in the images.

One simple way to apply this heuristic is to interpret the camera as the filmmaker's sight. Consider, for example, Jordan's *Visions of a City*, a collection of city street scenes reflected in windows, bumpers of cars, bottles, and so on. The sound track consists of soft, vaguely Eastern music, until we hear the noise of traffic near the end. The film has something like a protagonist in the figure of a young man who walks the streets and looks around. Using the character-as-filmmaker heuristic we can see this young man as the filmmaker's stand-in by interpreting his looking around as analogous to the filmmaker's collecting and editing of the images. But the would-be protagonist is pushed to the margins of the film; we see him repeatedly, but only in glimpses of his reflections. And the film does not explicitly attribute the imagery to the character's vision. Thus, the imagery is not wholly comprehensible as the vision of this character. The peculiar quality of these images (they are all reflections) suggests that we use the style-as-consciousness heuristic to understand them as the filmmaker's vision. This means, of course, that we will have to explain why the filmmaker might want to look at such things. In general, we may see the film as an expression of the filmmaker's interest in, or fascination with, these reflections. More specifically, we can see the film as an attempt to draw out the connections between disparate objects, like car bumpers and store windows, or as the filmmaker's novel way of looking at street scenes.

Our interest in the stylistic experimentation of the poetic avant-garde lies not in its ability to mimic the filmmaker's mere sight, but in its ability to replicate other, more profound aspects of the film-maker's inner life. To phrase this as another heuristic: interpret overt manipulation of film style as a representation of an altered mental state, such as a dream, memory, hallucination, or fantasy.

This heuristic is easiest to apply when a framing situation marks a segment of the film as a representation of the mental life of a character. In *Meshes of the Afternoon*, for example, a woman reclines in a chair, and we see a close-up of an eye closing. It is relatively easy to infer that what follows is her dream (although the end of this dream is not so unequivocally marked). This explicit (though open-ended) framing situation yields two kinds of useful information: it identifies whose mental life we are seeing, and what mental state is producing the imagery. It is useful to know whose mental life we are seeing because what we know about the character's concerns can help us make sense of his or her mental life. In *Meshes of the Afternoon* we learn only a little: we see that the dreamer is a woman, and we see her perform several seemingly inconsequential actions before falling asleep: she picks up a flower, she glimpses a figure in black; she unlocks the door to a house and enters; she takes the tone arm off a spinning record. This does not give us a clear picture of her fears or desires, but even this minimal framing situation aids our comprehension. We will make our interpretation of these images consistent with what we take to be the concerns of a woman in her twenties who might enter a middle class home and take a nap. The same images would be interpreted quite differently if they were framed as the dream of a man who had broken into the house and fallen asleep. Knowing what *kind* of mental imagery we see also aids comprehension. If, as in *Meshes of the Afternoon*, the segment is framed as a dream, we expect material from the dreamer's life to be re-worked to express her fears and desires. Again, the same images would have a quite different effect were they framed as a drunken stupor.

A framing situation that tells us whose mental life we are seeing and what mental state is producing the imagery provides a great deal of useful information. But in the poetic avant-garde cinema, framing situations are rarely so explicit. For example, Brakhage's *The Way to Shadow Garden* (1954) identifies the source of the mental imagery but does not tell us what kind of mental image we see. The film concerns a young man who, preparing to go to bed, is tormented by some powerful but ill-defined anxiety. He puts out his eyes with his fingers and staggers out of his room. As he is writhing in the doorway, the image switches to negative and the abrasive sound we have been hearing is replaced by slightly more soothing sound. The young man moves into the garden outside, and we see shots of the flowers, apparently sometimes from his point-of-view, but always in negative. On one hand, the images of the garden in negative are rather clearly attributed to the young man. When the camera pulls away from him in the film's last shot, the image switches back to positive. But on the other hand, nothing explains what kind of experience the images in negative represent. They are not his literal sight because he has blinded himself. He does not go to sleep, nor has he taken drugs. In the film's penultimate shot, we see him looking into the camera, suggesting that through his blindness, he has recovered some kind of alternative vision. The nature of this vision remains mysterious, but the film invites us to contemplate what other mode of being or seeing might be symbolized by the images in negative. (Following the discussion in chapter 1 on the importance of alternative kinds of vision in Brakhage's work, we can use the character-as-filmmaker heuristic to understand the young man's blindness and his recovery of sight as analogous to Brakhage's quest for an authentic, original style of filmmaking. And, if we are so inclined, we can use this analogy to interpret details of the film that otherwise remain mysterious. The young man's anxiety is thus Brakhage's anxiety about his creative powers; the gouging of his eyes is Brakhage's forceful rejection of conventional film form; and so on.)

The Way to Shadow Garden leaves open the question of what kind of mental imagery is symbolized by the footage in negative, but it does identify a character as the source of this imagery. Often in the poetic avant-garde, such anomalous imagery is not even given a source. Where we do not have even a minimal framing situation, we have to rely on internal cues to interpret novel or distorted imagery as a representation of an altered mental state. Of course, this is often difficult because most mental states do not have a definite structure or definite subject matter. A dream, for example, could be about any subject and take just about any form. This looseness is one reason such mental states are attractive models for the poetic avant-garde film: they provide a measure of coherence, but countenance a wide range of experimentation. Nevertheless, we can sometimes infer which mental state is represented on the basis of internal cues.

Tom Chomont's *Oblivion* (1969) is one such film poem with no framing situation. In four minutes we see a rapid-fire montage of images, some as short as two frames. Many images are altered: some are upside-down or backwards, some are superimposed, and some are made by printing a color positive through a high-contrast black-and-white negative. This latter technique produces an effect something like solarization: the deepest shadows are reversed to glowing white, and the colors in the middle and highlight areas appear more saturated (Fig. 3.4). The film has a definite erotic overtone, due partly to the heightened color and grain of the altered images, but due also to images of the naked or partly naked body of a man. A few times we glimpse images of the man's genitals and of hands stroking his body (Fig. 3.5). On the basis of these erotic images, the heightened sensuality of the altered film images, and the overall tempo of the film, J. J. Murphy (1979) sees *Oblivion* as a representation of a masturbation fantasy: "The tempo of the film builds and then releases—almost as if to prolong the erotic pleasure—as the surges of tension rise toward orgasm, which

Fig. 3.4

Fig. 3.5

is, after all, the 'oblivion' of the film's title'' (122). Let me reiterate that Murphy is able to comprehend the film as a representation of a particular kind of mental state—a masturbation fantasy—without any explicit framing situation. But the few suggestive cues he finds in the film underdetermine this interpretation. I do not say this to dispute Murphy's analysis; *Oblivion* is one of those films that encourage play with what I called free interpretation sets in chapter 2. My point is that in order to see the film as a masturbation fantasy Murphy must use cues in the film, as well as the style-as-consciousness heuristic.

The equation of aspects of film style, especially camerawork, with the filmmaker's consciousness has a long history in the poetic avant-garde cinema. We have seen that Tyler suggests such an equation. Brakhage makes the link between cinema and a kind of vision the cornerstone of his theory and filmmaking. But the most extensive historical examination of this notion is found in P. Adams Sitney's *Visionary Film*. For Sitney, the representation of human consciousness is the central trope of the American avant-garde cinema. And he sees the history of that cinema as the search for progressively more direct forms of representing consciousness. Thus, in Sitney's view, the difference between *The Way to Shadow Garden* and *Oblivion* is a question of the formal evolution of the avant-garde film. Trance films, such as *The Way to Shadow Garden*, are relatively primitive in that their representation of consciousness requires the mediating figure of a character. On the other hand, in lyrical films, such as *Oblivion*, consciousness is represented directly, without being framed and mediated by a specific character.

The historical trajectory traced by Sitney has important consequences for the ways viewers make sense of the poetic avant-garde film. The evolution from the trance film to the lyrical film suggests a gradual shaping of the viewer's strategies of comprehension. Viewers attribute the imagery in the trance film to the consciousness of the filmmaker only transitively. The film gives us the consciousness of a character; then the character-as-filmmaker heuristic equates the character's vision with that of the filmmaker. But as this trance figure became more marginal in films like *Anticipation of the Night* and *Visions of a City*, a style-as-consciousness heuristic (proposed by Tyler and Brakhage at the end of the 1950s) attributes the distortion and alteration of the imagery directly to the filmmaker's consciousness. By the time Murphy wrote about *Oblivion* (in 1979), any experienced avant-garde film viewer could use the style-as-consciousness heuristic to make sense of overt manipulations of film style by attributing them to some sort of altered perception or consciousness. I am not challenging Sitney's argument concerning the evolution of the form of the avant-garde film.[6] I am only pointing out that this history is not merely an evolution of film form, but an evolution of the ways viewers make sense of the poetic strain of the avant-garde cinema.

Coherence of Detail

Heuristics derived from the personification of filmmakers and film style provide viewers with ways to begin to make sense of the images and sounds in a poetic avant-garde film. But viewers must still work out the details. At the local level, viewers must integrate details into meaningful units. And at the global level, viewers must integrate these meaningful units into large-scale schematic structures.

At the local level, the film poem requires many of the same comprehension strategies as do other kinds of films. In particular, viewers must be prepared to use general world knowledge to infer the links between one shot and the next.[7] Often these links are causal. Consider, for example, a shot of a smoking gun followed by a shot of a person lying on the floor. Given what we know about guns and about where people typically lie down, we infer that the person has been wounded by the gun. Causal links between successive shots are common, and especially useful, in all sorts of films, including avant-garde films. But links inferred on the basis of world knowledge are not exclusively causal. Successive shots might show different aspects of the same object or situation. Or they might show various examples of the same concept. Or two things that are opposites. It is probably impossible (and unnecessary, I hope) to spell out every such relationship; my point is that in viewing avant-garde films we are constantly called upon to make inferences based on our knowledge of the world, just as we are in viewing any kind of film.

Of course, the avant-garde film also calls on us to make inferences about the relationship between adjacent shots in some more specialized ways. One set of common film-viewing heuristics lets viewers establish spatial relationships between shots on the basis of cues provided by the continuity editing system. The poetic avant-garde film does not make full use of the continuity editing system. It does, however, make heavy use of several continuity devices that establish spatial and temporal links, such as the match-on-action, the frame cut and the eye-line match. In commercial narrative films, these devices are strong cues of spatial or temporal continuity. But in the poetic avant-garde, they are just as likely to be signs of fantasy, thought, memory or other subjective experience. Eye-lines are particularly important cues of subjectivity in the poetic avant-garde, as they are in much film viewing. The poetic avant-garde is filled with images of characters looking, because ''vision'' is a common theme. But eye-lines do not always establish literal sight, and viewers must be prepared to understand the eye-line match as a mark of subjectivity.

Other continuity devices suggest subjective states as well. For example, near the end of *Meshes of the Afternoon*, successive close-ups of Maya Deren's feet show her stepping on a beach, then grass, mud, concrete and finally a carpet. Though her movements continue smoothly from shot to shot, the space changes radically. Since our knowledge of geography and architecture tells us that the spatial and temporal continuity suggested by Deren's movements is impossible, we must explain the relationship between these shots some other way. In most poetic avant-garde films, such impossible inter-shot relationships are consistent with a character's subjective state—in *Meshes of the Afternoon*, this sequence is one of several indications that the body of the film is a dream. We might phrase the poetic avant-garde's continuity heuristic as: be suspicious of the spatial and temporal continuity suggested by devices of continuity editing, and be prepared to interpret such juxtapositions of shots as the subjective experience of the character.

One of the most fundamental and useful strategies for establishing local coherence in any kind of film is establishing coreference between shots. In other words, viewers must establish whether what they see in one shot is the same thing seen in the adjacent shots. At its most basic, this means that after seeing one shot we check to see if the next shot is of the same thing shot from a different distance or angle. We might see a long shot of a person, followed by a medium close-up of the person. If we recognize the coreference of these two shots, we can integrate them into a single meaningful unit, some shots of a person. Coreference is often more complex. Imagine this sequence: flowers by a picket fence; an old-fashioned fire truck moving slowly down the street; more flowers; children at a corner by a crossing guard; a man watering his lawn. The objects represented in each of these images are not exactly the same, but we can integrate these diverse images into a unified representation of a peaceful, small town (in which David Lynch's film *Blue Velvet* is set). The processing advantage is clear: once we establish the coreference of multiple shots, we need remember only the single, overarching representation.

When objects and spaces are clearly seen and part of familiar schemata, as they usually are in commercial narratives, establishing coreference is not difficult. In the poetic avant-garde film, however, establishing coreference is more challenging. Identifying objects and spaces in the images is harder because images may have been altered by a wide range of techniques: special optical effects, such as superimposition; extremely rapid editing; unsteady camera movement; scratching or painting directly on the film. Avant-garde filmmakers also tend to present less than obvious aspects of the things they are showing. They do not necessarily shoot objects from angles that present the most familiar, recognizable view. And they do not choose to show the parts of scenes or actions that we usually associate with those scenes or actions. For example, at the beginning of *Anticipation of the Night*, Brakhage introduces the figure who will function intermittently as the protagonist with close-ups of his hands, shots of his shadow (Figs. 3.6, 3.7) and a glimpse of his reflection in a window. It would be easy to miss the coreference and see instead shots of hands, shots of a wall, and shots of a window. In the avant-garde, viewers must look aggressively to establish coreference. As a heuristic, we might put it this way: establish coreference whenever possible, even by using what might seem to be minor elements in an image.

There are other strategies for dealing with the kind of fragmentation seen in *Anticipation of the Night*. As many writers have pointed out, the avant-garde film is characterized by spatial fragmentation and rapid cutting. This is true, but it does not explain the role fragmentation plays in the film. Fragmentation is not a goal in itself, used only because it differs from the commercial narrative; it is the by-product of a representational system that is dominated by specific

Fig. 3.6

Fig. 3.7

types of metonymy and metaphor—what I will call the avant-garde's *radicalized rhetoric*.

Metonymy is a rhetorical figure in which an object or event is represented by an image of something that is causally or spatially associated with it. This is a very common device in narratives. Representations of the individual events that make up the links in the narrative's chain of causes and effects are extremely malleable in all kinds of narratives. If one of the events is a trip, for example, the narrative might represent it by including lots of detail: packing bags, hailing a cab, getting into the cab, telling the driver to go to the airport, buying an airline ticket, boarding the plane, and so on. In fact, the sequence is infinitely expandable. More commonly, though, it is also reducible: a single shot of the character in an airplane allows the viewer to infer the whole trip. This form of metonymy is a very common technique for presenting everyday events in an economical way: one image is made to stand for a whole range of events spatially or causally associated with it. But metonymy can be used in more dramatic ways, too. In Fritz Lang's *M* (1931), young Elsie Beckman is stalked by a child murderer who buys her candy and a balloon before he kills her. The actual murder, however, is not shown; we must infer it from a shot of her balloon tangled in power lines. We can call this *radical metonymy*:[8] instead of seeing a central part of the event, or something closely associated with the event, we see only a marginal detail, and the inference we make is more difficult and less certain. In most modes of narrative filmmaking, such inferences are ultimately confirmed. In *M*, Elsie's murder is confirmed in the next scene.

In the avant-garde film, metonymy is often radical, and metonymic inferences often go unconfirmed. For example, consider again the segment of *The End* (1953) in which we see a man pass through a turnstile at Golden Gate Park. This image metonymically represents his suicide, because we associate the Golden Gate Bridge with suicide. There is no direct confirmation that the character has killed himself, though every other segment of the film ends with the death of its main character. Thus, when confronted with the radical metonymy characteristic of the poetic avant-garde, we must be prepared to make bold inferences and live without confirmation.

Poetic avant-garde filmmakers also make use of metaphor. In this rhetorical device, an object or event is replaced not with an image causally or spatially associated with it, but with an image that shares some of its semantic features. For example, in *The End*, a character's struggle to escape is metaphorically represented by images of flying birds and a close-up of an arm straining to lift a dumbbell.

There are a number of differences between metaphors in the poetic avant-garde film and those in other modes of filmmaking. First, in the poetic avant-garde these metaphoric images tend to be non-diegetic. In the example from *The End*, the image of the arm with the dumbbell is not part of the character's fictional world. Most metaphors in commercial narrative films are diegetic, making them less disruptive. If viewers miss the metaphor, they can still interpret the image as an element of setting, since it is part of the fictional world. And if they do notice the metaphor, the narration still remains relatively inconspicuous. Poetic avant-garde films typically do not create a consistent fictional world; to the extent they do, intrusions like non-diegetic metaphors are not only permitted but encouraged. In addition, metaphors are much more common in the poetic avant-garde than they are in most modes of commercial filmmaking.

The avant-garde film also uses *radical metaphors*: we see the metaphorical replacement but not the original narrative event. In a non-radical metaphor, to use the terminology introduced by I. A. Richards, we see both the tenor and the vehicle, both the original object or event and the image that metaphorically stands for it. To use a well-known example, near the end of Eisenstein's *Strike* (1925), we see both the Cossacks' attack on the workers *and* the slaughter of the bull. The metaphor emphasizes the innocence of the workers and the brutality of the attack, but the narrative sequence would be comprehensible even if we were to miss the metaphor, because all the key events are explicitly shown. But because a radical metaphor shows only the vehicle and not the tenor, missing the metaphor poses a more serious threat to comprehension. In *Reflections on Black*, a blind man "sees" several couples' abortive attempts to interact. The last episode ends with a shot of a coffee pot boiling over, but there is no explicit resolution of the personal relationship. The ending would seem arbitrary if not for the metaphorical value of the closing image. The shot of the coffee pot metaphorically suggests the release of the sexual tension that is built up in each episode but never explicitly released or resolved. This is a radical metaphor; we never see what literally happens to the characters. But whether the coffee pot metaphor represents the successful union of one of the couples, or is an ironic comment on the failure of these couplings, the film provides a measure of closure only through a metaphorical reading of the last images.[9] As this example suggests, the interpretation of the poetic avant-garde's radical metaphors is more difficult, more important to comprehension and less certain than the interpretation of metaphors in most other modes of filmmaking.

So far we have discussed the ways viewers of the poetic avant-garde establish local coherence through the conceptual, or semantic, structure of the images. In the poetic avant-garde film, local coherence also derives from patterns in the images' *surface* structure, the configuration of colors, shapes and movements that the perceptual system usually interprets as a representation of a three-dimensional scene.

At the local level, establishing surface coherence is not especially complicated. We simply do not have many familiar schemata for relationships among the colors, shapes and movements in images. We are exquisitely sensitive to the relationships among the events in a causal chain, but we recognize relationships among the surface qualities of images only if they are very simple. In fact, the only relationships we are especially prepared to notice are simple repetition and stark contrast, though we may sometimes be able to detect very basic progressions.[10]

Often, then, the surface structure of one image is simply repeated by the next, in what has become known as the graphic match. A graphic match occurs when the two-dimensional array of colors, shapes or movements of one image is shared by the array of the image immediately following it. For example, in *Anticipation of the Night*, Brakhage cuts from a close-up of crumpled white bed sheets (Fig. 3.8) to the white feathers of a bird (Fig. 3.9), matching the shots on the basis of their color and texture. The impact of such matches can be extremely powerful. According to Constructivist theories of perception, when first exposed to a picture, we see it very briefly as a two-dimensional array before we process it as a representation of a scene. If this brief experience is immediately followed by a straight cut to a graphically similar shot, there is a ''bottom-up'' jolt to the perceptual system caused by the juxtaposition of the as-yet-unprocessed array with the previous image. But the effect is also extremely local, since the exact configuration of the two-dimensional array is forgotten very quickly—usually in half a second or less (Hochberg and Brooks 1979). If the graphically similar images do not follow immediately, the effect is greatly diminished. And in most cases, the graphic similarity between two images will probably not be noticed at all if they are separated by intervening images.

Fig. 3.8

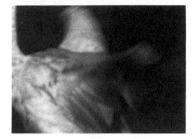

Fig. 3.9

Surface coherence can be established by contrast as well as by similarity. Such contrast is especially noticeable when it involves the brightness values of the images, as when a filmmaker cuts from an extremely bright image to an extremely dark one. In parts of Brakhage's *Window Water Baby Moving*, for example, images of almost pure white—shots of a window—alternate with black leader. Strong contrasts can also be created by alternating between color and black-and-white. Baillie's *Quixote* is primarily black-and-white, but in the middle of the film there is a passage of lush color footage. The film returns to black-and-white until the final image of the film, a close-up of a face bathed in red light. The contrast between the bright red image and the black-and-white footage that precedes it serves both to emphasize this final image and to connect it to the earlier color segment of the film.

Surface coherence need not be strictly limited to similarities and contrasts of the images' two-dimensional arrays. It can also be established on the basis of three-dimensional shapes in the scene. After the two-dimensional array is processed, but before the image is integrated into a more global structure, the image is represented in memory as a three-dimensional space filled with three-dimensional volumes. Patterns among these three-dimensional volumes are as important to the avant-garde film as the graphic match is. We can call the structure based on the color, shapes and movements of these three-dimensional shapes the *scenographic structure*. An object's appearance in a two-dimensional photographic image depends on the point from which the photograph was taken. Thus, an automobile tire will appear in the two-dimensional array as a circle when photographed from the side, but will appear as roughly rectangular when photographed from the front. Viewers (at least those who know a little

Fig. 3.10

Fig. 3.11

Fig. 3.12

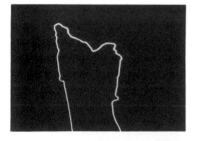

Fig. 3.13

Fig. 3.14

about tires) can understand almost any photograph of a tire, from whatever angle, as a representation of an object with a tire's characteristic donut shape. Thus, an image of an object can make a scenographic match with an image of a similarly shaped object, even if the two images do not make a graphic match.

An interesting moment of play with the difference between graphic and scenographic space is found in Pat O'Neill's *Down Wind* (1973). A shot of two copulating rhinoceroses (Fig. 3.10) is followed by a shot of a huge rock (Fig. 3.11). The rock image only vaguely matches the rhinoceros image, since they share only a large dark central shape. What follows is a barrage of short shots (about one-half second each) as the camera moves around the rock in a circle. After the camera has moved approximately 180 degrees, we see that from the other side, the shape of the rock quite closely matches that of the rhinoceroses (Fig. 3.12), though it "faces" the other direction. The circling of the rock shows that a single scenographic structure can produce images with many different graphic structures. And, the ultimate matching of the rock and the rhinoceroses shows that two scenes with very different scenographic structures can produce similar graphic structures, *if* they are photographed from the proper angles. As the section continues, we see a staccato circling of another similarly shaped rock. Then an irregular white outline on a black background is intercut in four-frame flashes (Fig. 3.13). The film's play with outlines and silhouettes encourages us to identify the object represented by the white outline—perhaps it is yet another irregularly shaped rock. The white line is then revealed to be the outline of a pair of gloved hands (Fig. 3.14). Once again, the film forces us to recognize the separation of graphic structure—the white outline—from the three-dimensional objects that produce it—the pair of hands.

It may be impossible to spell out every strategy viewers use to establish coherence among the details of the poetic avant-garde film, but in this section I have tried to suggest some of the main ones: infer causal links between apparently unconnected images; interpret impossible spatial and temporal links as marks of subjectivity; look aggressively for coreference; watch for radical metaphors and metonymy; and look for graphic and scenographic connections between adjacent images.

Coherence Overall

In the last chapter, I suggested that comprehension consists of matching discourse to schemata. We have seen some ways viewers do this at relatively local levels; viewers also try to establish the overall coherence of a film by matching details to global schemata. So, exactly how do viewers figure out the overall structure of the poetic avant-garde film?

Probably the most common approach to analyzing the overall organization of the poetic avant-garde film is to compare it to lyric poetry.[11] In the first part of this chapter, we examined some ways in which the poetry analogy helps viewers make sense of poetic avant-garde films. But as useful as it is in some ways, this analogy fails to help viewers derive the overall structure of the poetic avant-garde film. The problem is that lyric poetry is not distinguished by a particular structure, but by an *approach* to structure that leaves open the possibility of almost any global structure whatsoever, or even none at all (Frye, 270–281). Just as a lyric poem can take virtually any subject, it can take virtually any shape. Thus, the lyric poetry analogy leaves the basic question of how viewers make sense of the film's global level unanswered.

Just as it is not possible to catalog every connection a viewer might draw between two shots, it is not possible to catalog every overall schema a viewer might find in a poetic avant-garde film. But we can ask what *kinds* of overall schemata viewers may expect to find.

As a way of beginning to sort out the kinds of schemata one finds in the poetic avant-garde, let me point out that some schemata are more detailed, complete, and highly structured than others. For example, compare the schema for eating in a restaurant to the schema for a cocktail party. Both are general outlines that fit a wide range of particular cases. But the restaurant schema specifies a sequence of actions that must take place in a particular order, even though the actions themselves may be performed in a variety of ways: entering, ordering, eating, paying. On the other hand, the cocktail party schema is less detailed, less structured. It entails the arrival of guests and their later departure. But in between it specifies only an open set of usually present elements, not an ordered sequence of mandatory actions.

We might therefore think of global schemata as being arranged in a hierarchy, from the most complete, highly structured schemata down to the sketchiest, most open-ended schemata. As we might expect, the poetic avant-garde film's global schemata tend to be of the open, sketchy variety. The poetic avant-garde cinema tends to favor situations like orgies or aimless journeys rather than situations that follow predictable sequences. Nevertheless, the hierarchy of schemata suggests a heuristic for viewers aiming to optimize the coherence of the poetic avant-garde film: match the details of the film to a highly structured schemata; if this fails, try progressively sketchier schemata until one matches.[12]

Among the most highly structured global schemata are narrative schemata. Of course, the analogy between film and poetry does not encourage us to look for narrative in the poetic avant-garde film. Nevertheless, the search for narrative organization is fundamental to viewers of the poetic avant-garde film for several reasons. First, contrary to much of its own rhetoric condemning the commercial narrative film, the poetic avant-garde film is not completely non-narrative. Jonas Mekas's call for the ''plotless film'' in the early 1960s was actually a call for narratives of a certain type—more like those of the international art cinema than those of Hollywood. And many of the films produced up to the early 1960s are quite clearly narratives: *Meshes of the Afternoon*, *Reflections on Black*, Robert Frank and Alfred Leslie's *Pull My Daisy* (1959), Ron Rice's *Senseless* (1962). Even films that we may not think of as primarily narrative still have prominent narrative elements, such as characters who appear intermittently, as in Brakhage's *Anticipation of the Night* and *Dog Star Man* (1961–64).

A second reason avant-garde film viewers try to find narrative structure in these films is that searching for causal links between events is a fundamental part of our mental lives. It is such a useful means of understanding the world and managing to get around in it that it would be surprising if we would give up this search for causal links just because we are watching an avant-garde film. And research on discourse processing bears this out. A number of studies show that readers have greater perception and recall of detail when texts are structured as narratives (Mandler and Johnson, 1977). These studies also show—and this is even more interesting—that readers will try to impose a narrative structure when one is not evident in the text.

A third reason viewers tend to start by trying out narrative structures as they search for matching global conceptual structures is that narrative is so effective a means of anticipating and remembering the details of discourse. Narrative schemata tend to be more fully detailed than other kinds of schemata. Thus, it makes sense to try matching a narrative schema to the film; if this fails, one can resort to schemata that are less detailed and that will therefore establish coherence for fewer local details. I am not arguing that viewers can make any film into a narrative film. I am saying that viewers will try a narrative reading first, even if it is difficult, and then look for other organizing structures.

But even if a poetic avant-garde film has prominent narrative elements, it is not likely that a global narrative structure will establish coherence for all—or even most—of the local detail. In some ways, the narratives of the poetic avant-garde really are like the narratives of the international art cinema. As in the art cinema, the characters in the poetic avant-garde film are not generally goal-directed, as they would be in the commercial narrative film. In fact, the characters of the avant-garde are probably less goal-driven than art cinema characters, who usually have to deal with some reasonably specific personal crisis. The poetic avant-garde character's goal is often only to wander around (*Senseless*), or to look at things (*Visions of a City*), or to get away from some vague problem (several episodes of *The End*, *The Way to Shadow Garden*). Consequently, the narrative may be structured as an aimless and unpredictable trip, or as a search for something unknown. David Brook's *The Wind Is Driving Him to the Open Sea* (1968) intertwines two such apparently aimless searches. We see a young man wandering; he rides a bus, walks through woods, and so on. Images and sounds interpolated into this loose narrative suggest that he is looking for love, or for some sort of hero or role model. The film also seems to be a search for "Chandler," a mysterious man we never see. But through a series of interviews with Chandler's acquaintances, we get an ambiguous and contradictory portrait of the man. As the examples of Chandler and the wandering young man indicate, the characters in the poetic avant-garde narrative are often solitary loners: interaction between characters (which helps us understand character goals in the commercial narrative) is kept to a minimum in the poetic avant-garde. Of course, in trance films, such as *Reflections on Black*, characters are often unable to interact with the few characters they do encounter. Rather than watch characters pursue goals, our task might be to figure out what these goals might be. Sometimes, instead of considering the character's goals, we need only share the sights they see on their journey, as in *Visions of a City*.

The narratives of the poetic avant-garde also tend to be highly fragmented. Causal links between episodes are weak, so that we do not always understand why one episode has finished or why locations have changed. When a consistent storyline does not seem to establish coherence between episodes, the string of episodes may be interpreted as elucidating various aspects of the character's personality. For example, in *Blonde Cobra* (1959–63), Ken Jacobs assembled footage of Jack Smith shot by Bob Fleischner and audio tapes recorded by Smith. The loosely structured film seems to be a random sample of the Smith persona's stories, memories and anxieties, until the film ends with the death of that persona. If the film does not have a single protagonist, we can interpret the episodes as elucidating various aspects of the milieu that the film is about. For example, Maclaine's *The End* has six separate stories, but taken together, they form an inventory of anxieties about the bomb. The avant-garde narrative also tends to be frequently interrupted, either by the introduction of other unrelated storylines (*The End, The Wind Is Driving Him to the Open Sea*) or by non-narrative digressions. *Anticipation of the Night* is just one example of many poetic avant-garde films that are interrupted by long passages of play with the formal qualities of nearly abstract images.

In the absence of even a minimal storyline, the viewer can establish some degree of overall coherence by mapping musical analogies onto the structure of the film. One of the most common musical forms used in this way is the *theme-and-variations* pattern.[13] In this global conceptual structure, a film introduces a concept and subjects it to a series of permutations. For the viewer, comprehending this form is simply a matter of tracking the similarities and differences of the sections of the film. Often the theme-and-variations form will incorporate something like an exposition-development-recapitulation format, in which the theme introduced at the beginning will return at the end in something close to its original form. For example, Brakhage himself described his *Mothlight* (1963) as a series of three ''round dances'' with a coda. The film was created without a camera by affixing small natural objects, such as seeds, grass, and moth wings, to a strip of clear film stock. By carefully placing similar objects in the same spot in successive frames, Brakhage is able to produce a relatively stable image on the screen. On the other hand, when he affixes disparate objects to successive frames, or when he places objects randomly in the frame, the image moves frenetically. By alternating between stable and frenetic images, and by grouping similar objects in certain parts of the film, Brakhage creates the cyclical theme-and-variations pattern we can see in the film.

If viewers are unable to match even quasi-musical schemata to the film's global level, they can still make a general appraisal of the film's overall mood or atmosphere. Viewers may use such *atmospheric schemata* along with other schemata; a consistent mood, however, may be the sole global schema. In such films, meaning is built up gradually through the connotations of the images, and the order of the images is not especially important. Baillie's *Castro Street* (1966), for example, might best be described as a poetic documentary of an area we might call an industrial wasteland; the objects photographed are primarily factories and trains. But Baillie manipulates the images to bring out their sensual qualities. The overall organization of the film is rather obscure, but the discovery of such formal beauty in objects we normally consider ugly creates a consistent, if somewhat ambivalent atmosphere. Appealing to atmospheric coherence alone provides a kind of global schema of last resort: in the absence of any other kind of overall coherence, viewers can always establish this kind, if only by labeling the film as "spooky" (Brakhage's *Fire of Waters* [1965]), "sad" (*New York Near Sleep for Saskia*), or even "chaotic" or "random" (Brakhage's *Aftermath*).

As we saw in the last chapter, discourse processing is predominantly semantic, and surface details tend to be forgotten as soon as they can be integrated into larger, more meaningful structures. Yet the patterning of the surface is central to many kinds of art. Readers of poetry do not simply decode its meaning, they look for the way the surface features are patterned with rhyme, rhythm, alliteration and so forth. So it is with the poetic avant-garde film: to disregard the plastic qualities of the images is to disregard a major part of the experience of the film. Thus, we are faced with a contradiction: human discourse processing seems designed to discard central features of the work.

Obviously there are some exceptions to the rule that surface detail is used only provisionally and then forgotten. Artists seem to be able to learn to see a three-dimensional scene as flat, as an aid to representing the scene on a two-dimensional surface. With enough practice, people are able to memorize poetry. After several viewings of a film, some viewers can recite passages of dialogue along with the characters. Even after only one viewing, some striking scenes, images or even sequences of shots are remembered by many viewers. And, we have already seen that the surface structure of images can provide at least local coherence. The question here is, to what extent and under what conditions might the surface structure of a film provide coherence at more global levels?

In the earlier discussion of local coherence, I suggested that the graphic match was one of the primary ways through which surface structure could establish local coherence. A graphic match can structure a film at more global levels if it is repeated. In Charles Wright's *Sorted Details* (1980), graphic matches structure the entire film. Each shot of the 13-minute film is linked to the next by some similarity of color, shape or movement (Figs. 3.15, 3.16, 3.17).

A number of studies suggest that memory for surface information is actually better if the global schema is random or open-ended

Fig. 3.15

Fig. 3.16

Fig. 3.17

(Gernsbacher 1985). Since *Sorted Details'* global schema is what I have termed ''atmospheric''—the images are all drawn from urban landscapes, but there is no narrative or pointed theme—no detailed global structure other than the extended graphic match accounts for inter-shot relationships. This helps make the film's global *surface* structure very prominent, even after only one viewing.

Sorted Details notwithstanding, effects that depend on the similarity of this surface information tend to be very local because the processing of the raw two-dimensional array of shapes is so quick. But the viewer of the avant-garde film looks for scenographic structure as well as graphic structure, and the scenographic structure, since it is based on information that is more durable in memory, can more easily provide global coherence. As my brief analysis of the rocks and rhinoceros imagery in *Down Wind* suggested, O'Neill's film is structured by a series of graphic and scenographic motifs, so that the film has a *global* surface structure, even though it does not seem to have a clear overall meaning.

We might also ask if some films consist purely of surface structure. Strictly speaking, the answer is no—at least not in the sense that viewers simply look at the two-dimensional array and do not process it further. Even in films that are labeled ''abstract'' or ''graphic'' there is still a significant amount of processing beyond the literal surface. Virtually any differentiated surface suggests some depth relationships, even if it does not represent a space inhabited by objects. And beyond the construction of depth, we tend to see differentiated surfaces as comprising ''bodies'' that we structure by giving meaningful qualities, such as wholeness, energy and balance. Further, we structure these qualities over time so that even the most abstract film has structures like the quasi-musical schemata mentioned above.

Research on the role of surface information in discourse processing helps explain why, to a large degree, the poetic avant-garde is a cinema of local effects rather than global structure. Put simply, some films develop richly textured local detail at the expense of a coherent overall structure. When viewers are unable to establish global coherence with highly structured global schemata, the processing of local detail is attenuated (Gernsbacher 1985, Thorndike 1977). Stuck on local detail, the viewer must consider integrative strategies that rely on features of the individual images—features that might be missed in a film that made it easy to integrate local detail into global structure. Thus the apparent overall incoherence of many poetic avant-garde films actually helps viewers see more of the details. It has even been suggested that some avant-garde films are ''eye-training'' exercises meant to increase the viewers' sensitivity to their visual environment.

There are institutional factors that encourage this attention to the surface structure of the images. First, the films of the poetic avant-garde tend to be short. Of course, there are financial reasons for this, but short films present different opportunities as well as different limitations to the filmmaker. One of these opportunities is to encourage greater attention to the surface features of the images. Second, multiple viewing seems to be assumed as an ideal by many writers on the avant-garde, even as they admit that multiple viewing is not usually available to "regular" viewers, as opposed to critics and teachers (MacDonald 1988). Perception and memory for surface detail is aided by rehearsal: just as our appreciation for the surface structure of a poem increases the more we read or study it, so multiple viewing of the avant-garde film increases our ability to notice graphic and scenographic structure.

The avant-garde film is hardly unique in emphasizing surface structure through graphic and scenographic patterning. What distinguishes these patterns in the poetic avant-garde is their independence from the film's overall meaning. Outside the avant-garde, graphic or scenographic matches may sometimes be prominent, but ultimately they will be subordinated to the dominant narrative they are made to serve. But the poetic avant-garde is open to free improvisation with the colors, shapes and movements in the images, not because of what such improvisations might mean, but because of the way such play with pattern and disorder can engage the viewer.

Final Examples: *Window Water Baby Moving* and *Marasmus*

We have examined a number of devices and strategies viewers can use to make sense of the poetic avant-garde film. For the purpose of my analysis, I have artificially separated them, but in practice viewers must be prepared to apply them together. Viewers begin to hypothesize about the overall organization of the film at the same time they try to connect details into small chunks at the local level. Of course, this considerably increases the difficulty of the task of making sense of the film.

Noël Carroll (1981) refers to the kind of editing typical of the poetic avant-garde as *polyvalent montage*, and his description suggests the challenge it poses for the viewer: "Essential to how polyvalent montage is practiced by contemporary avant-gardists is the tendency to incessantly shift the rationale of the cutting to new associative pathways, both over the course of the entire film and even from shot to shot. Polyvalent editing is a kind of overtonal montage in spades because either the tonal dominant is always changing, or because there is no tonal dominant" (73). Individually, none of the heuristics I have proposed in this chapter is hard to apply. But the lack of "tonal dominant" means that viewers must be prepared to use any of the heuristics at any time, and this can make establishing coherence quite a challenge.

It is impossible to predict how these various devices and strategies will interact in every particular case. But we can begin to explain the ways these heuristics interact in the pragmatic terms set out in chapter 2.

Recall that film viewers assume that films will be "cooperative," in the sense that the films will be relevant and clear unless some competing principle motivates their apparent deviation from the co-operative principle. Recent work by Dan Sperber and Dierdre Wilson suggests that it is neither necessary nor possible to spell out all the possible motives for a speaker's deviation from a general cooperative principle. According to Sperber and Wilson, pragmatic effects are best explained as applications of a single principle: *optimal relevance*. As Sperber and Wilson point out, relevance is a matter of degree; some statements convey a great deal of relevant information, others only a small amount. Furthermore, this relevant information is derived only through the expenditure of varying degrees of mental effort by the receiver. Sperber and Wilson suggest that receivers do not merely assume that the sender's utterances will be relevant, they assume that the relevance of an utterance will be proportional to the effort it takes to process it. In other words, *optimally relevant* utterances compensate the receiver's processing efforts with appropriate amounts of relevant information. If an utterance is difficult to process, it ought somehow to reward the receiver with some additional benefit. Thus, the viewer of the avant-garde film must be prepared to explain not only seemingly "uncooperative" material but seemingly sub-optimally relevant material as well. In other words, the very difficulty of making sense of a poetic avant-garde film sets viewers searching for principles that motivate that difficulty.

We can always invoke the brute avant-garde principle by interpreting the difficulty of an avant-garde film as a gesture intended to shock viewers out of their complacent viewing habits. But this principle does not establish coherence among the film's elements; it only makes the film relevant to a particular social context in which the film can be seen as a provocation. As a means of concluding this discussion of the poetic strain of the American avant-garde, let me demonstrate the interplay of other, more subtle, comprehension strategies with two final examples: Stan Brakhage's *Window Water Baby Moving*, a 12-minute film about the birth of Stan and Jane Brakhage's first child, and Betzy Bromberg and Laura Ewig's *Marasmus* (1981), a more recent work that uses the style and structure of earlier film poems.

A common, but not universal, feature of avant-garde film screenings is that viewers get an introduction to the films they will see, either from the filmmaker, from a printed program, or from a teacher. Thus the potential viewer of *Window Water Baby Moving* may well know that the film is about the birth of a child. Nevertheless, the opening of the film poses problems for the viewer, who must sort out a complex coreference problem and at the same time generate some hypotheses about the overall organization of the film.

First, the coreference problem. The title of the film is both cryptic and highly descriptive; it literally lists the things we see in the film's opening, but does not immediately suggest a coherent topic or subject for the film. Also, it elides the crucial fact that the baby we will see moving is as yet unborn, and that the protagonist of the film is not a baby, but Jane, the baby's mother. Thus, as the film begins, the viewer cannot be certain which images and details are the most

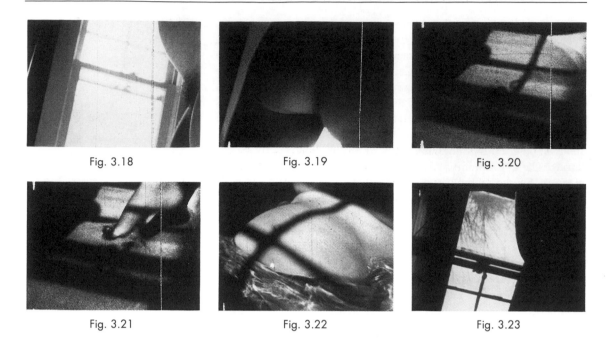

Fig. 3.18   Fig. 3.19   Fig. 3.20

Fig. 3.21   Fig. 3.22   Fig. 3.23

significant. However, we are particularly ready to identify human agents in all forms of discourse, so when we see Jane's body, we tend to assume that the film will be about her. But the framing of the initial shots of Jane cuts against our seeing her as clearly the protagonist. Rather than showing her face, the images show her first in silhouette and at the margins of the frame, with the window of the title prominent in the center of the frame (Figs. 3.18, 3.19). And when we do see Jane more clearly, when she is in the bath, the light from the window falls so that the shadow of the window panes occupies the exact position the window had in the previous shots (Figs. 3.20, 3.21). After Jane is shown in the bath (Fig. 3.22), Brakhage uses a shot of the window *upside-down* (Fig. 3.23), so that the position of the window panes approximates the position of their shadows on Jane's belly. In these opening images, Jane is more marginal in the frame, but we are inclined to focus our attention on human agents; we would likely consider the window a marginal element of the setting, but its prominence in the frame, and in the title, makes it more central. These contradictory cues reveal a tension between the film's documentary impulse and its formal experimentation. Viewers must therefore be prepared to approach the film from these two perspectives at the same time.

At the beginning of the film, we try to generate some hypotheses about the global organization of the film. Among the first shots are images of Jane, late in her pregnancy, emphasizing her swollen belly. Given her prominence early in the film, we hypothesize that she will function as a character, and that the film will have a narrative organization—at least in part. The advanced state of her pregnancy implies a sequence of actions: a labor and delivery of a child. This is confirmed by the rest of the film. The film's major segments—though not its local detail—follow a predictable trajectory: images of Jane pregnant; Jane's labor; the delivery of the child; the delivery of the afterbirth; the baby lying on Jane's breast. The film is somewhat atypical of the poetic avant-garde in that the narrative implied by the initial state of its character accounts for so much of the global structure.

At the local level, however, the film is not nearly so tidy. The temporal order of the images is scrambled. There are long stretches of black inserted within and between major segments. The editing is rapid, and the camera moves erratically over the scene. Some shots are upside down. The coherence of these local details cannot be established by appealing to the overall narrative. In fact, if we take the film to be about Jane's pregnancy and the birth of her child, these features of the film's style are violations of the optimal relevance principle, and this apparent violation needs to be justified by an appeal to other organizing principles.

A significant degree of local coherence is provided by the surface structure of the images: graphic matches and stark contrasts between adjacent shots are apparent throughout. Shots of Jane's round belly are matched to other round shapes such as her breasts and the baby's head. In one passage, Brakhage cuts together a series of shots of Jane's belly from a variety of angles; because of the roundness of her belly, they all match graphically (Figs. 3.24, 3.25, 3.26). In the first segment, shots of a sunlit window are matched to shots of the window's shadow falling on Jane's belly. Images of the doctor's hand on the baby's head (Fig. 3.27) are matched to Stan's hand on Jane's belly (Fig. 3.28), which are, in turn, matched to images of Jane's hand clutching her pillow during labor. Jane's face during labor (Fig. 3.29) is matched to shots of her face while bathing (Fig. 3.30) and after the birth. Scenographic matches based on the three-dimensional qualities of the elements in the scene abound as well. The juxtaposition of shots compares Jane's eyes to her mouth to her vagina (Figs. 3.31, 3.32, 3.33). The water in her bath is juxtaposed to puddles of blood shed during delivery.

These scenographic matches suggest metaphorical coherence through which various openings are equated. We understand the juxtaposition of Jane's mouth and vagina and the window because all are openings. This provides not only local coherence, but additional global coherence as well. Because these openings and passageways metonymically suggest transitions, these openings become metaphors for the very process of birth itself.

The style-as-consciousness heuristic helps explain aspects of the cinematography of *Window Water Baby Moving*, particularly if we know a bit about Brakhage's ideas about filmmaking. For Brakhage, a child's unschooled and uncontaminated perception is a model for the avant-garde film. This helps account for the stark contrasts between the sections of black film and bright images: they evoke the baby's experience of emerging into the light for the first time. Brakhage's

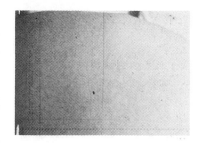

Fig. 3.24

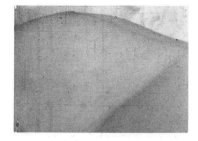

Fig. 3.25

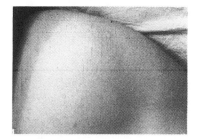

Fig. 3.26

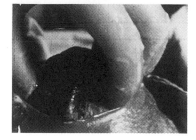

Fig. 3.27

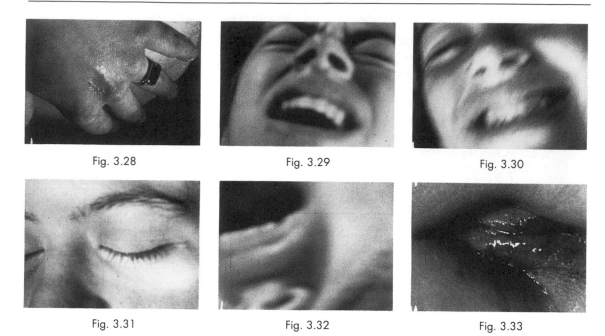

Fig. 3.28   Fig. 3.29   Fig. 3.30

Fig. 3.31   Fig. 3.32   Fig. 3.33

aesthetics are also predicated on the idea that this child-like perception, unbounded by the conventions and taboos of adult perception, can help us achieve a profound, unmediated engagement with the world. Thus, Brakhage rejects the taboos and conventions that inhibit more conventional childbirth films and lavishes attention on things we do not normally look at, and that might make us uncomfortable: we get extreme close-ups of the placenta and long close-ups of Jane's vulva even before the baby's head appears.

The temporal shuffling of the images also points up another contrast between *Window Water Baby Moving* and more conventional childbirth films. Brakhage cuts from the most intense and explicit images of the delivery to erotic images of Jane in her bath, of Stan's hand caressing her belly, and of Stan and Jane kissing. In addition to providing opportunities for graphic matches between the images of the delivery and the erotic images, these temporal reorderings highlight the sexual aspects of childbirth, aspects utterly repressed by more clinical films on the subject.

Window Water Baby Moving is a dense, complicated film whose structure and style will remain obscure for many viewers. But by establishing coherence on the basis of the surface structures of the images, the metaphorical connections among images, and the symbolic value of the events represented, the apparent violations of the principle of optimal relevance are recuperated. The film rejects conventional film form, but not because such a rejection is valuable in itself. In historical terms, the unconventional form of *Window Water Baby Moving* shows how the poetic strain synthesizes the intense subjectivity of the trance film and the graphic organization of the abstract cinema. Or, as Parker Tyler might have put it more poetically, *Window Water Baby Moving* uses the facts of childbirth only as starting points, as elements of a composition, for a total form expressing a complete human experience.

Betzy Bromberg and Laura Ewig's *Marasmus* is one of many films of the 1980s that are quite evidently indebted to earlier film poems like *Window Water Baby Moving*. We see, for example, the characteristic experimental approach to film technique: the film switches among color, black-and-white, and negative film stock and is filled with images shot through color filters. The film is also heavily edited, and the juxtaposition of shots highlights a wide variety of associative connections. We see graphic matches of colors, shapes and movement, as well as a wide variety of conceptual links.

Fig. 3.34

The film exploits a fundamental structural tension between a quasi-narrative and an improvised theme and variations on a set of motifs. The film shows two women in several settings: the interior of a high-rise office building, an industrial park, and a near-desert wilderness. These images and a dense sound montage make it rather clear that the film is about the place of women in a patriarchal and technologically threatening culture. The film's peculiar title, which is the name of an advanced state of malnutrition common to children living in poverty, also poses the question of children's place in such an environment.

Fig. 3.35

According to Bromberg, the filmmakers had no plans for a narrative while they shot the film (interview with the author, 24 April 1992). The project began as a set of filmed backgrounds for a dance piece. When that project fell through, the filmmakers decided to use the footage they had shot of Bromberg's body shrouded in plastic (Fig. 3.34) as the basis for their own film. The filmmakers themselves play the women in the film—each filmed the other—and shooting proceeded as a free improvisation with a set of props in a number of locations they liked. That first image of the shrouded body became the conceptual center of the film, playing a key role in both the narrative and the improvised theme-and-variations structure.

Fig. 3.36

Part of the coherence of the film is due to the consistent cinematography. The camera is almost always hand-held, and it regularly moves in to extreme close-up on the faces—especially the mouths—of the women. The editing juxtaposes these images, drawing parallels and accentuating contrasts between the two women.

The theme-and-variations structure is worked out primarily with a set of transparent barriers. In addition to the plastic shroud, we see plastic bubble wrap held over a face (Fig. 3.35), transparent plastic gloves (Fig. 3.36), and a sheet of glass against which Ewig's face is pressed (Fig. 3.37). Another prominent barrier image has one of the women holding a piece of brush in front of her face (Fig. 3.38). The barrier motif is also articulated by the cinematography. Bromberg and Ewig frame a number of images through horizontal slits, as in our first view of the shrouded body (Fig. 3.39), in an image of Bromberg shot

Fig. 3.37

Fig. 3.38   Fig. 3.39   Fig. 3.40

Fig. 3.41   Fig. 3.42   Fig. 3.43

through a set of glass shelves (Fig. 3.40), and in an exterior shot through a set of blinds.

The thematic meaning of these motifs is profoundly ambivalent. Certainly the barrier imagery suggests the women's confinement and their separation from each other—not to mention their death. But the plastic shroud image also functions as an image of birth. When Ewig moves the camera close to Bromberg's shrouded body, her hand reaches in from off screen and begins to rip an opening in the plastic (Fig. 3.41). As the film progresses, the figure is re-born, and the transparent shroud begins to suggest a womb (Fig. 3.42).

But birth is itself treated somewhat ambivalently in the film. The delivery from the plastic shroud suggests some sort of transcendence (Fig. 3.43). But in one remarkable passage, birth is cast in a less appealing light. A flat, lifeless voice on the sound track intones, "It's a boy. Congratulations." We see a tiny baby doll held up and brought to the camera (Fig. 3.44). Then we cut to a close-up of Ewig eating (Fig. 3.45) and we hear a loud crunching noise. As the shot continues we see that Ewig is eating peanuts, but the juxtaposition of these images and sounds rather humorously links childbirth and cannibalism.

It would certainly be stretching a point to call the film a narrative, but it is impossible to avoid at least a partial narrative interpretation of the film. The film represents the women as struggling not only with technology and patriarchy, but each other. The women are represented as opposites: Ewig is dark, and is depicted as somewhat sinister; Bromberg is lighter and plays the less threatening role of the figure in the shroud, and a number of times she is shown relaxing in the sun. Interactions between the two characters are rare. Because Bromberg and Ewig shot the film themselves almost entirely with a hand-held camera, one of them must always be behind the camera. This prevents them from appearing on screen together throughout most of the film, with two exceptions. Early on, a figure in black strikes a figure in white with a sword (Fig. 3.46). This, of course, provides a rudimentary narrative context for the recurring image of the woman in the plastic shroud. Near the end of the film, we see the women together a second time, this time wrestling behind a translucent screen (Fig. 3.47).

Fig. 3.44

The thematic ambivalence we saw in the meaning of the barrier motif also plays a role in the narrative. Between the two moments of open conflict, there are repeated images of attempts to breech the barriers that separate the character and the camera. We see a hand opening the plastic shroud. A hand reaches out to stroke Bromberg's hair. A hand reaches out to the hand of the dark figure behind the brush. If we remember that the second character is behind the camera, these images suggest an interaction between the two women that stands in stark contrast to the images of conflict enacted when they are shown on screen together. Bromberg suggests that one way to understand the interchange between the women-as-filmmakers and women-as-characters is to see the film as a kind of reflexive autobiography, in which the give-and-take of the filmmakers' collaboration is metaphorically worked through in the story of the two women. As we have seen, this too is part of the tradition of the film poem, wherein the struggles of the characters are refracted versions of the filmmaker's creative process.

Fig. 3.45

So far, I have concentrated on drawing links between *Marasmus* and the early film poem: *Marasmus* uses the formal strategies of the early film poem, and in part uses the subject matter of Brakhage's films about childhood and childbirth. Of course, there are also obvious differences. Brakhage documents actual births, whereas Bromberg and Ewig represent birth and childhood more allusively. But the most telling difference lies in the ways Brakhage and Bromberg and Ewig make childhood meaningful by using it as a means of exploring some other thematic terrain.

Fig. 3.46

One aim of Brakhage's cinema was to chronicle daily life, especially his own family life. One of the reasons children were such a useful subject for Brakhage is that they emblematize his notion of the artist. The naive, uncorrupted vision of children is one of Brakhage's metaphors on vision—an analogy for the creative vision of the artist. Childbirth represents the beginning of a brief moment of purity, soon to be lost to the corruption of language and socialization. Brakhage's film poems about childhood are not merely records of family life; more importantly, they attempt to render glimpses of childhood vision. For Brakhage the child is an artist in miniature, achieving naturally the kind of personal vision Brakhage labors to render on film.

Fig. 3.47

In *Marasmus*, childbirth and childhood are no longer strictly private matters. The title of the film introduces childhood metonymically, by identifying it as a political issue rather than a private experience. Children, particularly those living in poverty, are, like the women in the film, threatened by patriarchy and industrial technology. The ambivalence with which childbirth is represented suggests not only the filmmakers' anxieties about raising children in an inhospitable environment, but the precarious position of women, on whom a disproportionate share of the burden of child-rearing still falls.

The politicization of private experience is not a universal feature of new film poems; there are plenty that remain resolutely personal. But in a significant number of new films that use the formal strategies of the film poem, private spaces and events—avant-garde home movies, if you will—open out to the examination of the public realm. For example, in Nina Fonoroff's *Department of the Interior* (1986) and Inez Sommer's *Still Life with Postcards* (1988), as in *Marasmus*, the details of private life are no longer metaphors for personal vision; they have become metonyms for a set of political issues.

4

Brakhage, Abstract Expressionism and Interpretive Schemata

In 1961, filmmaker and critic Charles Boultenhouse suggested that Stan Brakhage's erratic camera movement was the cinematic equivalent of the rapid brushwork of the Action Painters. Since then scarcely anyone writing about Brakhage's work can avoid linking it to Abstract Expressionism. Few critical opinions in the avant-garde are as widely held as this one, but it is repeated more often than it is thoroughly examined. Since this notion is so fundamental to our understanding of both the poetic and minimal strains of the avant-garde cinema, I would like to explore the link between Brakhage's work and the aesthetics of Abstract Expressionism.

This brief excursion is important for two reasons. First, the link between Brakhage and the Abstract Expressionists provides an important *interpretive schema* for the poetic strain of the avant-garde film. Interpretive schemata provide a means of making sense of works of art that frustrate normal discourse processing skills. As Brakhage abandoned the trance form and developed the lyrical form in which characters played increasingly marginal roles, his work became harder to comprehend. This interpretive schema, drawn from common critical ideas about Abstract Expressionism, thus became increasingly important to Brakhage's work. And as we will see in chapter 5, interpretive schemata—derived in part from the one used for making sense of Brakhage's work—are even more important to the ways viewers make sense of the films of the minimal strain.

Second, by the late 1960s, Brakhage's work was taken to be a norm for the avant-garde film, and the minimal strain was commonly seen as a reaction against this norm. This common view of the relationship between Brakhage and the minimal strain uses the analogy between Brakhage's work and Abstract Expressionism. As Regina Cornwell put it: "Viewing a Brakhage projected next to a Warhol of this period would be very much analogous to looking at a Pollock or a DeKooning next to a Warhol silkscreen" (1979b, 78). Thus, understanding the terms of the Brakhage/Abstract Expressionism analogy is vital to an understanding of the evolution of the American avant-garde film.

What I am calling interpretive schemata are, like cognitive schemata in general, patterns of acquired knowledge. Specifically, they are *procedural* schemata, well-learned sequences of actions used to perform a task—in this case, assigning meaning to artworks whose basic comprehension is problematic. The notion of interpretive schemata is based on a distinction between first-order and second-order skills, between comprehension and interpretation. Or, as others have put it with regard to literature, between a kind of general *linguistic* competence and a more specific *literary* competence (Culler 1975, 113–30). Most often, second-order thematic interpretations presuppose successful first-order comprehension of a series of events. For example, interpreting the theme of a novel, an aspect of literary competence, requires linguistic competence that enables the reader to understand the setting, the activities of the characters, and so on. But this first-order comprehension is frustrated by many avant-garde works, including Brakhage's lyrical films. Nevertheless, even when basic comprehension is frustrated, viewers can make sense of such films by using interpretive schemata to ascribe thematic meaning to them. I want to make clear, however, that interpretive schemata are *not* simply the means through which *any* interpretation is made: they are special procedures invoked to make sense of works whose basic comprehension is problematic.

I use the term "schemata" here to distinguish interpretive schemata from other principles of comprehension such as the strategies and heuristics I laid out in the last chapter. The terms "strategy" and "heuristic" suggest flexible procedures that are adapted to the problem at hand. For example, I suggested that one useful heuristic for the poetic strain was to interpret overt manipulation of film style as a representation of an altered mental state, such as a dream, memory, hallucination, or fantasy. This heuristic guides the viewer, but it remains rather open-ended. It provides clues about what might count as a solution, but it does not give step-by-step instructions on how to achieve it. "Schema," on the other hand, suggests a procedure that, once invoked, is more mechanically applied. Interpretive schemata allow viewers to attribute specific meanings to readily identifiable features of works of art.

The most extended treatment of Brakhage's relationship to Abstract Expressionism is in P. Adams Sitney's *Visionary Film.* The gist of Sitney's argument is that the association between Brakhage's films and Abstract Expressionist paintings is grounded in their shared formal qualities.

Making specific connections between Brakhage and the Abstract Expressionists is complicated by the heterogeneity of Abstract Expressionist work. Unlike the Futurists or Surrealists, the Abstract Expressionists were not a cohesive group of artists who saw themselves as a movement and laid down their common fundamental principles in manifestoes. And in formal terms, their work is rather diverse. As art historian Charles Harrison puts it, ''the term 'Abstract Expressionism' is misleading, embracing as it does at one extreme the work of Willem de Kooning which is rarely 'abstract', and at the other the work of Barnet Newman, which is not characteristically expressionist'' (1974, 168).

Harrison's point is well taken, but there are nevertheless rough similarities among the works of the Abstract Expressionists.[1] The features common to all Abstract Expressionist works are: a loose, evident brushwork deployed in a shallow space. Brakhage's films do not have actual brushwork, and similarities between the imagery in his films and Abstract Expressionist works are extremely infrequent; consequently, the argument for a formal similarity between the films and the paintings rests heavily on this shallow space. There is no doubt that many of the strategies Brakhage used in his late 1950s movement toward the lyrical film and greater abstraction flattened the space in his films. Out-of-focus cinematography, scratches on the film emulsion, and extremely rapid and indecipherable camera movement all block the representation of deep space and emphasize the surface of the image. But Sitney not only notes this tendency to ''affirm the flatness and whiteness of the screen,'' he identifies Brakhage's space as Abstract Expressionist (1979, 142). Actually, it is quite different.

The shallow space of the Abstract Expressionists was achieved by extreme painterliness and loose brushwork in a (usually) non-figurative framework. A broad, ragged brushstroke cutting a swath across the canvas in one of Franz Kline's black-and-white paintings, for example, does not *depict* anything in the usual sense. The roughness of the edge of the brushstroke accentuates the surface of the canvas because the physical material—paint—is dripped or running on it. The viewer does not see a depicted scene, only running paint dried on a surface. However, the Abstract Expressionist's space is not completely flat. The surface effects, like running paint, are often layered, as in Pollock's drip paintings, and the overlap is a cue to certain depth relationships: this drip is on top of that one, so it appears closer. Also, human perception of color projects depth onto almost any articulated surface: light values advance, dark ones recede, and warm hues like red project out more than cool hues like blue. In the final analysis, the painting will have depth relationships, but they may be ambiguous (an overlapping cue may contradict a color cue, as when a normally receding blue patch overlaps the normally advancing red) or just plain shallow. The space is never very deep because devices that render the impression of deep space, especially linear perspective and the modeling of form with light and shadow, are never used. Thus, in spite of the great variations between one Abstract Expressionist painting and another, some form of shallow (but not flat) space is common to all.

The space in Brakhage's *Thigh Line Lyre Triangular* (1961)—an often-cited case and Sitney's key example—is different from the space of any of the Abstract Expressionists. Brakhage ac-

Fig. 4.1

curately, if mystically, describes its two-part structure: "Only at a crisis do I see both the scene as I've been trained to see it (that is, with Renaissance perspective, three-dimensional logic, colors we've been trained to call a color, and so forth) and patterns that move straight out from the inside of the mind . . ." (1963, n.p.). The paint and scratches that Brakhage adds to the film *are* flattened and surface-bound just like the loose brushstrokes in Abstract Expressionism. But as Figure 4.1 shows, the scratched and painted surfaces of *Thigh Line Lyre Triangular* also carry photographic images, complete with modeled forms, elements of perspective and illusionistic space. Sitney cites images like this as having an Abstract Expressionist space, and he compares them to de Kooning's *Woman with a Green and Beige Background* (1966, Fig. 4.2). But in de Kooning's figurative work, the representation is integrated into the surface; the very same brushstrokes that flatten the picture space also build the representation, and they build it without the use of modeling or perspective. Brakhage, on the other hand, maintains both surface and depth. Granted, Brakhage avoids the central point perspective we think of as prototypical of Renaissance perspective. In Brakhage's work we rarely see the converging orthogonals characteristic of Renaissance perspective because Brakhage very rarely shows a wide view of an architectural space. But the images still have many consistent depth cues, particularly forms modeled with light and shadow. The result is that, beyond the surface-bound scratches and paint, the photographic images fall back into a three-dimensional space that is deeper than anything we see in Abstract Expressionism.

Brakhage's spatial construction is clearly not an exact replica of the Abstract Expressionists'; still, many passages of his films do not carry photographic images with deep space. Some do have a simple, shallow space. But at this level of generality, whatever formal qualities link Brakhage to Abstract Expressionism also link him to broader tendencies in twentieth-century painting. A tendency toward a flattened pictorial space has been a common feature of painting since the Impressionists. And if it is a feature of Abstract Expressionism, it is also certainly a feature of the "post-painterly" geometric abstraction which replaced Abstract Expressionism as the dominant school of American painting. And as for the two-part space of *Thigh Line Lyre Triangular*, it is actually closer to the space of Miró's Surrealist painting of the 1930s and 1940s than to Abstract Expressionist space. In Miró's work of this period, such as *Painting* (1933, Fig. 4.3), softly inflected color backgrounds suggest an atmospheric space, and crisp, dark lines and shapes lie on the surface.

If Brakhage's work invites comparison with such a wide range of painting styles, why has it been linked so exclusively with Abstract Expressionism? The link was not simply the idea of an eager and imaginative critic; Brakhage himself eagerly cultivated the notion and tried to extend and deepen the connection in his *Metaphors on Vision* as well as in many of his later writings. In fact, even in the 1961 essay that Sitney credits with being the first to acknowledge Brakhage's link to Abstract Expressionism, Boultenhouse was citing *Brakhage's* opin-

Fig. 4.2. Willem de Kooning, *Woman with a Green and Beige Background,* 1966. Oil on paper on masonite, 28 ½" × 22 ¾". Grey Art Gallery & Study Center, New York University Art Collection, Gift of Longview Foundation, 1973. © 1992 Willem de Kooning/ARS, New York.

ion (Boultenhouse 1961). Insofar as there is a source for this idea, it is the filmmaker himself.

There are two major reasons why Brakhage might try to associate his work with Abstract Expressionism. First, it lent legitimacy to his films. By the early 1960s, Abstract Expressionism had not only the approval of the museum establishment but the official sanction of the state. Throughout the 1950s and early 1960s, Abstract Expressionist work was widely exported to Asia and Latin America as well as Eastern Europe, all with the active support of the United States Information Agency (Cockroft 1974, 39–40). Brakhage embraced Abstract Expressionism not at the height of its impact on the art world, but at the height of its public acceptance.

Brakhage did not need the prestige that Abstract Expressionism had to offer within the realm of the avant-garde film; he was easily the most thoroughly covered filmmaker in the pages of *Film Culture.* But the 1960s were years of transition for the avant-garde film, and by 1963—the year Andy Warhol won *Film Culture*'s independent filmmaker award—it was clear that the art world proper and the world of the avant-garde film were drawing closer together. In this emerging relationship, the avant-garde film could find new publicity and a new audience as well as a new legitimacy. But while *Film Culture* and Jonas Mekas's column in the *Village Voice* eagerly embraced the film work of visual artists like Warhol, Bruce Conner, and later Paul Sharits and Michael Snow, the arms of the art world were less than completely open to the filmmakers of the avant-garde.

Fig. 4.3. Joan Miró, *Painting,* 1933. Oil on canvas, 68 ½″ × 6′ 5 ¼″. Collection, The Museum of Modern Art, New York, Loula D. Lasker Bequest (by exchange).

There are many reasons for the art world's reluctance to accept the films of the avant-garde. First, the financial benefits of film collecting are severely limited. Second, the style and subject matter of the early 1960s avant-garde film were out of step with the cooler attitudes of the geometric abstraction that had come to prominence since the heyday of Abstract Expressionism. And finally, the avant-garde film, like Pop Art, was tainted by its association with popular culture; some critics rejected it as amateurish or non-artistic.[2]

Brakhage's prominence in *Film Culture* carried little weight with the opinion makers of the art world. When *Art in America* began to extend coverage to filmmakers,[3] Brakhage, of all the major figures of the avant-garde, was easiest to overlook. He had not been one of the twelve filmmakers to receive a 1964 Ford Foundation grant, and the coverage was almost exclusively limited to those filmmakers who had received the Foundation's seal of approval. Also, Brakhage did not establish his reputation as an artist before he moved into film, as

Robert Breer and Conner did, and as later Structural filmmakers like Sharits and Snow would. Finally, *Art in America* may have preferred to avoid discussing Brakhage's films because they were sexually explicit, containing nudity, sex and scenes of childbirth rendered in the most unglamorous detail.

But the second and stronger motivation for Brakhage's associating himself with the Abstract Expressionists is that it aided in their comprehension. In cultivating spontaneity and accident, he went to extremes: his work was a radical alternative not only to the Hollywood mode but to the well-known abstract styles of Len Lye and Harry Smith as well. In other words, his films, in comparison to the rest of the poetic avant-garde, posed monumental problems of comprehension.

These problems grew most acute for Brakhage as he moved away from the trance form, in which a protagonist encounters a series of more or less comprehensible situations, and into the lyrical form, which has no traditional characters and few comprehensible actions. I am not suggesting that the trance films of the 1940s and 1950s are not often quite puzzling. But the existence of human agents—even very enigmatic ones—allows viewers to start with some of the same strategies they use for understanding most narrative discourse. By so minimizing characterizable human agents (in films that are nevertheless not totally abstract), Brakhage's later films frustrated his viewers' basic skills of comprehension. Brakhage and the critics who wrote about his work did what every film critic tries to do: they constructed a framework within which a body of work is made meaningful. But for Brakhage's mature work some such framework was not an informative nicety that fleshed out an interpretation—it was a prerequisite to understanding the films. Brakhage and these critics did not have to fabricate this framework from scratch. Instead, they borrowed an interpretive schema that had already been in active use for a decade in the criticism of Abstract Expressionism, paintings that had earlier posed the same problems of comprehension as Brakhage's work. When first exhibited, the works of the Abstract Expressionists were incomprehensible to many. Even among art critics of relatively sophisticated tastes, befuddlement seems to have been a widespread reaction to the work of these new American painters.[4] Enter the *Action Painting schema*.

First articulated by critic Harold Rosenberg, the Action Painting schema holds that the viewer reads the marks on the canvas as traces of more important, earlier gestures by the painter. In the 1952 *Art News* essay on Abstract Expressionism in which he coined the term "Action Painting," Rosenberg argued: "At a certain moment the canvas began to appear to one American painter after another as an arena in which to act—rather than as a space in which to reproduce, re-design, analyze or 'express' an object, actual or imagined. What was to go on the canvas was not a picture but an event" (1960, 25). The value of this event—and here Action Painting theory betrays its Surrealist ancestry—stems from its spontaneity and its ability to express psychic states not fully controlled or even understood by the artist. As Rosenberg wrote in his 1957 essay on Hans Hofmann:

> If the ultimate subject matter of all art is the artist's psychic state or tension (and this may be the case even in nonindividualistic epochs), that state (e.g., grief) may be represented through the image of a thing or through an abstract sign. The innovation of Action Painting was to dispense with the *representation* of the state in favor of *enacting* it in a physical movement. The action on the canvas became its own representation. This was possible because an action, being made of both the psychic and the material, is by its nature a sign—it is the trace of a movement whose beginning and character it does not in itself ever altogether reveal (e.g., the act of love can, according to Freud, be mistaken for murder). (55)

It is because of his erratic, "gestural" camerawork that Brakhage has been indelibly marked as an Abstract Expressionist. But once again, the connection is not as apt as many writers imply.

According to the widely, though not universally, accepted Action Painting schema for the interpretation of Abstract Expressionism,[5] the painter's gestures are the seat of aesthetic value because the canvas is identified with the act of creation. Even though the work was always a surrogate for an ephemeral action, it was considered a fairly direct surrogate because the canvas was viewed in substantially the same form as it was painted. The traces left by the action were fairly deep; seeing an Action Painting, it is fairly easy to imagine the process of its production. This is the feature of Abstract Expressionism—what Rosenberg called the "extinguishing of the object"—that makes the "action" more important than the "painting." (As we will see, the emphasis on the process at the expense of the object produced is particularly influential in the criticism of the minimal strain.)

The screen or the frame of a film is not an arena the way the canvas is. Filmmakers can certainly engage the film material directly by writing or scratching on the emulsion, but such marks on the film strip are not displayed as the brushstrokes are: marks on the film are flashed by the viewer, greatly mediated by projection. For this reason, comparing film stills to paintings can be misleading. In projection the images are dramatically transformed if the frame-to-frame differences are very great, as they are in *Thigh Line Lyre Triangular*, where Brakhage scratches and paints the surface of the film. And where the frame-to-frame differences are smaller, as they are in sections of *Mothlight* (1963) where seeds are carefully placed in the same position frame after frame, the production process requires such care that it precludes the kind of gestural spontaneity that was so important to Action Painting theory.[6]

In spite of these differences between Brakhage's films and Action Painting, most critics have taken Brakhage's cues in applying the Action Painting schema to his work. Brakhage, trying to close the gap between his films and the Abstract Expressionist canvases, described his working method, emphasizing the role of his body movements:

> I took images as I could, according to feeling. So that as I've trained myself to hold this camera so that it will reflect the trembling or the

> feeling of any part of the body; so that it is an extension, so that this
> becomes a thing to ingather the light . . . (1963, n.p.)

Applied to Brakhage's work, the Action Painting schema is this:
interpret any otherwise unexplained camera movement as evidence of
the filmmaker's presence and as an expression of his psychic agitation
as he responded to the filmmaking situation. Thus, using the Action
Painting schema, the rapid, erratic camera movement in *Window
Water Baby Moving* (1959) can be interpreted as a sign of the filmmaker's emotional response to the birth. Of course, in *Window Water
Baby Moving*, such an interpretation is confirmed by other elements
of the film, especially the shots of Brakhage's face. But in *Thigh Line
Lyre Triangular*, in which the filmmaker's image does not appear, the
Action Painting schema provides the sole means of judging the filmmaker's attitude toward the events shown. In general, this schema
becomes important to poetic avant-garde films whenever the attitudes
and emotions of the filmmaker or characters are not shown in more
direct ways, for example, through legible images of facial expressions.

Interpretive schemata generally ascribe a specific meaning to
specific features of films, such as emotional agitation to erratic camera
movement. But interpretive schemata can be used with varying degrees of finesse, and they can sometimes be adapted to account for new
elements of films. For example, David James (1989) adapts the Action
Painting schema to explain the style of Carolee Schneemann's *Fuses*
(1964–68), a film poem documenting the filmmaker's lovemaking
with James Tenney. In James's account, the response of the filmmaker
to the erotic situations shown in the film is inscribed not in the
camerawork, but on the film stock itself:

> The urgency in which the lovers' individual lineaments are sub-
> sumed inheres as thoroughly in Schneemann's physical encounter with
> the material of film as it does in her encounter with the body of James
> Tenney. Emerging as the totalizing, polymorphous, introverted energy
> and self-absorbed hypersensuality of the sexual activity of the pro-
> filmic, the erotic power of *Fuses* overflows into the filmic, is repro-
> duced there as a filmic function. For the physical passion traced pho-
> tographically is returned upon in Schneemann's excitation of the
> physical body of the film in editing—the touch of her hand on the film's
> flesh in her painterly and sculptural work on the emulsion. (320)

As we might phrase this expanded version of the *Action Filmmaking
schema*: interpret indirect evidence of the filmmaker's bodily movements as the trace of a physical response to the events represented in
the film. Or as Rosenberg would put it, consider the film not as a space
in which to reproduce an object, but an arena in which to act. Ironically, what is sometimes taken to be the most direct embodiment of
the filmmaker's psychic state in the physical material of film, is
actually a critical stance, a style of interpretation produced by the
interaction of the American avant-garde cinema with the world of the
American visual arts.

We have seen that while the comparison between Brakhage and
Abstract Expressionism is apt, the analogy is not really based on

shared imagery, shared spatial structure, or even similar working methods. Rather, constructing the analogy with Abstract Expressionism is a means of making sense of Brakhage's films. Brakhage and the Abstract Expressionists posed similar problems for viewers, and critics resolved these problems with similar interpretive schemata. And, once in play, those same interpretive schemata can help make sense of other poetic avant-garde films. In the next chapter we will examine other interpretive schemata drawn from the visual arts, those used to make sense of the minimal strain of the American avant-garde film.

5

Rounding Up the Usual Suspects: The Minimal Strain and Interpretive Schemata

In 1963, the New York painter who had scandalized the art world with his ''artless'' renderings of soup cans, Coke bottles and Green Stamps turned his attention to the movies. Andy Warhol had earlier had some difficulty in gaining a foothold in the New York art world: established painters regarded him and his work with suspicion; galleries were reluctant to show his work. But once he achieved a measure of success as a painter, the world of the avant-garde film was open to him. Within a year Warhol had won *Film Culture*'s Independent Film Award for five of his films: *Kiss*, fifty minutes of close-ups of a woman kissing various men; *Haircut*, thirty-three minutes of a man getting a haircut; *Eat*, forty-five minutes of Pop artist Robert Indiana nibbling at a mushroom; *Sleep*, six *hours* of a man sleeping; and *Empire*, eight hours of the Empire State Building.[1] It might be overstating the case to say that *Sleep* and *Empire* were to the avant-garde film what Stravinsky's *Rite of Spring* was to music fifty years before, but Warhol's films—especially his early silents—were signposts of significant changes in the American avant-garde cinema.

Warhol's appearance marks the beginning of the avant-garde's increasingly intimate association with the contemporary visual arts. The most obvious manifestation of this association was the development of a strain of minimal filmmaking within the avant-garde cinema. The films of the minimal strain rejected the heightened subjectivity of the film poem and its standard stylistic devices: erratic camera movement and cutting, allusive metaphors, improvisational form. Instead, these early minimal films—especially Warhol's, but others' too—presented an increasingly prolonged and impassive stare at the most inexpressive of bodies and objects. A less obvious, though equally telling, emblem of the link with the visual arts was the gradual disappearance of the film poem metaphor from *Film Culture*'s critical rhetoric.

These aesthetic dislocations were framed by institutional changes in the avant-garde mode of filmmaking. Increasingly, the filmmakers who rose to prominence after Warhol had backgrounds in the visual arts: Canadian Michael Snow had been a minimalist painter; Tony Conrad had been a performance artist associated with the Fluxus group; Paul Sharits, educated as a painter, was also associated with the Fluxus group; Bruce Conner and Robert Breer began their careers as artists and continued to produce highly regarded Pop sculptures as well as films.[2] And not only artists but art critics turned their attention to film. In the pre-Warhol era, only *Film Culture* offered regular coverage of the avant-garde film; during the mid 1960s, a number of art journals published articles on current work in the avant-garde film. The most important of these was *Artforum*. Established in the early 1960s to promote West Coast art, *Artforum* moved to New York in the middle of the decade. Also about this time, Annette Michelson became its film editor. From this platform she was a major force behind the consideration of the avant-garde film in the context of radical work in the visual arts.

From our perspective, however, the most important point about the avant-garde's turn toward the visual arts is that it deranged the viewer's ability to make sense of the avant-garde cinema. The implicit viewing procedures that had evolved for the poetic strain do not work for the minimal strain. Viewers cannot easily interpret these films as the expression of some aspect of the filmmaker's subjectivity. And yet the problem is not establishing basic coherence, as we found with Stan Brakhage's lyrical films. After all, it is relatively easy to match an appropriate schema to an eight-hour film of the Empire State Building.

The problem with Brakhage's work is discovering coherence. With the minimal strain, the problem is discovering relevance: how can one meaningfully relate such films to the concerns of the community that views them? The films of the minimal strain apparently violate the principle of optimal relevance. They do not seem to reward the viewer's attention and effort with appropriate amounts of relevant information. Our question then becomes, what competing principles might account for this apparent irrelevance? In this chapter, we will examine how the art world supplied these principles in the form of new interpretive schemata for the avant-garde cinema.

Sitney's "Structural Film"

The most influential attempt to come to terms with the aesthetics of the avant-garde's minimal strain is P. Adams Sitney's 1969 *Film Culture* essay, "Structural Film." This essay launched the avant-garde's liveliest controversy of the 1970s.[3] In the face of a torrent of criticism, "Structural Film" has been reincarnated in print twice, and Sitney has elaborated its ideas in additional articles and lectures.[4] Yet in spite of the widespread reaction against the essay, it continues to set the agenda for most discussions of the minimal strain of the avant-garde film.

"Structural Film" is an appropriate foundation for a discussion of the interpretive schemata applied to the minimal strain of the avant-garde film, but not because Sitney invented them. The basic interpretive schemata brought to bear on the Structural film were already developed by the early 1960s and were in common use in the visual arts by the time of the publication of Sitney's essay. And not only did Sitney not develop these schemata, he used them only selectively. As we will see, Sitney's view of these films is somewhat idiosyncratic, which in large part accounts for the storm of criticism that surrounds "Structural Film." This criticism can be seen as an attempt to revise Sitney's position by bringing it into line with prevailing interpretive schemata.

What makes Sitney's work so unusual among critics of the avant-garde film? As readers of his study of the history of the avant-garde, *Visionary Film*, will be well aware, Sitney sees his project as an attempt "to isolate and describe the visionary strain within the complex manifold of the American avant-garde film" (1979, x). This "visionary strain" is no minor subset of the avant-garde; his contention is that the avant-garde film in the United States is closely associated with the concerns of Romantic poetry.

Sitney's interpretation of the American avant-garde is modelled on his teacher Harold Bloom's treatment of the English Romantic poets (1961). Bloom argues that the example of the French Revolution encouraged the English poets at the beginning of the nineteenth century to have utopian social aspirations, even though revolution was thwarted in England. At the same time, this utopianism was inflected with Protestant theology that stressed independence and individualism. Thus the poet's inspiration came from within, rather than from above or from the group, and his vision was intensely personal. Unlike Bloom, Sitney does not explain the visionary quality of the American avant-garde as motivated by its historical context, but he nonetheless sees the avant-garde in Bloomian terms. As such, its primary concern, according to Sitney, is the representation of the human mind in all its depth, especially the minds of artists, whose powers of imagination and vision enable them to see the conflicts raging within themselves and between them and society.

Visionary Film charts the evolution of these concerns through what Sitney identifies as the major phases of the American avant-garde. The visionary strain begins in the "trance" film, in which a protagonist struggles with internal conflicts that have been projected onto an imaginary world. In the next phase, the lyrical film, the protagonist disappears as the filmmaker uses film to represent his or her personal vision of the world more directly. In the "mythopoetic" film a new kind of protagonist appears: not the hypnotized protagonist of the trance film who struggles with internal problems, but a mythic figure who struggles with the problems of the individual confronting the world and society.

It is against this background—films concerned with the struggles of individuals with themselves and the world—that Sitney saw Structural film suddenly emerging. Sitney argues that from the 1940s to the mid-1960s visionary filmmakers like Gregory Markopoulos, Sidney Peterson, Kenneth Anger and especially Brakhage developed more condensed and complex forms to express themes of the self. He called this the *formal* film. But since the mid-1960s, filmmakers with a new sensibility had emerged. "Theirs is a cinema of structure," he wrote, "in which the shape of the whole film is predetermined and simplified, and it is that shape which is the primal impression of the film" (368). The basic difference is that the formal film is complex, whereas the Structural film is simplified. Sitney elaborates this distinction:

> A precise statement of the difference between formal and structural organization must involve a sense of the working process; the formal film is a tight nexus of content, a shape designed to explore the facets of the material. . . . The structural film insists on its shape, and what content it has is minimal and subsidiary to the outline. Four characteristics of the structural film are its fixed camera position (fixed frame from the viewer's perspective), the flicker effect, loop printing, and rephotography off the screen. (369–70)

In the most complete and recent version of "Structural Film," in *Visionary Film*, the suddenness of the emergence of Structural film is toned down; Structural film is seen as a development out of the formal film, and not as a reaction against it or a complete break from it. According to Sitney, the Structural film develops from the lyrical film the way the lyrical film developed from the trance film. The trance film was concerned with the psyche of its protagonist, but its first-person aspects—shots from the protagonist's point of view—were qualified and mediated by the entrance of the protagonist as a character in the film. By not showing the protagonist, Brakhage's lyrical film more faithfully captures the first-person quality of the visionary's struggle. Sitney explains that in the lyrical film, "we see what the film-maker sees; the reactions of the camera and the montage reveal his responses to his vision. . . . Without that achievement [Brakhage's work] and its subsequent evolution, it would be difficult to imagine the flourishing of the structural film" (370). Structural film, too, withholds the protagonist in favor of an increased awareness of the camera. For Sitney, the difference is only that the simplified structure is a representation of the human *mind*, not human vision. In Sitney's argument, the Structural film was a break from earlier "formal" film in so far as it uses different organizational strategies to slightly different ends. At the same time, it is a development consistent with the *overall* project of the American avant-garde. In an often cited (and sometimes misquoted) passage, Sitney explains this project: "If, as I have claimed, the often unacknowledged aspiration of the American avant-garde film has been the cinematic reproduction of the human mind, then the structural film approaches the condition of meditation and evokes states of consciousness without mediation; that is, with the sole mediation of the camera" (370).

That the minimal strain is the latest phase in the Romantic trajectory of the avant-garde is hardly the consensus view of the history of the American avant-garde. In practice, Sitney's description of the visionary strain grew into an interpretation of the entire history of the avant-garde as the development of a kind of American Romanticism. For some, this totalizing view of history is suspect, and these suspicions are especially acute regarding the Structural film, which most critics see as essentially Modernist and opposed to the Romantic aesthetic. For this reason, responses to "Structural Film" took pains to situate these films in the context of recent Modernist work, especially in the visual arts, which the writers felt was the most proximate and relevant context. In so situating these films, critics brought to bear the interpretive schemata developed for works in the visual arts.

The criticism of "Structural Film" has not been aimed uniformly at all parts of the essay but has centered on a few passages. Sitney's attempt to identify, define and explain a tendency of mid-to-late 1960s avant-garde filmmaking has three basic components: theory, history and criticism. Of these, the critical portion is by far the longest. Of the eighty-two paragraphs in the latest and longest version, in *Visionary Film*, sixty are devoted to critical analyses of the work of four filmmakers: Michael Snow, Paul Sharits, George Landow and Hollis Frampton. This criticism *per se* has never been very controversial. No one disputes Sitney's interpretation of the individual films. For example, Sitney maintains that Snow's work is a metaphor for human consciousness. Regina Cornwell goes so far as to complain that this perception blinds Sitney to other aspects of the films, but no one has tried to argue that Snow's work is *not* a metaphor for consciousness. Sitney's criticism is somewhat out of the mainstream, but it is his historical and theoretical claims that have been the target of most of the criticism of the "Structural Film" essay. This is not really surprising, since even in the longest version this part of the argument is very brief and not very thoroughly developed.

The essay's historical section consists of a survey of the work of Andy Warhol and a comparison of the Structural film to the work of Brakhage, Markopoulos and Anger, whom Sitney uses as examples of the earlier, "formal" avant-garde. This section has been severely criticized by almost every writer who has responded to Sitney. The complaints generally argue that Sitney has underemphasized or ignored the work of many filmmakers—notably the Fluxus artists and European filmmakers[5]—and developments in the other arts—notably Minimalism in the visual arts.[6] We might defend the brevity of Sitney's historical survey on the grounds that it was never intended to catalogue exhaustively the precursors to Structural film, but only to survey certain key developments. Still, many have accused Sitney of prejudice in selecting his historical evidence to support his contention that Structural film fits the Romantic trajectory he was working so hard to establish.[7] And in the process of selecting this evidence and presenting it as the dominant strain of the American avant-garde of the late 1960s and 1970s, he has consigned a large portion of the non-Structural avant-garde film to oblivion.

The theoretical portion of the essay is also very brief and consists primarily of an attempt to define "structural," and this attempt at a definition has received even more criticism than his sketch of its history. In ''Structural Film,'' Sitney offers two definitions of the concept. One is very concrete. The Structural film, Sitney writes, has four typical characteristics: a fixed camera position, the use of the flicker effect, loop printing, and rephotography. As his detractors were quick to point out, Sitney offered these defining traits with the disclaimer that they were neither necessary nor sufficient conditions for a film to be deemed Structural. That meant that some Structural films might not use any of these techniques and that even films that *did* use one or more of these might not be Structural after all. What sort of definition could this be? For some, this alone was enough to show that the notion was nonsense (Jenkins 1978). But these four typical traits were offered as a kind of family resemblance description of what Structural films might look like, not as a theoretical explanation of the class of films. The four traits make a rather flimsy definition, but as critical hints, they work quite well. Not only do they happen to appear in many Structural films, they are regularly cited and summarized even by writers who find them unacceptable as a definition of a genre.[8]

If we remove the criticism, the history and the loose ''operational'' definition of Structural film from Sitney's essay, there is not much left for his abstract theoretical definition. In the passages where he most explicitly defines Structural film, he identifies it as ''a cinema of structure in which the shape of the whole film is predetermined and simplified, and it is that shape which is the primal impression of the film'' (368). Or, ''the structural film insists on its shape, and what content it has is minimal and subsidiary to the outline'' (370). Every writer who addresses Sitney's ''Structural Film'' points to one or the other of these passages as the key to his definition.

One common complaint against this definition is that it uses imprecise terms. According to Malcolm Le Grice, the label Structural is misleading, since it has nothing to do with the intellectual movement of French Structuralism, and ''the loose concept of shape is of little help'' in defining the concept (1977, 87). Paul Arthur (1978–79), too, criticizes Sitney's use of the catch-all term ''shape'': by defining the Structural film as one with a prominent ''shape,'' Sitney's definition is nearly circular because the terms ''structure'' and ''shape'' are nearly synonymous. And Regina Cornwell (1979b) makes the same charge of vacuousness against his definition of the ''formal'' film, arguing that on the basis of Sitney's definition it is impossible to distinguish it from the Structural film.

Jenkins, Le Grice, Arthur, and Cornwell all raise intelligent objections to Sitney's formulation of Structural film. But what is most significant in their responses to Sitney is not their critique of his work, but their articulation of an alternative view of the minimal strain of the American avant-garde cinema. To put it generally, this alterative sought to make sense of the minimal strain of the avant-garde cinema by incorporating it into the Modernist project, as that project was envisioned in the 1960s and 1970s. In what follows, I will have occasion to point out what now appear to be shortcomings of this alternative. In so far as these critics adopted the view of Modernism that was then so pervasive in thinking about the visual arts, they adopted its blindnesses as well as its insights.

The minimal strain was incorporated into the Modernist project via three interpretive schemata, two of which were adapted from contemporary thought about the visual arts.

The first, the *phenomenological schema*, was not widely applied to the visual arts before being adapted to avant-garde film. It was developed in the film criticism of Annette Michelson, who was strongly influenced by the phenomenology of Edmund Husserl and Maurice Merleau-Ponty. She in turn exerted considerable influence over criticism of the avant-garde film, not only as film editor for *Artforum* but as a teacher at New York University, where she trained many of the critics of the avant-garde film. According to the phenomenological schema, the critic interprets the film as presenting itself to the direct perception of the viewer. Alternatively, the film is interpreted as the embodiment of some fundamental feature of consciousness.

The second interpretive schema for the minimal strain was the *art-process schema*, derived from the aesthetics of composer and teacher John Cage. Cage's advocacy of the blurring of the boundaries between ''art'' and ''life'' was very influential on 1960s art in many media. For him, any material organized in any way could have aesthetic value, and traditional aesthetic forms needlessly restricted the range of options open to the artist. According to the art-process schema, the production of an innovative film is seen as a demonstration of the rigidity of the conventional process of filmmaking.

The most common of these interpretive schemata is the third, the *anti-illusion schema*, derived from the work of Clement Greenberg. In large part, Greenberg's influential art criticism provided the theory behind Minimalism itself. In the brief essay ''Modernist Painting,'' Greenberg argued that the Modern artwork has tended to purge itself of all qualities not essential to its medium. Painting is pigment on a flat surface, and any representation of depth is an impurity. As we will see, this notion had immense appeal, especially to critics of the avant-garde film. According to the anti-illusion schema, any film image with limited depth cues is interpreted as an assertion of the inherent qualities of the film medium.

The Phenomenological Schema

Unlike Arthur and Cornwell, Michelson never criticized Sitney in print. In fact, Michelson's and Sitney's analyses of Michael Snow's *Wavelength* (1966–67) are quite similar. But their understanding of Brakhage's work, which they both saw as the appropriate background to Snow, demonstrates that their views of the avant-garde are radically different.

In 1966, Annette Michelson called Brakhage's invocation of the Action Painting schema ''an uncritical parody of Abstract Expressionist orthodoxy'' (42). As Michelson points out, Brakhage lays claim to being an ''Action Filmmaker'' only by falling back on what was at that time a rather tired reading strategy. For Sitney, Brakhage had joined the Abstract Expressionists to throw off the bonds of convention. Sitney saw it as an act of courage, and an artistic achievement of the highest order; its political ramifications were of little concern to him. But Michelson, for whom politics was paramount, saw his association with Abstract Expressionism as capitulation: Brakhage might have escaped the tyranny of Renaissance perspective, but by submitting to the authority of the established powers of the art world, the radical point of his work was blunted. By the late 1960s, Brakhage's stock had risen with Michelson, who reappraised his work in *Artforum*. Michelson had objected to the use of the Action Painting schema, but now she valorized other aspects of his work (especially what I called his "total liberation theory" in chapter 1) by using a new interpretive schema of her own: the phenomenological schema.

The evolution of Michelson's phenomenological perspective on the avant-garde can be traced in a series of articles she published in *Artforum* between 1968 and 1973. These articles are an extended analysis of three central figures in film theory: Andre Bazin, Sergei Eisenstein and Brakhage.[9] But the most influential articulation of Michelson's approach is her essay "Toward Snow" (1971), a landmark of film criticism in which her phenomenological approach is applied to the avant-garde's minimal strain.

Michelson begins her analysis of Snow's work by noting that certain films explore the nature of consciousness in "a striking, a uniquely direct presentational mode" (1971, 172). For Michelson, Snow's work is the paradigm case of the link between cinema and consciousness, and his films represent "an inquiry into the modes of seeing, recording, selecting, composing, remembering and projecting" (183). Again, as with Brakhage's link to Abstract Expressionism, note that Snow himself cues the phenomenological reading of his film: Michelson undergirds this reading with earlier comments by the filmmaker himself.[10] For Michelson, the clearest example of a film that directly presents experience is Snow's *One Second in Montreal* (1969), in which "the flow of time is somehow inscribed in the filmic image, immediately given, perceptible in our experience of it" (177). This brings Snow's film close to the work of Brakhage, which, as she phrases it, "aspires to present itself perceptually, all at once, to resist observation and cognition" (176). This new temporality is the basis of one aspect of the phenomenological schema: any long take without appreciable dramatic action can be read as the inscription of time on the image. Alternatively, it can be read as being presented for our fascinated contemplation—though not our analysis.

For the most part though, Michelson's analysis of *Wavelength* depends not on the direct inscription of aspects of experience on the image, but on a pair of metaphors that suggest how the film represents consciousness as well as directly presenting it. As Michelson writes at the beginning of her essay, "There is a metaphor recurrent in contemporary discourse on the nature of consciousness: that of cinema" (1971, 172). She amplifies this notion by citing a commentator on Husserl:

> Phenomenology is an attempt to film, in slow motion, that which has been, owing to the manner in which it is seen in natural speed, not absolutely unseen, but missed, subject to oversight. It attempts, slowly

and calmly, to draw closer to that original intensity which is not given in appearance, but from which things and processes do, nevertheless, in turn proceed. (173)

And as cinema is a metaphor for consciousness, *Wavelength* is the paradigm case. "The film," she writes, "is the projection of a grand reduction; its 'plot' is the tracing of spatio-temporal *données*, its 'action' the movement of the camera as the movement of consciousness" (175).

But this is only the first half of the metaphorical reading of *Wavelength*, for if it figuratively represents consciousness, it also figuratively represents cinema. The overall structure of the film is a gradual zoom that slowly narrows the field of view. Yet this zoom is not continuous but "stammering" in that it is interrupted by superimpositions, color flashes, shifts of the film stock from positive to negative, and a number of identifiable events. From this Michelson concludes that "the effects of these perceptions is to present the movement forward as a flow which bears in its wake, contains, discrete events: their discreteness articulates an allusion to the separate frames out of which persistence of vision organizes cinematic illusion" (174).

In practice then, the phenomenological schema has three components. First, any passage that is significantly longer than is required to understand the "event" depicted and that does not manipulate the temporal dimension of the action is read as the inscription of the flow of time on the film. Second, aspects of the film are interpreted as the metaphorical embodiment of some fundamental feature of human consciousness such as its immediacy or its continuity. And third, aspects of the film are interpreted as metaphorical representations of cinema itself.

The "direct perception" notion is easily applied by many critics, though rarely does it serve as the cornerstone of an analysis of a film. Usually the "point" of the film, its relevance to the viewing community, is established through another interpretive schema, while direct perception is brought in to account for the "pleasure" of the film by speaking in terms of its "sensuous qualities" or its being "perceptually engaging." For example, Richard Bartone's analysis of Larry Gottheim's *Four Shadows* (1978) relies heavily on the Greenbergian play between two- and three-dimensional representation. But Bartone also suggests that the task of the viewer of this film is like the task of the filmmaker, who must "simply open his senses to the world's immediate impressions without the intervention of logic or intelligence" (1979, 169).

The metaphorical corollaries of the phenomenological schema, on the other hand, are the least "schematic" of the interpretive schemata for Structural film, since selecting features of the film that metaphorically embody cinema or the mind often involves significant problem-solving activity. Also, unlike the direct perception notion, these metaphors may serve as the foundation for an analysis of a film since they have been deemed "significant" enough to account for the relevance of a work. In fact, although Sitney does not generally use the interpretive schemata of the art world, the "metaphors for consciousness" component of the phenomenological schema is quite evident in his analysis of the Structural film. Michelson's phenomenological interpretation is the "official line" on Snow, and Sitney cites her article extensively in the final version of "Structural Film." But the metaphor for consciousness is more than just a quick way for Sitney to address *Wavelength*; it is the dominant trope of his survey of the American avant-garde film. He puts it plainly: "the often unacknowledged aspiration of the American avant-garde has been the cinematic reproduction of the human mind" (1979, 370).

The similarity between Sitney's and Michelson's treatments of Snow is striking. Not only is the "metaphor for consciousness" the centerpiece of both their analyses, but each has approvingly cited the other's essays on Snow.[11] Ultimately though, such similarities mask the fundamental differences in their approaches to Modernist art. For Michelson, Snow's work has political import as a sophisticated critique of illusion.[12] For Sitney, Snow's work was not a critique of illusion, nor was it particularly political in any way. His use of the "metaphor for consciousness" interpretation was as a means of locating Snow in the Romantic trajectory of the American avant-garde.

Michelson concludes her discussion of Snow's work with the suggestion that it is circular and tends toward tautology in that the perception of each film involves a recognition or even a reconstruction of the processes that produced it. Ironically, this suggestion recalls the Action Painting schema that Michelson had criticized in 1966. But whereas Michelson had dismissed this critical move as conservative, in his 1978 reappraisal of "Structural Film," Paul Arthur uses this kind of reconstruction of the film's production as the second major interpretive schema for the minimal strain of the avant-garde film.

The Art-Process Schema

For critic Paul Arthur, the single most important implication of the films produced in the wake of Warhol's work was that the experience of film viewing had been radically changed. Arthur's assertion that these films produced a new relationship between the viewer and the film object is the focus of his two-part essay "Structural Film: Revisions, New Versions, and the Artifact" (1978–79). The usual charges of imprecision are made against Sitney: the description of Structural film as having a simple shape that is the primal impression of the film is just too vague. As a consequence, for Arthur, Structural film is a grab-bag that includes or excludes films willy-nilly, regardless of what the viewing experience is really like. To correct this, Arthur sets out to demonstrate more precisely what the viewer does with a Structural film.

For Arthur, an important early example of a film that requires a new kind of viewer is Brakhage's *Mothlight* (1963). The film is not a conveyor of meaning either in the transparent commercial narrative mode, or in the metaphorical associative mode of the earlier avant-garde, what Sitney had called the ''formal'' film. Instead, *Mothlight* belongs to a new class of films, those that direct attention away from the screen and to the physical object in the projector. How is the viewer's attention so directed? Arthur suggests four potential causes: a high rate of information change on the screen; poor legibility; a cognizance of the film's facture; and most tellingly, an *intuition* that a look at the film strip would help to explain the other three features. What Arthur identifies as a cognizance of the film's facture is the second major interpretive schemata for the minimal strain, the art-process schema.

Arthur agrees with Sitney that *Mothlight* has ties to the old ''formal'' film insofar as affixing small objects to the filmstrip is part of Brakhage's effort to devise new means of creating subjective and personal imagery. But it is also, Arthur suggests, part of the Modernist effort to destroy the illusionism of art. Brakhage and the Structural filmmakers do not suppress the material nature of the film strip in the way that films with understandable images do. Instead these film-makers *examine* the status of the film object. And viewers, once their attention is drawn to the object by these films, recognize the dual nature of cinema as simultaneously an artifact and a performance.

According to Arthur, this turning of attention to the object underlies not just films that make use of innovative materials but most of what Sitney calls Structural film because the viewer makes similar moves with any film whose structure is predetermined and simplified. A film with a minimally changing image and a regular editing rhythm cues the viewer to reconstruct the film's production. As Arthur puts it:

> The relations produced in the viewer as concern the process of ordering are maintained by a kind of mental, temporal placement as he/she tries to retrace the operative procedures. Through this mechanism, the viewer imagines the succession of production stages which could logically ''explain'' the terms of the immediate filmic situation . . . Understanding at what point (or points) a system was applied to production can be a key element in establishing the degree or pattern of viewer-distanciation and reflexivity. (1979, 124)

In other words, the viewer attends to the projected images only provisionally; the viewer uses these images to reconstruct the steps the filmmaker took to produce them, and these procedures are the point of the film. Just as Harold Rosenberg argued was the case for Abstract Expressionism, and as Brakhage argued was the case with his early work, the screen is no longer a place for images but an arena in which to act.

By resurrecting the actions of the filmmaker as the seat of the film's value, Arthur makes himself Rosenberg's heir;[13] but the way he interprets these actions makes him a descendent of John Cage. For Rosenberg, the actions of the artist were spontaneous gestures driven by emotions the artist may not even understand. But for Cage, the action of the artist is a more deliberate act, even if the act provides a framework for random events. Though Cage is not explicitly cited in Arthur's essay, Cage's work and theories are an important background to Arthur's treatment of Structural film.

Though Cage himself was a composer, his aesthetic theories published in his book *Silence* (1961), and his teaching posts at Black Mountain College in the early 1950s and The New School for Social Research in New York in the late 1950s, gave him enormous influence over all the arts in the 1960s. He was an extreme advocate of innovation and the lifting of constraints of any kind from the artist. He suggested two basic strategies for this liberation: the inclusion of a wide range of raw materials, and the development of new compositional procedures.

Cage was a student of Arnold Schoenberg, the founder of serial music. Schoenberg had come to believe that the possibilities of tonal composition had been exhausted after centuries of dominating Western music. The octave is divided into the twelve notes of the chromatic scale; in traditional tonal composition, only a few of these are emphasized. By concentrating on this smaller subset of notes, tonal compositions have a familiar, musical sound, but for Schoenberg, this familiar sound had become aesthetically lifeless. In the alternative he developed, atonal serialism, each of the twelve notes of the chromatic scale receives equal emphasis and the composition as a whole is structured through intricate mathematical patterns. As far as Cage is concerned, Schoenberg's importance lies in the fact that he made new sonic and compositional patterns available to the composer and thereby expanded the range of experiences available to the listener.

But for Cage, even Schoenberg restricted the composer too much for, after all, atonal music still consists of notes played by the same traditional instruments. Cage wished to expand the range of acceptable musical material to include not only the twelve notes of the chromatic scale but any sound made by any means. For example, Cage modified traditional instruments. In his pieces for prepared piano (beginning in 1938), Cage inserted foreign objects into the piano so that when the performer struck the keys, the piano's hammers would not cleanly strike the strings but would instead strike the objects. Or, when the strings were struck, their vibrations would set the objects in motion and the objects in turn would strike other strings. Cage went even further and composed music without traditional instruments. In *Imaginary Landscape No. 4* (1951) the "instruments" are a dozen radios, each tuned to a different station. The most notorious example of Cage's effort to expand the range of sound available for musical composition is his *4′ 33″* (1952), a piece for any instrument during which the performer is to sit in silence for four-and-a-half minutes while the audience listens to the ambient sound of the concert hall.

Cage was concerned not only to include new and unusual sounds in his music but also to introduce new compositional strategies. Once again he followed Schoenberg's lead away from tonal music, only to find the principles of serialism too restrictive as well. Instead, Cage relied heavily on chance combinations of sounds through a system of coin tossing he derived from the *I Ching*. His 1951 *Music of Changes* is composed this way, but again, since it uses a traditional instrument the sound produced is not totally unpredictable. In his *Imaginary Landscape* piece for radios however, not only were the settings of the radios determined at random, the programming received by the radios was unpredictable. In fact, since the piece was first performed late at night, most of the radio stations were off the air and only a few of the radios made any intelligible sound.

These strategies of including a wide range of materials and using a wide range of procedures to structure the materials rested on two aesthetic principles. The first principle holds that much material that makes up our everyday world has aesthetic value. This attitude was very influential on the art of the 1960s. The inclusion of previously unsanctioned material is a fundamental feature of assemblage art. In Robert Rauschenberg's *Monogram* (1959), for example, we find such oddities as an old tire and a stuffed goat. The Pop Artists, though sticking to paint and canvas for the most part, included images that were previously "inartistic," such as Andy Warhol's Campbell's soup cans, car accidents and electric chairs. This Cagean principle also found application in the avant-garde film, for example in Brakhage's inclusion of tiny pieces of debris in his *Mothlight*, and in Conner's use of found footage.

The second aesthetic principle is just as prevalent in 1960s art and even more important to the avant-garde film since it has become an important interpretive schema for the Structural film. Cage's advocacy of, and emphasis on, novel compositional principles relocates aesthetic value by removing it from the object produced and affixing it to the process that produces it. As with the Action Painting schema, the viewer begins by reconstructing the process that the artist used to produce the work. But then, according to the art-process schema, instead of interpreting the work as an expression of an intense psychic state, the viewer compares this process to the reigning artistic norms and reads the work as a comment on the conventional and repressive nature of those reigning norms. The point of "retracing the operative procedures," to use Arthur's phrase, is that it leads to an awareness of the nature of the film process so that viewers might be less susceptible to films that hide the processes of their production.

Having seen that the Action Painting schema used for Brakhage's work can be adapted to the demands of the Structural film by reworking it into the art-process schema, we should not be surprised to see Brakhage's work itself reinterpreted with this "adjusted" interpretive schema. Arthur transforms Brakhage from an example of the reigning norm of the "formal" film, against which the Structural filmmakers revolted, to a precursor, or even a founder, of the new movement. In fact, in part one of Arthur's revision of "Structural Film," Brakhage is shown not only to have been at work on the same set of problems as minimal filmmaker Tony Conrad but also to have provided many of the same answers. The art-process schema thus fits Brakhage's *Mothlight* perfectly. Arthur writes: "The accession of new or little used materials became a way of deflecting or defeating the authority—economic and esthetic—of industrial mediation by appropriating aspects of image-making previously ensconced in mechanically-fixed operations'' (1978, 10). In other words, Brakhage used innovative materials to make images in ways that did not depend on how cameras were typically designed and used by the commercial film industries. This action is not merely artistically innovative, it is a political act that resists ''the authority . . . of industrial mediation,'' that is to say, capitalism. Arthur finds similar political implications in Tony Conrad's *Articulation of Boolean Algebra for Film Opticals* (1975). The film consists of a series of horizontal stripes crossing the entire film strip. Since these stripes cross both the image and the sound track, the same stripes create both the sound and the image. But because the sound head is twenty-six frames away from the gate from which the image is projected, the sound and image are out of sync. Arthur finds this composition to have progressive political effects: ''The film induces speculation on the projection apparatus and its capacity to divergently present identical units of information. Hearing and seeing become disjoined from their usual complementary role in the film experience and the spectator is led to a recognition of sound/image conjunction as mechanical convention'' (1978, 11–12).

Arthur's essay is a pioneering attempt to come to terms with the way the minimal strain challenges film viewers. But as a theory of the viewer, the art-process approach has some limitations. First, it casts the role of the viewer in passive terms, making the viewer subordinate to the film. Conrad's film has the power to ''induce speculation,'' while its viewer must be ''led to a recognition.'' We might question whether the realization that sound and image may not be synchronous is the kind of recognition that any viewer needs to be led to. Viewers would likely have seen some films with disjointed sound and image tracks, whether conventional documentaries with voice-over narration or work by Godard, Resnais or Duras, all of whom are known for experimentation with sound/image relationships. Arthur's point might be that none of these filmmakers lead us to contemplate the *projection* apparatus. True, but if viewers did not already know the basics of projector mechanics, there is no way that they could conclude that the sound/image disjunction was produced by the separation of the sound head and the gate in the projector.

Arthur's essay, particularly part two, is an exemplary discussion of the minimal strain of avant-garde filmmaking in the context of Modernist visual art. But though Arthur cites an impressive list of artists in various media working on Modernist projects, his film analyses appeal to a background of ''usual'' film practice. *Boolean Algebra* looks less innovative next to Peter Kubelka's *Arnulf Rainer* (1958–60), which, according to another critic's application of the art-process schema, conducted ''a major rediscovery and investigation of the basic elements of film'' (E. Simon 1972, 33) a decade and a half earlier. And when it comes to demonstrating the conventional nature of our aesthetic criteria, both films were anticipated by Duchamp's readymades. Only against the background of the classical Hollywood cinema can the avant-garde invariably be seen as a cinema of radical innovation; consequently, the tradition of the commercial narrative film is constantly (though sometimes implicitly) invoked as if it were a perpetually and universally reigning norm.

The question of the reigning norm during the rise of the Structural film rather neatly distinguishes Sitney from critics like Arthur who use the art-process schema. For Arthur, the Structural film is an act of aesthetic and political resistance. By selecting the Hollywood film as the reigning aesthetic norm and an exemplar of capitalism, Arthur makes Conrad and Brakhage both aesthetically and politically revolutionary. In comparison, Sitney's view of the avant-garde film is apolitical and evolutionary. He did not see the avant-garde as the continuous revolt against the reigning norm, nor did he interpret the work of any filmmaker as a demonstration of the bankruptcy of the commercial film. Thus, Sitney rarely sees the avant-garde film against the background of the Hollywood film. In the context of the minimal strain, I am inclined to see this as a virtue. But as David James (1989) and Dana Polan (1985) show, in the context of other work in the avant-garde cinema, avoiding the relationship between the avant-garde and Hollywood must be reckoned a problem.

The Anti-Illusion Schema

In his introductory essay to the catalog of a traveling exhibition of American avant-garde film, John G. Hanhardt set out to define the project of the American avant-garde by distinguishing it from the European art film. While art films do question "the established codes of filmmaking, . . . they do not engage the material of film and the illusion of space . . . with the same specific regard as does the avant-garde film" (1976, 20–21). By citing the exploration of the material of film and the illusion of space, and making it the defining quality of the avant-garde film, Hanhardt invokes the most important and common interpretive schema in the avant-garde. According to this schema, derived from the art criticism of Clement Greenberg, any element on the screen that does not produce an impression of three-dimensional space is read as a demonstration of the inherent flatness of the cinematic image. This inherent flatness is valorized over the "deceptive" deep space commonly associated with the commercial narrative cinema. If, as recent film theory had suggested, the representation of depth has negative ideological consequences, then the completely flat image would avoid them. Even further, when juxtaposed with representations of three-dimensional space, the flat image can be seen as a critique of that representation and thereby not only avoid its ideological consequences but counteract them.

Greenberg had great influence on the avant-garde film, for his essays not only chronicled the visual art of the twentieth century, they set the agenda for Minimalism. By analyzing the art of this century as the progressive solution to a set of representational "problems," his work suggested future developments as well as analyzing work already produced. He was also able to give prominence to those artists who continued to address these problems. This he did not only as the author of the widely read "Modernist Painting" (1961), but as the curator of "Post-painterly Abstraction" (1964), one of the earliest exhibitions of Minimal art. Thus to the extent that the aesthetics of Structural film were the aesthetics of Minimalism, they were the aesthetics of Clement Greenberg. Though Greenberg's aesthetics were by this time largely apolitical, the work produced under his aegis was easily appropriated by the more political film scholars who by the 1970s began to look to the avant-garde for an alternative to the politically flawed commercial narrative.

What was this aesthetic that was so influential on the art of the 1960s and so attractive to film scholars? Greenberg's aesthetic theory begins from what he takes to be a fundamental law of art in the modern era: each artistic medium aspires to a state of purity wherein its works are purged of all characteristics that are inessential to the medium itself. For example, the medium of painting consists of pigment applied to a two-dimensional support. Representational imagery, for centuries considered a natural and even essential aspect of painting, is not only no longer necessary, but is to be avoided in advanced art. The most advanced or highly developed paintings are those that not only reject representation and display their two-dimensionality but reject the slightest hint of a represented third dimension. Painting is pigment on a flat surface; by definition it must be this, and according to Greenberg, modern painting should be *only* this.

This condensed paraphrase of Greenberg's aesthetic theory reduces it to the point of parody. But it was just this reduced version of his work that gained currency among critics of Structural film, especially in the work of Regina Cornwell. The anti-illusion schema is the dominant critical strategy in her work, and like many others she seems to have derived it from Greenberg's essay "Modernist Painting." This essay, originally delivered as a radio talk, is a concise and unequivocal account of the essentialist side of Greenberg's theory. But while "Modernist Painting" may represent an important aspect of Greenberg's work, it comes nowhere close to an outline of a program of criticism. As Greenberg explained in a postscript that accompanied a reprint of the essay, merely because a given work excludes all qualities inessential to its medium in no way suggests that the work be valorized. To say that a painting is flat identifies it as part of a contemporary aesthetic trajectory but in itself does not constitute a judgment of value.

Greenberg's "American-Type Painting" (1955, revised 1958), a longer, less polemical and less often cited essay, offers a more complete picture of his formalist criticism. In it, he analyzes the work of the color field Abstract Expressionists, and he goes far beyond the simple claim that their work rejects the representation of a third dimension. In turning away from contrasts of light/dark value as the basis for their compositions and toward contrasts of hue, they developed a new "shallow, atmospheric, breathing" space. Whether this is really a new kind of space is certainly open to debate, but this argument is more sophisticated than the simplistic valorization of flatness that is too often attributed to Greenberg. In fact, Greenberg himself expressed no small amount of distaste for art that might be considered a simpleminded application of the essentialist tenet. In "Recentness of Sculpture" (1967), Greenberg makes the point that being abreast of the times is no substitute for "inspiration" and "sensibility." Greenberg here may be smuggling an impressionistic standard of taste into his aesthetics, but he is certainly not equating flatness with achievement—either artistic or political.[14]

The critics of Structural film, on the other hand, often apply the anti-illusion schema without analyzing the representation of depth in the film under consideration. Cornwell's "Some Formalist Tendencies in the Current American Avant-garde Film," for example, is virtually a catalog of Greenbergian readings. She writes that in Ernie Gehr's *History* (1970), "the images created by the grain, shifting and changing in time, only suggest film's virtual three-dimensionality, but constantly reaffirm its actual two-dimensionality" (1972, 111). There is no analysis of how the film's images suggest three-dimensionality in the first place, let alone how they do this at the same time they reaffirm two-dimensionality. With a broader Greenbergian framework that conceives of avant-garde films as demonstrations of other essential properties of the medium, she can easily expand her interpretations to other features of the film process in addition to the flatness of the screen. In Gehr's *Wait* (1968), the filmmaker's "method emphasizes that film is actually composed of individual frames with only the illusion of movement" (1972, 112). Sharits's work demonstrates other facets of the medium:

> S:TREAM:S:S:ECTION:S:ECTION:S:S:ECTIONED (1970), Sharits's latest work, seeks to explore film as a strip, or as Sharits explains it, "film as a line in time," drawing the viewer's attention to it as it passes vertically through the projector. Normally one doesn't notice this, and only becomes aware through an occasional and accidental scratch which appears on the screen, made as the film passes through the projector gate. (1972, 112)

Like Arthur, Cornwell sees these films along basically pedagogical lines. Using the anti-illusion schema, she interprets Structural film as a vivid demonstration of the true nature of cinema, which is concealed by the "normal" film.

British filmmaker and theorist Peter Gidal sees what he calls the "Structural/Materialist" film in similar terms: "Structural/Materialist film attempts to be non-illusionist. The process of the film's making deals with devices that result in demystification or attempted demystification of the film process" (1976, 1). Gidal took a very hard line on this, and the extremity of his view distinguishes the Structural/Materialist film from the Structural film:

> The specific construct of each specific film is not the relevant point; one must beware not to let the construct, the shape, take the place of the "story" in narrative film. Then one would merely be substituting one hierarchy for another within the same system, a formalism for what is traditionally called content. (1976, 1)

For Gidal, any "beautiful" image, any trace of narrative or even an engaging shape was a politically reprehensible version of "illusionism." Thus, in his eyes, much of the American Structural film was just as ideologically complicit as the Hollywood film.[15]

Even though Gidal dismisses the American Structural film, his theory of the Structural/Materialist film appeals to the same interpretive schemata that American critics used. The anti-illusion schema is very apparent in his appeal to the "tension between materialist flatness, grain light, movement, and the supposed reality that is represented" (1976, 1). The other schemata play a role in his theory, too. His notion of "materialism" relies heavily on something like the art-process schema: "If the final work magically represses the procedures which in fact are there in the making, then that work is not a materialist work" (1976, 6). But if the awareness of these procedures conjures up images of the creating artist, this, too, would be illusionistic. Gidal rejects the notion that cinema can represent consciousness as Michelson and Sitney had suggested:

> Film cannot adequately represent consciousness any more than it adequately represents meaning; all film is invisibly encumbered by mystifactory systems and interventions which are distortions, repressions, selections, etc. That a film is not a window to life, to a set of meanings, to a pure state of image/meaning, ought to be self-evident. (1976, 10)

But Gidal's antipathy for representation ultimately leads him to suggest that the politically progressive film must provide an experience that is not so far from the direct perception of the phenomenological schema: "Filmic reflexiveness is the presentation of consciousness to the self, consciousness of the way one deals with the material operations; filmic reflexiveness is forced through cinema's materialist operations of filmic practice" (1976, 10). For all its differences with the Structural film, Gidal's version of the "anti-illusion project" draws heavily on the concepts that were being applied to the American avant-garde films that he rejected as illusionistic.

Greenbergian Formalism is usually considered the paradigm of apolitical art criticism. Why was it so attractive to scholars of the avant-garde film, for whom politics had become a central concern? About the time that Greenberg was publishing his Formalist theories in essays like "American-Type Painting" and "Modernist Painting," Roland Barthes was writing the essays that would make up *Mythologies* (1957). Barthes's criticism of popular culture events and artifacts shares a remarkable formal similarity to Greenberg's work on high culture. In the 1957 essay "Myth Today," Barthes summarizes his notion of myth: "Semiology has taught us that myth has the task of giving an historical intention a natural justification, and making contingency appear eternal. Now this process is exactly that of bourgeois ideology" (1972, 142). Thus for Barthes, myth does exactly the opposite of what Greenberg suggests modern art does. To paraphrase Greenberg in Barthesian vocabulary, modern art has an anti-mythical or anti-ideological function: it demonstrates that aspects of works that were previously accepted as natural and necessary were actually cultural and contingent. It is only a myth of pre-modern painting that it must represent objects in space; modern painting, like Barthes's criticism, removes the mask of the natural from the cultural.

The parallel between the anti-ideological criticism of contemporary film theory and Greenbergian Formalism is made even more dramatic since the features of films that contemporary theorists condemned as ideologically dangerous are exactly those features of representational art that Greenberg dismissed as inessential. In a series of essays written around 1970, French film theorists set out to explain the ideological effects of the style and technique of the commercial cinema.[16] Each theorist denies that the roots of cinema are to be found solely in the technological innovations of the mid-to-late nineteenth century. Instead, they trace these roots to the development of capitalism and linear perspective in the Renaissance. The claims these writers make about the mechanisms through which perspective representation affects viewers share little with Greenberg's theory. For example, in ''Ideological Effects of the Basic Cinematographic Apparatus,'' Jean-Louis Baudry invokes psychoanalytic mechanisms in his argument that the representation of perspective space encourages the spectator to submit to capitalist ideology. Nevertheless, the French theorists, like Greenberg, take pains to point out that what seemed to be a natural feature of pictorial representation is not really inevitable.

Films made under the indirect influence of Clement Greenberg had already disposed of those features that the ideological critics found most objectionable. For Greenberg, a law of Modernism had led artists to reject representation in favor of an examination of the features of their media; these artworks had already put into practice the theories of the French intellectual scene even before post-structuralism mandated a critique of representation. The coincidence of the concerns of Barthes (and the post-structuralists) and Greenberg ensured that the films of the minimal strain of the avant-garde were met by film scholars who had a critical method to which the films appeared to yield their secrets. For Sitney, of course, the Greenbergian concern with the ''laws'' of Modernism and the theories of the French were generally beside the point in dealing with the Romantic avant-garde. In Sitney's eyes, the Structural filmmakers were interested in cinema's essential qualities only in so far as they helped express the nature of consciousness. But for a critic like Cornwell, who saw Structural film as part of the Modernist trajectory, Sitney's terminology suggests links to the French intellectual scene that she was only too eager to exploit. In fact, she suggested renaming it Structuralist film in order to make that connection more explicit (1979b, 90).

The most common way to exploit this connection was to use French Structuralism as Cornwell did, to politicize the avant-garde film in a relatively painless way. Serge Guilbaut (1983) argues that the success of American art after World War II required the development of a painting style that was not only distinctive and abstract—and could therefore be seen as an ''advance'' on Surrealism—but was apolitical—so that it might evade attacks by Cold War ideologues. It could therefore receive the support of agencies of the United States government and the growing private art market. Minimalism is not explicitly political, and in its early years the absence of overtly political material may have worked to the advantage of its practitioners. But as the Vietnam war escalated and resistance to it grew, an apolitical stance was harder to maintain, so that after the traumatic events of 1968, credible avant-garde art *had* to be political. Modernist interpretive schema criticism of Minimalism and Structural film resolved this dilemma by making the artworks political by suggesting that they addressed not the politics of American military involvement in Asia, but the "politics of illusion." This justified the concerns of these artists and gave their work relevance without causing major dislocations in the evolution of film or painting styles and without jeopardizing the institutional support for this work which was only first being secured.

A Last Example

So far this analysis of the interpretive schemata as they have been brought to bear on the minimal strain of the avant-garde cinema has concentrated on several survey articles intended to explicate a general tendency in the American avant-garde film. But what about the criticism of individual works? Besides further demonstrating the pervasiveness of the interpretive schemata approach, an extended analysis of a single film seems an appropriate test of the power of these schemata.

Wanda Bershen's 1971 *Artforum* article on Hollis Frampton's *Zorn's Lemma* (1970) is the first major analysis of a work that has since become one of the most important examples of the Structural film. Bershen's early analysis was groundbreaking: later criticism of the film elaborated, but did not fundamentally alter, the claims she made in 1971. In the next chapter, *Zorn's Lemma* will serve as an important example in my attempt to articulate an alternative kind of analysis of the minimal strain of the American avant-garde. Bershen's analysis will serve here as an example of the interpretive schema approach.

Like many critics of the avant-garde film, Bershen takes her cues from the filmmaker. She openly cites Frampton's notes for the film on only a few specific points, but in large measure her analysis is an elaboration of Frampton's own interpretation as given in these notes (which are located at the Anthology Film Archive).

The anti-illusion schema plays a minor role in Bershen's analysis. Her interpretation of the very end of the film shows its influence: "Finally even that image [of a snowy field] fades to a rectangle of white light, the minimum definition of cinema" (45).[17] For the most part, her analysis rests mainly on the art-process schema and the phenomenological schema. Since she uses the art-process schema, she must begin with an invocation of the dominant cinema:

> Most conventional narrative films (and, indeed, the film-poem forms previously mentioned) place their viewers within the complex web of their own feelings and responses. Structural films do just the opposite by refusing the viewer all such pleasures, thus producing rather a rude

confrontation. What *is* this thing that calls itself a movie? That is the underlying question posed by structural cinema. (42)

To her credit, Bershen does cite the tradition of the earlier avant-garde, though she privileges narrative cinema as the most relevant background. And she, too, sees the film's function as primarily pedagogical. Structural films, she writes, isolate aspects of the phenomena that make up cinema, and "after a time the evidence gleaned from such explorations may enlarge our understanding of each phenomenon and its interactions with the others" (42). The educational task of the film includes the Cagean demonstration of the limitations of dominant filmmaking:

> Having established itself as belonging to the generic category of "film," *Zorn's Lemma* proceeds to totally ignore normal movie conventions. Not only does the structure lie bare, unclothed by any vestige of "content," but that structure is self-constructed. The film maker has provided a set of conditions and allowed them simply to take their course as if programmed by a calculating machine. A 24-letter alphabet at 24 f.p.s. provides the entire structural frame of the movie. . . . Rather than an inventor or "maker" he is a kind of "engineer," a director of forces which already exist in his world. The 24-letter alphabet is man-made, while the 24-f.p.s. film speed is a requirement of film machinery. Philosophically this suggests a considerably less egocentric concept of the artist than has prevailed even in the earlier decades of our own century. (44)

Having reconstituted the labor of the artist and identified the difference between the action of this filmmaker and the one that makes "normal movies" as a question of "egocentrism," Bershen can leave it to the reader to infer that Frampton has changed our notion of the artist for the better and has left the "normal movie" looking parochial and conservative in his wake.

The art-process schema is used here even in the face of several major obstacles. To begin, the invocation of "normal movie conventions" is inconsistent with the background Bershen had already provided. She began her article with a discussion of the tradition of Structural cinema that she dates from 1964, and introduced *Zorn's Lemma* as a synthesis of some of its concerns. Yet, in order for the art-process schema to work, the film must be seen against the background of the undefined "normal movie conventions." Against the background of post-1964 avant-garde film (or post-1964 art in any medium), *Zorn's Lemma* would not suggest a "less egocentric concept of the artist." Her reconstruction of Frampton's production of the film is also skewed. Even against the background of normal movie conventions it is hard to see how his use of a twenty-four-letter alphabet and the twenty-four fps film speed suggests in any way that he has relinquished control of the film's composition. After all, most filmmakers shoot at twenty-four fps and we are not inclined to think that this implies that their works are "self-constructed." What Frampton *has* done is to use the number 24 to structure features of his film, a choice that is in no way "dictated" to him by his medium. The assertion that the twenty-four-letter alphabet is "man-made," and is therefore not a product of Frampton's manipulation, would also be surprising to anyone who usually thinks of the alphabet as having twenty-six letters. Bershen suggests that Frampton used the Roman alphabet, but this cedes to Frampton the "egocentric" power to select the alphabet he wishes to use, in this case, one that fits his already chosen twenty-four-unit schema. Furthermore, no version of the Roman alphabet had exactly twenty-four letters.[18]

The point of this exercise is not merely to refute Bershen's interpretation (though I think it does that, too). Rather, it is a demonstration of the cost at which such an art-process interpretation is maintained. *Zorn's Lemma* does not lay bare its determination by forces outside the purview of the artist. Frampton is an intellectual bricoleur who not only borrows texts and structures but *transforms* them as he needs. By ignoring these transformations, Bershen actually masks and naturalizes the choices Frampton did make. And in suggesting that the film addresses "normal movies," Bershen ignores the relationship between the film and a wide range of art in the 1960s that established a set of norms to which the film *does* conform.

Having used the art-process schema to identify the historical implications of *Zorn's Lemma*, Bershen uses a set of phenomenological metaphors to make a specific interpretation of the film's meaning: "The film proposes a possible construct, a model in mathematical or scientific parlance, for the component parts and dynamic of the specific perceptual experience of film-viewing" (42). Later, Bershen makes the more familiar phenomenological interpretation that the film metaphorically represents aspects of the machinery of film, in this case, the theater. The film's last section consists of a very long take of a man, a woman and a dog walking away from the camera across a snowy field. She says of the end of the film: "Finally we are left the silent, snowy screen, a last resting place before being thrust out once more into the unsettling glare of 'reality' which lies in wait outside all movie theaters. We begin in the dark and end in light, a suggestive metaphor for the experience proposed by this film" (44). Bershen makes her most important point by relying on the other phenomenological metaphor, that the film represents the human mind. Just as Michelson argued that Snow's film represents the movement of human consciousness, Bershen reads Frampton's film as retracing the evolution of human knowledge:

> Spoken language was the first step and written language the final one away from the immediacy of "real experience."
>
> *Zorn's Lemma* thus begins with spoken language, progresses to written language (the relief alphabet in gilt letters) and arrives in Section II at the central problem, of linguistic (representing symbolic) versus visual (representing immediate) experience. (45)

This interpretation of *Zorn's Lemma*'s as an attempt to represent "real" experience leads Bershen to make the simpler phenomenological claim that our experience of portions of the film is equivalent to our experience of the world itself. Regarding the footage of events that replaces the words in Section II, she writes: "In that we cannot know the outcome of these events and must 'live through' them, they are equivalent to 'real' experience. . . . We are being asked increasingly to process 'raw data,' as we do from moment to moment all of our lives" (45). This trajectory from symbolic to immediate experience makes the end of the film the most "immediate" of all:

> The final section of the film, predictably, approaches the limit between "cinema" and "real life." Its spoken text is manipulated so that it functions only rhythmically, *not symbolically*. Simultaneously the long-held image of a snowy field, empty of symbolic content and barely illusionistic, comes as close to an experience of "real" space and "real" time as is possible on film. (45)

The phenomenological schema can be coherently applied to long takes with very little action because the viewer self-consciously experiences the flow of time during them. But Bershen's phenomenological interpretation of other aspects of this final section raises some troubling questions. First, in what sense is the image of the snowy field "barely illusionistic"? It actually represents a very deep space of hundreds of yards; this might be considered one of the most "illusionistic" shots in the film. Second, how can the spoken text function "only rhythmically, not symbolically" if Bershen can quote it in support of her interpretation as she does earlier in the essay? As with her use of the art-process schema, a reading consistent with the phenomenological schema is maintained only at the expense of an inconsistent treatment of the elements of the film. Modernist interpretive schema criticism, like any criticism, selects and accounts for only a limited number of an artwork's features. But Bershen's analysis demonstrates that Modernist interpretive schema criticism not only views films selectively, it often distorts the features it purports to explain. And, it distorts them in a predictable way that is no longer interesting.

Seven years after the "Formalist Tendencies" article, Cornwell published "Structural Film: Ten Years Later" (1979), in which she acknowledges that the repeated application of the anti-illusion schema is reductive and that consciousness of the flatness of the screen is not a sufficient basis for a theory of film. Her charge of reductionism was aimed more at Paul Sharits than herself, but she nonetheless offers an apparent alternative to the reductionism that "came out of a search for an ontology of film in the late 1960's and the early 1970's" (1979b, 90). Once again using Gehr's *History* (1970) as a test case, she writes:

> Gehr's film provokes a musing on the very impossibility of the existence of a work such as it at any historically earlier time. . . . Hand-in-hand with its non- and anti-narrative tendency is its general rejection of metaphor and symbol in place of an *immediate experience of film as an object* whether it is composed of representational or of abstract imagery or moves between the two. Loop-printed and serial imagery, long camera takes on stationary objects or static scenes, simple bipolar

or more complex mathematical orderings, are *ways of stressing the object*. (Cornwell's emphasis, 1979b, 90)

She begins by using the art-process schema to identify the film as anti-narrative, and moves into a straightforward phenomenological stance from which the film is immediately experienced. Far from suggesting any real alternative, she has simply replaced one interpretive schema with two others.

Cornwell's inability to escape the endless recirculation of interpretive schemata is a symptom of her preoccupation with the processes of film *production*. Even Paul Arthur, who of all the critics of Structural film most explicitly addresses the viewer, sees the viewer's task as the reconstruction of the film's creation. And this preoccupation with film production is, in turn, a symptom of an undeveloped theory of the viewer of the avant-garde film. As Sitney put it in his original formulation, the Structural film has minimal content and "insists on its shape." Yet for all the discussion of his definition, the crucial question, "how does a film insist on its shape?" has gone unanswered. It is to this question we now turn.

6

Film that Insists on Its Shape: The Minimal Strain

Sitney's definition of the Structural film as one that "insists on its shape" was not very widely accepted in the avant-garde's critical environment. As we saw in the last chapter, other writers invariably criticized this formulation as imprecise or even meaningless. But Sitney's definition takes an important step toward acknowledging the importance of the viewer's experience. In this chapter, I develop this underemphasized aspect of Structural film by suggesting some ways that a film might indeed "insist on its shape."

Attempts to refine Sitney's definition have generally concentrated on explanations of the Structural film's production. Consistent with the widely held view that it was primarily a reflexive examination of the features of the film medium, Structural film was classified and explained on the basis of the technical procedures used to create the film. But these classifications tend to disregard the viewer's experience. Works that share a technical procedure—even when that technical procedure is very evident—can offer radically different viewing experiences.

Consider one of the most complete taxonomies of Structural film, found in the concluding chapters of Malcolm Le Grice's *Abstract Film and Beyond* (1977). In it, films are categorized based on which phase of the film production process the filmmaker chooses to emphasize (e.g., shooting, printing or projection) or on the techniques used by the filmmaker (e.g., repetition, flicker or fixed camera position). According to this taxonomy, Hollis Frampton's *Artificial Light* (1969) is akin to Fred Drummond's *Shower Proof* (1969) because they both subject a single passage of film to a series of printing effects. Thus categorized, the point of both works seems to be to encourage the viewer's awareness of the printing process, a facet of film production that is usually concealed. *Shower Proof* repeatedly subjects its basic image set to a single procedure—high contrast duplication—so that the growing contrast gradually obliterates the image; *Artificial Light* subjects its basic image set to an unsystematic variety of techniques including hand tinting, scratching the emulsion, superimposition, and

Fig. 6.1

Fig. 6.2

Fig. 6.3

negative reversal. For Le Grice, both films are "about" the printing techniques that produced their images, even though one offers a systematic degradation of image quality and the other offers unpredictable variations on a theme. In fact, from this perspective, both films are similar to J. J. Murphy's *Print Generation* (1973–74) and to Michael Snow's *Wavelength* (1967). Since *Print Generation* is created through contact printing, and *Wavelength* features a prominent zoom, all these films are "about" particular film techniques and lead the viewer to an awareness of processes normally concealed in film production. Whatever the similarities in how these films were produced, however, there are great differences in the experiences they offer to the viewer.

My aim in this chapter is to analyze the kinds of experiences the films of the avant-garde's minimal strain provide. Modernist interpretive schemata provide a means of ascribing meaning to these films. But to come to terms with the viewer's whole experience, we must examine the perceptual and cognitive processes through which the viewer grasps their structure.

The Simple Schematic Film

I have no illusions that a single model can explain the viewer's comprehension of every film that at one time or another has been labelled Structural. Sitney's inclusion of flicker films especially muddies water that was not very clear in the first place. Whereas the viewer's conscious puzzling out of the global structure of films like *Zorn's Lemma* (1970) is clearly a top-down process, the viewer's experience of the flicker effect is a paradigm case of bottom-up perceptual processing. That is, the perception of rapidly flickering and intense colors is not very well explained as a hypothesis-driven search for the best solution to a problem, but rather in terms of the relatively low-level processing of the retina. Much of our response to the work of flicker filmmakers like Tony Conrad and Paul Sharits depends on phenomena like afterimages and flicker fusion that are best explained neurologically rather than cognitively.[1]

I will concentrate on an important sub-group of the Structural film, what I call *simple schematic films*. To put it in the discourse processing terms we have been using, a simple schematic film is a film whose global template schemata—those that structure the film as a whole—are exceedingly simple and very prominent. Let me begin to refine this general definition with an example, George Brecht's *Entrance/Exit* (1965). The film begins in darkness. The camera's aperture gradually opens and the image of an entrance sign appears (Fig. 6.1), grows brighter (Fig. 6.2), and is finally obliterated by over-exposure (Fig. 6.3). Then, over the course of approximately six minutes, the white screen gradually darkens to black. Finally, a dim exit sign appears, grows brighter and is ultimately obliterated by overexposure at the end of the film.

The simple schematic film is not always quite this elementary, but the Brecht film does demonstrate two of its most important features. First, its global template schema is very simple. The global template schema of *Entrance/Exit* is the gradual lightening and darkening of the screen. Though it is caused by a change in the f-stop setting of the camera, the viewer need know nothing about photography to have a schema for the changing of light/dark values. Thus the template schema is simple not only in the sense that it does not involve many elements, but in that it does not require any special knowledge of photography, film or the history of art. Any person would have the template schema to match the film's global structure.

Second, at the local level, the simple schematic film demands very limited prototype matching. Brecht's film has only two images that must be identified, so the viewer's efforts are focused on the global level of the film. Limited prototype matching of the simple schematic film helps explain how three of the four techniques Sitney suggested were typical of the Structural film (fixed camera position, loop printing, rephotography, and flicker effect) help make the film's shape prominent. Sitney's detractors complain that this is an ad hoc collection of features with only coincidental connections to the film's form. But three of them invariably limit prototype matching. The repetition of images, whether through rephotography as in Ken Jacobs's *Tom, Tom, the Piper's Son* (1969, revised 1971), or through loop printing as in Franklin Miller's *Stores* (1974), reduces the number of hypotheses the viewer must generate at the film's local level because there are fewer images to process. Similarly, fixing the camera position eases the viewer's task of identifying the spatial relationships between shots. These three techniques tend to direct the viewer's attention and mental effort at deciphering the film's global structure.

The global template schemata of the simple schematic film does not require specialized knowledge of photographic processes, but a viewer completely unfamiliar with this type of film might lack appropriate viewing strategies for films that do not include a narrative or any sort of characters. The history of the simple schematic artwork therefore plays a crucial role in our understanding such films: the development of this form, in a wide range of media, gradually shaped the strategies used in making sense of this kind of artwork. Sitney was wrong about one aspect of the history of the Structural film when he introduced the term in 1969: a cinema of structure had not "suddenly emerged" but was only one facet of a long tradition in the arts. This tradition does not supply explicit rules for the comprehension of these works, but with precedents from other media, viewers have much clearer expectations about the kind of experience the work will provide.

The Evolution of the Simple Schematic Artwork

The simple schema dates from the early days of Modernism, though it has precedents throughout the history of art, as *The Sense of Order*, E. H. Gombrich's study of decorative art, shows. The deepest roots of the simple numerical schema in the Modernist era are in advanced music, in both European serialism and American experimental music. For example, composer Arnold Schoenberg's compositions from the early twentieth century have a sophisticated mathematical integrity, but their structures are imperceptible to all but the most highly trained listeners. As he began his career, Schoenberg came to believe that the possibilities of Western tonal music had been exhausted; the heavy emphasis on a limited number of tones on the scale too severely restricted the composer's freedom. In 1908, he composed his first atonal work, wherein each of the twelve notes of the chromatic scale received equal emphasis. In 1923, he refined this atonality through the serial technique. A serial work begins with a tone row, a series of the twelve chromatic tones arranged in any order as long as each note is played once before any can be repeated. Other composers, notably Olivier Messiaen and his students Pierre Boulez and Karlheinz Stockhausen, followed Schoenberg's development of this structuring system for pitch with total serialism, in which the other musical parameters—loudness, duration, timbre, attack—were similarly organized. As far as our interest in the simple schematic artwork is concerned, Schoenberg's key innovation was to make melodic and expressive qualities secondary to the systematic permutation of the tone row.

American experimental musicians are a more proximate source for the avant-garde film's experimentation with simple schematic structures. Total serialism generated works of such complexity that only the most trained listeners (and perhaps not even they) could perceive the tone row and the permutations to which it was subjected. But American composers, in large measure following the lead of John Cage, used mathematical schemes to generate compositions that were simpler, more redundant, and, as a consequence, had global structures that were easier to perceive. The Fluxus composers, such as LaMonte Young, George Brecht and George Maciunas, were heavily influenced by Cage's course at the New School for Social Research in 1958, and they engaged in a wide range of "musical" experiments that emphasized the Duchampian aspects of Cage's aesthetics. Young's *Composition 1960 No. 5*, for example, consisted of turning butterflies loose in a concert hall. These composers did not restrict their experiments to music: they engaged in publishing, performance art and filmmaking. As Maciunas pointed out in his comments on Sitney's "Structural Film," some of the Fluxus works anticipated Warhol's celebrated work, making them important but often overlooked precursors to Structural film. In addition to Brecht's *Entrance/Exit*, other Fluxus work bears directly on the simple schematic film. George Maciunas's *10 Feet* (1966) is ten feet of film stock long (lasting about seventeen seconds), and the only images are numbers that mark the passing of each foot of film. Robert Watts's *Trace* is a filmed X-ray of a person swallowing liquid. But sometimes even these simply constructed works had a prankish side: Yoko Ono's *Four* (1965) consists of straight-on close-ups of buttocks as their owners walk on a treadmill (Fig. 6.4).

The simple schema has precedents in European fiction, too—though, as in serial music, the complexity of its early incarnations

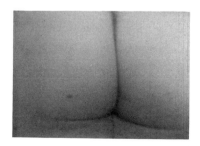

Fig. 6.4

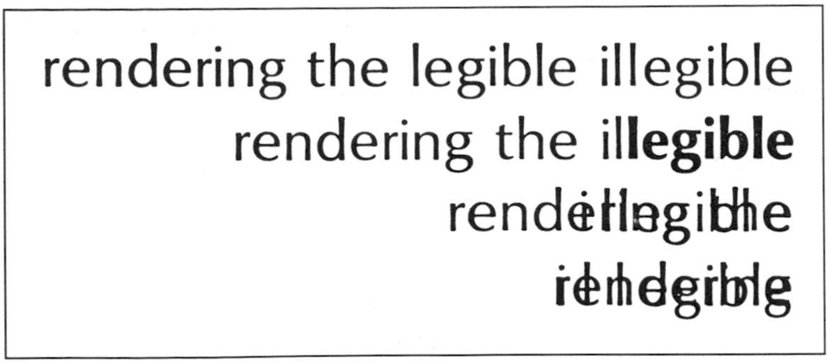

rendering the legible illegible
rendering the il**legible**
rend**e**lł**e**gi**b**l**h**e
r**e**łh**e**gi**b**l**g**

Fig. 6.5. Claus Bremer, 1963.
Reprinted with permission.

makes the schemata very difficult to perceive. New Novelist Michel Butor's *La Modification* (1957) is structured with mathematical patterns, but discovering them, let alone perceiving them, requires an almost perverse attention to the details of the narrative. *La Modification* is the story of a single train journey by Paris businessman Léon Delmont. A series of flashbacks and flashforwards dominates each of the nine chapters of the Butor novel as the protagonist remembers his marriage and an affair and fantasizes about his future life with his mistress. As Patrice Quéréel notes in her monograph on *La Modification*, the arrangement of these flashbacks and flashforwards gradually evolves from chapter to chapter according to a complex but meticulous pattern (1973, 18). Still, however carefully plotted these patterns are, they are neither simple enough nor prominent enough to be easily perceptible.

Simple schemata in poetry are more prominent than the patterns in the French New Novel. Though the term ''Concrete Poetry'' was coined only in 1953,[2] poetry whose structure is at least as prominent as its meaning has many precedents in literary Modernism. Stéphane Mallarmé's *Un Coup de Des Jamais N'Abolira le Hasard* is often cited for its innovative typographical structure; the Russian Futurists, the Italian Futurists, and the Dadaists are cited for their emphasis on phonetic patterning at the expense of meaning. In the 1950s and 1960s, this tradition was revived and extended, especially by Brazilians Augusto and Haroldo de Campos and Swiss Eugen Gomringer.[3] The term Concrete Poetry has been applied to a wide range of poetry, not all of which uses the simple schema. A prototypical concrete poem would be one whose typographical layout evoked its meaning. Simplistic examples of this device (like a poem about a tree in the shape of a tree) are not held in high regard,[4] but typography can evoke meanings in more sophisticated ways, as in the translation of a poem by Claus Bremer shown in Figure 6.5.[5]

The work of a group of Parisian writers and mathematicians is related to Concrete Poetry, but it is more specifically concerned with what I call the simple schema. In 1960 this group organized what they called the *Ouvoir de Littérature Potentielle* (or OuLiPo as it is known, translated as the Workshop of Potential Literature) and began to

Liminal Poem

to Martin Gardner

O
t o
s e e
man's
s t e r n
p o e t i c
t h o u g h t
p u b l i c l y
e s p o u s i n g
r e c k l e s s l y
i m a g i n a t i v e
m a t h e m a t i c a l
i n v e n t i v e n e s s,
o p e n m i n d e d n e s s
u n c o n d i t i o n a l l y
s u p e r f e c u n d a t i n g
n o n a n t a g o n i s t i c a l
h y p e r s o p h i s t i c a t e d
i n t e r d e n o m i n a t i o n a l
i n t e r p e n e t r a b i l i t i e s.
Harry Burchell Mathews
Jacques Denis Roubaud
Albert Marie Schmidt
Paul Lucien Fournel
Jacques Duchateau
Luc Etienne Perin
Marcel M Benabou
Michele Metail
Italo Calvino
Jean Lescure
Noel Arnaud
P Braffort
A Blavier
J Queval
C Berge
Perec
Bens
FLL
RQ
.

Fig. 6.6. Harry Mathews, reprinted from *Oulipo: A Primer of Potential Literature,* by Warren Motte, Jr., by permission of the University of Nebraska Press. © 1986 by the University of Nebraska Press.

produce poems by fitting meaningful combinations of words into preordained schemata. An elementary example is the snowball sentence, in which each word must have exactly one more letter than the word before. Figure 6.6 shows Harry Mathews's "Liminal Poem," a snowball sentence about OuLiPo itself (cited in Motte 1986, 25).[6] As is evident here, the schema dominates the meaning, and the work's impact comes from the fact that the unusual combination of letters has meaning at all. The schema's inflexibility warps syntax and meaning, pushing both to the background, while the simplicity of the schema guarantees that the pattern is perceptible.

In the late 1960s and early 1970s, Walter Abish used some of these same strategies to structure prose. Abish's novel *Alphabetical Africa* (1974) begins with chapter ''A'' in which every word begins with the letter A:

> AGES AGO, Alex, Allen and Alva arrived at Antibes, and Alva allowing all, allowing anyone, against Alex's admonition, against Allen's angry assertion: another African amusement.

In chapter ''B,'' Abish includes words that begin with B; in chapter ''C'' he uses words that begin with A, B and C, and so on. Like the OuLiPo work, much of *Alphabetical Africa*'s impact comes from the realization that the language is still meaningful in spite of the powerful constraint of the simple schema. The arbitrariness in the selection of the words makes the template schema very prominent, even though readers do not see the pattern all at once, as they do in the smaller OuLiPo works.[7]

By the late 1950s, the simple schema had also been introduced to the American visual arts by Jasper Johns. Johns is most widely known for his use of the iconography that became the staple of Pop Art: flags, targets, and common objects like beer cans and flashlights. The consistent association of his iconography with Pop Art has tended to overshadow the schematic aspects of his work, which are especially important in the gray alphabets series he began in 1956 and the gray numbers series he began in 1958 (Fig. 6.7). Johns used a similar simple schema to determine the contours of the imagery in both series. The paintings consist of rows and columns of letters or numbers. In a number painting, for example, the top row begins with 9, then continues with 0, 1, 2, and so on. Each subsequent row begins with the next digit—row two begins with and ends with 0, and so forth. The process of hypothesis generation and testing involved in the discovery of such a simple schema is undoubtedly very short and would not be especially interesting as an account of the viewer's total response to the work. Nonetheless, as in the OuLiPo works, the schematized elements of the work are the ones that are most effectively perceived and remembered.

By the mid 1960s, works with simple schemata were common in what was called *serial* or *systemic art*. Though systemic art was sometimes associated with Minimalism, the exploration of compositional procedures that systematically permuted sets of defined elements produced work that was far more intricate than the simple geometric abstraction that we usually think of as Minimalist. This exploration of the simple schema was carried especially far in the work of Sol LeWitt and Mel Bochner. LeWitt's early sculpture consisted of neatly fabricated lattices and grids with relatively few units. By 1966, his sculpture was still neatly fabricated, but instead of the small lattices, he was creating larger, more complex, works. His *Serial*

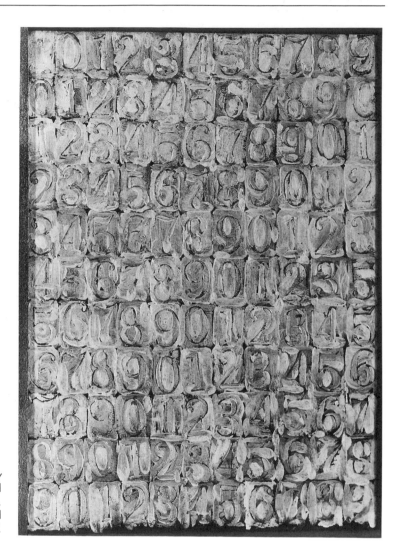

Fig. 6.7. Jasper Johns, *Grey Numbers*, 1958. Encaustic and collage on canvas, 67" x 49 ½". © 1993 Jasper Johns/Licensed by VAGA, New York, NY.

Project No. 1 (1966), for example, was a set of individual units, each composed of an inner form and an outer form (Fig. 6.8). Each form could be constructed either as an open framework or as a closed box. Each form could also be constructed in three heights—high, medium or low. Given these parameters—open/closed and high/medium/ low—LeWitt built every possible combination of the two forms, resulting in thirty-six units which he mounted together in an orderly array so that the compositional schema is apparent. And, what LeWitt did for geometry, Bochner did for arithmetic. In his *Three Ideas and Seven Procedures* (1971) installation, Bochner affixed a continuous strip of masking tape at eye level to the walls of several rooms of the Museum of Modern Art. With black felt tip he wrote numbers, approximately an inch apart, starting from 0, from left to right on the tape. He got to around 2,000 when he reached the end of the tape, at which point he changed to a red pen and repeated the numbering going back from right to left.

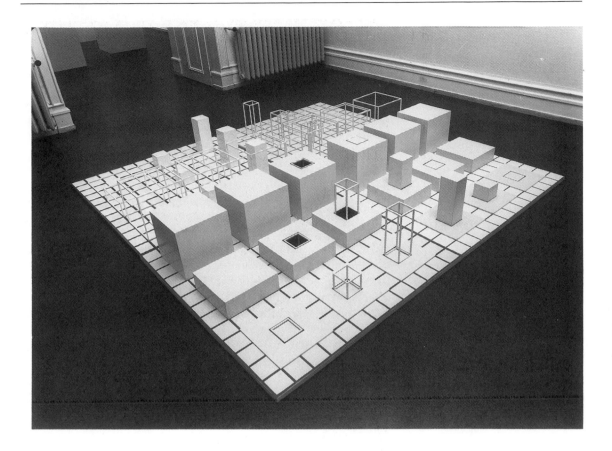

Fig. 6.8. Sol LeWitt, *Serial Project No. 1 (ABCD)*, 1966. Steel, 20⅛″ × 6′ 6¾″ × 6′ 6¾″. © 1992 Sol LeWitt/ARS, New York.

By 1960, the simple schema had been introduced to literature, music and the visual arts, and in each field it continued its prominence until well into the 1970s. It was subjected to a sustained and varied development and did not "suddenly emerge," even in film. Speaking generally of the simple schematic work in any medium, its use of overlearned template schemata has the effect of making the global template prominent. To analyze the perception of the simple schematic film in more detail, we must discriminate between various types of simple schemata.

Two Types of Simple Schemata

The simple schematic film may use two types of template schemata. If the units of the template schemata can be ranked in a progressive order, we can label it a *simple numerical schema*; if they cannot be so ranked, we can label it a *simple permutational schema*. Since the various exposures in *Entrance/Exit* could easily be ranked on a scale of light to dark, it is a simple numerical schema film. On the other hand, Larry Gottheim's *Four Shadows* (1978) is an example of a simple permutational schema film. The film consists of four four-minute sets of images, one for each season of the year. There are also four four-minute passages of recorded sound. The image sets are repeated four times so that every combination of sound passage and image set is included once. There is no obvious place to start, nor is there necessarily any order that ought to be followed in presenting the combinations. And no unit is more appropriate for the end than any other; the film is complete when all the combinations have been exhausted.[8]

Since *each* global template schema in the simple schematic film is either numerical or permutational, it is possible for a single film to use both types of simple schemata. Takahito Iimura's *24 Frames Per Second* (1975, revised 1978) is such a hybrid film. The film is constructed solely of black and white frames. It is divided into twenty-four sections, each of which has a permutational schema. The first section begins with the title "1/24." Following this are forty-eight twenty-four-frame sets: the first set is twenty-three frames of black with a single frame of white inserted somewhere; the next set is twenty-three frames of white with a single black frame. The film alternates between black-dominated and white-dominated sections until the inserted frame has occupied every possible position in the twenty-four-frame set. The second section begins with the title "2/24" and repeats the permutational schema with two frames of black among twenty-two frames of white. The film continues through section "24/24." Each section is permutational because it lists, in no particular order, all the possible positions for the inserted frames. At the most global level, the film is numerical because the number of inserted frames grows larger with each passing section, and the film ends when the number of inserted frames can grow no more.

Distinguishing between numerical and permutational schemata is not simply an academic exercise. Each type of global template schema has specific processing consequences for the viewer of the simple schematic film.

The most important cognitive consequence of the simple numerical schema is the increased tendency for the perceiver of one of these works to *spatialize* the form of the work, even though in film (and literature) the structure is actually temporal.[9] This kind of re-mapping of a temporal order into a spatial array is a common task for critics. Levi-Strauss's analysis of myth lays out the various elements of a myth in chart form; Raymond Bellour's analysis of *The Birds* (1963) carefully maps the detailed symmetries of the film. On a more limited scale, we do this in our everyday viewing and reading when we notice "circular" plots, "parallel" moments or the "linear" development of conflicts. It should come as no surprise that the tendency to spatialize the form of artworks is so widespread. According to John Anderson, this spatializing is a fundamental feature of mental representation, and even abstract qualities that have no natural spatial dimension are spatialized in memory if they can be related to some kind of ranking (1980, 78–79). In fact, Anderson argues that whenever it is *possible* to spatialize concepts, it is to our perceptual and cognitive advantage to do so (86).

Films with simple numerical schemata are especially easy to spatialize, even for naive viewers, from the very first encounter. One major reason for this ease is that the progressive relationship between the units of the work provides a kind of "ranking" that can be directly spatialized. Furthermore, the schemata we use to remember and predict the form of the work are often very familiar; in such cases, little effort is required to recognize them. When a work is based on a simple numerical progression, we quickly grasp the overall structure and can predict local details of the remainder of the work. As we process the work, we have a convenient schema for holding the entire structure in memory as a relationship between its parts.

In most reading and viewing, spatialization exploits the work's semantic level, such as the events of the narrative of a commercial fiction film. Surface features are remembered only briefly, partly because we have relatively few large-scale schemata for the perception of the surface levels of artworks (van Dijk 1979, 153). As we discovered in chapter 3, in the poetic strain of the avant-garde we often perceive surface features locally because the style lacks the transparency of the classical film. But global structures still escape us because we lack schemata that can aid our perception of the surface level. For example, the camerawork in a Stan Brakhage film is sometimes so rapid it blurs the image. Since it interferes with our ability to see what the image represents, the camerawork is very prominent. However, since the movement is not systematic, after the film the most we are likely to remember is that the camerawork contained rapid movements; we cannot spatialize the camera movement to the extent of remembering what kind of movements occurred in which part of the film.

The numerical schemata in the minimal strain of the avant-garde typically pattern the surface features of the work, such as the exposure change in *Entrance/Exit*. And since the surface features are so simply patterned, global surface structure is easily perceived and spatialized. In most reading, for example, we rarely remember surface details such as the initial letters of words. But given the simple numerical schema of the gradually expanding vocabulary of *Alphabetical Africa*, the initial letters of words are easily noticed and remembered, and the pattern of surface detail is the most prominent aspect of the text, and is easily spatialized.

We may distinguish not only between numerical and permutational schemata, but between two types of permutational schemata. If the work defines a limited set of possible elements, it has a *closed* permutational schema. The sections of *24 Frames Per Second* have closed permutational schemata because there is only a limited number of positions for the inserted frames, and every possible position is included in the film. If the permutational schema does not define a limited set of possible features, it is an *open* permutational schema. Frampton's *Artificial Light* has an open permutational schema because there is no limit to the printing techniques to which the original image set could be subjected.[10]

The numerical schema and the two types of permutational schemata differ in how easily they are spatialized and in the strength of the expectations they generate in the viewer. A numerical schema permits easy spatialization of the work's form, and the viewer has strong expectations about the trajectory of the work, even to the point of anticipating local detail. And, since the local details are so firmly fixed into the progression of the global template schema, the viewer has very strong expectations about when the work will end. The permutational schema does not permit easy spatialization because there is no way to ''rank'' the individual members of the permutational set. Though there is no direct spatialization of the work's form, the closed permutational schema does permit the spatialization of the work's ''conceptual space,'' the range of possible permutations of the work's elements. This conceptual space is often entirely mapped out by the work itself, as in *24 Frames Per Second* or LeWitt's *Serial Project No. 1.* In the closed permutational schema, the local details follow one another in no particular order, so expectations about the position of local details are relatively weak. But the viewer still has strong expectations about the work's conclusion because the gradual exhaustion of the conceptual space can be monitored. The open permutational schema generates the least specific expectations on the part of the viewers; they can predict neither the order of details at the local level, nor the work's conclusion. And accordingly, the open permutational schema carries the lowest processing benefits, and the global structure of these films is harder to perceive and remember.

Though comprehending the global template schemata in these films requires no specialized knowledge, the viewer of each type of simple schematic film is often aided by *explanatory articulation.* E. H. Gombrich developed this concept in his work on decorative art, where he found that the structure of a functional object is often highlighted by the deployment of decorative patterns. For example, decorative patterns may isolate and emphasize the lid or handles of a container so that these important functional elements may be quickly identified and more easily used (1979, 165). In the simple schematic artwork, explanatory articulations often identify, or at least suggest, the primary schemata structuring the work. This function is often served by descriptive titles. For example, the viewer's comprehension of *24 Frames per Second* is aided considerably by the titles that follow each section. Simple schematic works have explanatory articulations in their titles, in prologues and epilogues, in section divisions corresponding to changes in schemata, and so forth. Even though the schemata used by these works are simple and overlearned, explanatory articulation cues viewers that the search for the work's global template schemata is their primary task.

Strategies of Engagement

The concept of explanatory articulation and the processing benefits of the easily spatialized form have led me to emphasize how easily the viewer is able to identify the global template schemata of the simple schematic film. But we must not confuse the viewer's ease in processing these films with the aesthetic value of the works. Quite to the contrary, excessively simple works do not offer particularly interesting experiences to the viewer. The continued confirmation of a single hypothesis leads to boredom and inattention. If the film is to remain engaging, it must sustain the cycle of hypothesis generation and testing throughout. So far, I have been able to skirt this issue because most of my examples of the simple schematic film have been short, so that even a very simple structure can maintain the viewer's interest over the course of the film. But maintaining this interest over longer periods is a more complex affair. Longer simple schematic films have two basic strategies for sustaining and prolonging the problem-solving cycle: *solution inhibition* and *solution multiplication*.

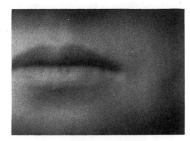

Fig. 6.9

Solution Inhibition

The strategy of solution inhibition works by triggering the generation of hypotheses without immediately providing direct confirmation of these hypotheses. This inhibition occurs at various levels. For example, Larry Gottheim's *Fogline* (1970) and John Lennon and Yoko Ono's *Apotheosis* (1970) prevent the viewer from identifying individual images, thereby inhibiting solutions at the level of the prototype schemata. Chieko Shiomi's *Disappearing Music for Face* (1965–66) permits the identification of its one image, but inhibits the correct hypothesizing of its global template schema. The film begins with a close-up of an apparently motionless mouth (Fig. 6.9). Though this continues for some time, we hypothesize actively (at least at first): is it a still photo, or is the person just not moving? Will we cut away? How long will this go on? Perhaps finally our attention flags, but after a couple of minutes, the position of the mouth has changed ever so slightly. We may hypothesize that the image is in motion; if we look at the screen to see the image move, our hypothesis will not be confirmed—even though it happens to be correct. After a few minutes more, we notice that the mouth has begun to stretch into a smile; finally, the smile is clear and the film ends (Fig. 6.10). The structure of the film is exceedingly simple. It is a single shot of a person smiling, shot with a very high-speed camera at hundreds of frames per second. However, the cryptic title provides no explanatory articulation, and no motion is ever apparent on the screen. Only after watching an extended portion of the film can we confirm our hypothesis that the image *is* moving, but at an imperceptibly slow speed.

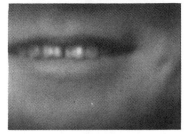

Fig. 6.10

The open permutational schema film almost invariably uses the solution inhibition strategy. As I suggested above, the local details of neither type of permutational schema can be precisely predicted because the permutational set is not explored in a particular order. And with the *open* permutational schema, the viewer is never completely sure what the filmmaker will do next, or for how long he or she will do it.

This uncertainty is exploited by a pair of open permutational schema films made by Hollis Frampton in 1969. *Carrots and Peas* and *Artificial Light* both subject a passage of film to a variety of printing and editing techniques: in *Carrots and Peas* the basic passage is a close-up of cooked peas and carrot slices; in *Artificial Light* it is an animated zoom out from the planet earth, followed by a series of about

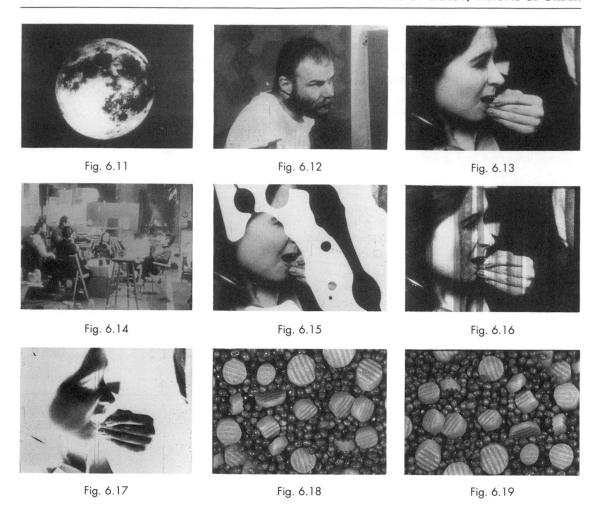

Fig. 6.11   Fig. 6.12   Fig. 6.13

Fig. 6.14   Fig. 6.15   Fig. 6.16

Fig. 6.17   Fig. 6.18   Fig. 6.19

fifty shots of Frampton's friends conversing. In neither film is there a progressive or cumulative effect to the various techniques applied to the basic footage, so the global template schemata of the films are not clear as one views them. Rather, the interest in the open permutational film lies in the moment-to-moment anticipation of novelty and repetition.

In *Artificial Light*, the basic set of images is constructed to facilitate this anticipation. The zoom out from the planet earth is itself an unusual and memorable shot (Fig. 6.11), but it is made even more so by its inclusion in a series whose other members are quick shots of mostly unfamiliar people (Figs. 6.12, 6.13). Several of these shots are more distinctive than others because of some small gesture, and the series ends with a brief establishing shot (Fig. 6.14); these distinctive shots become landmarks that we remember and anticipate as the cycle repeats. Because the time between the introduction of new printing techniques is short—one is introduced every forty-eight seconds—we are less likely to hypothesize narrative links between the shots, occupied, as we are, with the very prominent manipulation of the film stock.

We do try to confirm the hypothesis that the permutations do not alter the basic sequence of images with each cycle. We come to expect novelty, but we have fairly specific expectations about what *kind* of novelty is likely. Any given film, even a very short one, can be considered to be a very large set of individual features implying an equally large number of permutational sets. If, as I argue above, the permutational schema is not a willy-nilly assortment of these features, there must be some mechanism through which the viewer identifies the appropriate permutational set. As Gombrich argues, our best perceptual bet is that the present state of affairs will continue (1979, 2–3); with the second cycle of *Artificial Light*, the viewer can begin to narrow the candidates for continuity and identify a number of traits that have already varied. By the third cycle—which is ''normal'' in that it is right side up, positive and mostly unmarked with scratches and color—it is fairly clear that the shots themselves will not change, and that the permutational set being explored is the range of possible printing techniques, which are likely to vary each cycle (Figs. 6.15, 6.16, 6.17).

Frampton confirms our hypothesis that we will see a new printing variant with every cycle but twice disconfirms our hypothesis about the stability of the basic image series. Once he challenges our memory of the basic cycle by showing only one frame out of every twenty-four, leaving the rest black; and once he surprises us by reordering the shots themselves. Note that both of these variants occur later in the film, since their effect depends on our at least partially learning the order of the series, and our sensing that novelty will be introduced only in certain areas. Placing these variants at the beginning of the film would have complicated our efforts to hypothesize the appropriate permutational set (printing techniques) by venturing into another permutational set (variations on the order of the images in the set). Viewers would probably still be able to derive the central tendency of the film to manipulate printing technique, but the surprise of these two ''violations'' depends on viewers' high confidence in their hypothesis about the film's organization.

Carrots and Peas is an open permutational film similar to *Artificial Light*, but instead of a series marked by a few distinctive features, the basic unit in the main part of the film is a particularly monotonous close-up. The film begins with a pixilated sequence in which carrot slices and peas appear on the screen in various configurations, ultimately settling into an all-over kind of field composition, which is then subjected to a series of permutations. Its first variation is slight, but disquieting. Frampton first presents the field of carrots and peas *upside down* (Fig. 6.18), and this orientation is only clear after the correct version is shown to us (Fig. 6.19). Also in this film, Frampton trades on the optical power of the intense orange and green of the vegetables. One variation has a black-and-white print of the

Fig. 6.20

Fig. 6.21

Fig. 6.22

Fig. 6.23

image slightly tinted with pale colors. A few cycles later, Frampton cuts from a color shot to a plain black-and-white shot, and the retina's negative afterimage of the color shot projects red and blue onto the black-and-white peas and carrots. It is impossible to tell, unless the film is inspected frame-by-frame, whether the effect is created on the retina or photographically with Frampton's optical printer.

The open permutational film generally uses the solution inhibition strategy; its global template schema is not fully or explicitly defined, and the viewer's hypotheses about the film's organization are focused gradually over the course of the film. The solution inhibition strategy can also be used with numerical schematic films. J. J. Murphy's *Print Generation* (1973–74) is a simple numerical schematic film that uses the solution inhibition strategy on a much larger scale than the Frampton films or *Disappearing Music for Face*. Because it provokes such active hypothesizing while so effectively inhibiting the solution to the perceptual and cognitive problems it poses, the film is one of the most engaging of the avant-garde's minimal strain. It is all the more remarkable because it creates these complex effects through the use of a single global template schema.

Print Generation begins with a series of abstract patterns that gradually coalesce into a series of random, but clear, images. These images then gradually decompose into the same abstract patterns that began the film. Murphy created this structure by assembling a basic set of sixty one-second shots of miscellaneous home-movie footage, and contact-printing the set over and over, for a total of fifty generations. The odd-number generations formed one group and the even generations formed another. Murphy joined the two groups, thus making a symmetrical pattern of fifty cycles of the original sixty-shot series. The fifty generations of contact printing obliterate the original images, creating the abstractions that open and close *Print Generation*; the images are clear only toward the center of the film, where they are less removed from the originals (Figs. 6.20–6.35).

In accordance with our model of the perceptual cycle, the viewer's perception of the structure of *Print Generation* can be divided into two phases: the generation of hypotheses about what this structure might be and the testing of these hypotheses. *Print Generation* eschews explanatory articulation and thus inhibits the early generation of precise hypotheses about the work's form. The title of the film could prime appropriate schemata if it were placed at the beginning of the film, but Murphy has placed the title after the first round of twenty-five cycles. The title itself is ambiguous, so that even if viewers know the title, as is likely, they may misinterpret it because it sounds as much like a social phenomenon (such as the ''Me Generation'') as a photographic process. If misinterpreted, it again fails to prime the appropriate schemata. But the most important reason that *Print Generation* inhibits the generation of accurate hypotheses is that the imagery at the beginning of the film is so degraded. This has several consequences. First, it is very unlikely that viewers will interpret the changes in the patterns on the screen as a cut to a new shot, and the knowledge that the film is composed of discrete shots is a prerequisite to understanding the structure of the film. Second, even after several complete cycles, when viewers may begin to notice repetitions of the abstract patterns, the viewers will not hypothesize that the relationship between the repeated patterns is a gradual improvement of the image quality. They will be unable to make this particular hypothesis until at least one of the patterns is not only recognized as having been repeated, but begins to look like a recognizable image.

Fig. 6.24

Once this hypothesis is generated, viewers actively search for confirmation in the film. This confirmation takes two forms. First, patterns that have been tentatively identified will be checked for improving image quality and for reconfirmation of their identity. Second, patterns that have yet to be identified must be searched for clues that can in turn generate hypotheses about what they represent. That this is an active process can hardly be denied by anyone who has seen the film and experienced the almost desperate search for the solution to these small-scale perceptual problems.

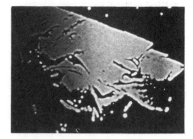

Fig. 6.25

The spatialization of form typical of simple numerical schematic works depends on the interaction of the local texture with the large-scale structure. Since the film perceiver is only in contact with a single point of the work at any one time, visualizing the spatial form of the work as a whole becomes a complex process. Viewers build a simple outline of the global structure from their interaction with the local texture, which is loaded with details perceived only in passing. In *Print Generation*, the play between the local texture and the overall structure is strangely paradoxical. After ten generations, the images are readable, though the fidelity is rather low. But as soon as the images can be read, attention shifts from the printing effect to the images themselves, as the viewer tries to engage the images by interpreting or connecting them. As the global template schema is confirmed, it fades from perception.

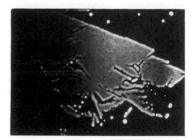

Fig. 6.26

The middle portion of *Print Generation* relies on the fact that when the viewers' hypotheses about the individual shots are consistently confirmed, as they are when all sixty images have become clear enough to understand, the viewers will begin to search for other organizational patterns. *Print Generation* strategically troubles our efforts to process the images that appear in the center of the work. Our perception of the subject matter of the work depends on our ability to schematize it, just as did our perception of the numerical pattern that structured the surface of the text. *Print Generation*'s images were selected and combined intuitively, or by principles that cannot be detected in the text. According to Murphy, all the footage he shot in Vermont is grouped together, as is the footage from New Jersey (interview with the author, 18 October 1984). In the fragments that show up in the film, all the locations look more or less anonymous. In essence, Murphy has stripped the schemata from the selection and combination of the basic sixty images of the film. As a result, no one can remember more than a few of the images or their order, but everyone clearly recalls the general shape of the film

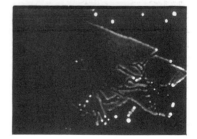

Fig. 6.27

Fig. 6.28

Fig. 6.29

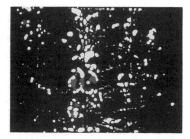

Fig. 6.30

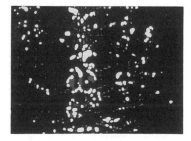

Fig. 6.31

because the simple schema of the gradually improving image quality provides a convenient way of remembering it.

The randomness of the image selection, or in my terms, its *de-schematization*, has a positive effect on our perception of the film, too. The only shot-to-shot relationship that helps us predict and remember the flow of images is the simple repetition of the cycle. Sixty abstract, unconnected images are far too many to hold in memory; at the beginning, each must be recognized anew each time it is presented. Gradually, and unevenly, some of the images grow clear. Those that move are readable sooner than those that do not; those with a few, simple shapes become clear before those that present a more even overall texture (compare Figs. 6.20–6.27 to Figs. 6.28–6.35). In the second half of the film, these same two factors help us remember certain images longer than others. But because of the de-schematized shot-to-shot relationships and the sixty-image overload, the solution inhibition effect is renewed as every image ultimately fades into oblivion. In spite of its mathematically precise structure and the fact that we have seen all sixty images, *Print Generation* maintains long passages of stubbornly indeterminate imagery, onto which the viewers, driven to hypothesize order or meaning wherever they can find it, project the most idiosyncratic and personal of interpretations.

Solution Multiplication

Though many filmmakers, writers and artists have produced simple schematic work, few have gone about it as confidently and as self-consciously as Hollis Frampton. In a grant proposal for *Magellan*, the twenty-four-hour film he had planned but not completed when he died in 1984, Frampton summarized the major concerns of his career up to and including *Zorn's Lemma* (1970):

> 1. Rationalization of the history of the art. "Making film over as it should have been."
> 2. The malleability of the sense and notion of *time* in film.
> 3. Establishment of progressively more complex *a priori* schemes to generate the various parameters of film-making, in order to eliminate subjective, thumbprint "composition."
> 4. The place and use of the written and spoken word in film.

Frampton could hardly have been more explicit if he had used the term itself: he was developing what I have called the simple schematic film. His first point may indicate only his faith in the revolutionary project of the avant-garde cinema, but points two and three directly address features of the simple schematic work. What he calls the "malleability of the sense and notion of time" is the tendency of the viewer to spatialize the form of the film. Later in the same proposal he elaborated on this notion, using his film *Zorn's Lemma* as an example:

> Previous schemes for ordering films had been almost entirely linear, involving mapping of elements along a single (one-dimensional) time-line. *Zorn's Lemma* uses a two-dimensional scheme (albeit a very

simple one) and I believe this represents a distinct innovation in the structuring of the cinematic artifact.

The details of Frampton's analysis of the spatialization of *Zorn's Lemma* are less important in this context than the fact that he thought viewers would experience the temporal arrangement of the film in a novel, spatial way.

Zorn's Lemma is Frampton's best-known film, and as Frampton suggested, it is more complex than *Artificial Light* or *Carrots and Peas*. It is also more complex than *Print Generation*, but like Murphy's film, it is an example of what I call the simple numerical schema film. Because of its progressive structure based on the alphabet, it is very easily spatialized: viewers have strong expectations about both the organization of details at the local level and the completion of its global template schemata. Frampton's third point, about progressively more complex *a priori* schemes, suggests that his work used the solution multiplication strategy: it prolongs the cycle of hypothesis generation and testing not by withholding confirmation of hypotheses, but by readily confirming one hypothesis only to quickly suggest another. In other words, whereas the viewer of *Print Generation* slowly solves a few perceptual puzzles, the viewer of *Zorn's Lemma* quickly solves many.

Zorn's Lemma has three parts. The first part is only a few minutes long and consists of black leader with a voice-over reading of a simple poem from *The Bay State Primer* used to teach children the alphabet. Each of the rhymed couplets in the film features a letter of the alphabet, not always at the beginning of the line, but as the initial letter of the subject of each couplet. For example, for "D" we have: "A dog will bite a thief at night." For "Y": "Youth forward slips, death soonest nips."

The second and longest part of *Zorn's Lemma* is comprised of a gradually evolving forty-five-minute series of one-second shots. It begins with twenty-four twenty-four-frame close-ups of metallic letters of the alphabet against a black background, followed by twenty-four frames of black. The alphabet has been abbreviated by omitting the letters "J" and "U."[11] Then follows twenty-four twenty-four-frame shots of words filmed from signs, windows, graffiti, and so forth, mostly from lower Manhattan (Fig. 6.36). For three more cycles, this series repeats, always in alphabetical order with one word for each letter of the abbreviated alphabet, except for "I," which in the second cycle is replaced with a word beginning with "J." Throughout the film, either "I" or "J" will be represented in any one cycle, and the use of an I-word or a J-word will alternate periodically. Similarly, "U" and "V" will only be represented one at a time, though instead of alternating, U-words will abruptly and permanently replace V-words later in the film. In the fifth cycle, a series of replacements begins when a shot of a fire is found in the place of the expected X-word. Irregularly (every one through ten cycles) another image replaces the shots of the words until every letter has been replaced. At this point, part two ends.

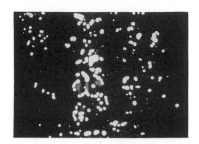

Fig. 6.32

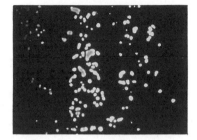

Fig. 6.33

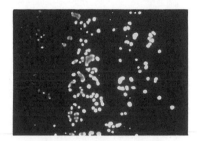

Fig. 6.34

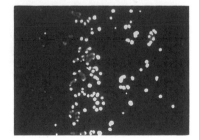

Fig. 6.35

Fig. 6.36

Fig. 6.37

The third and final part of *Zorn's Lemma* serves as a kind of retroactive explanatory articulation. It consists of what seems to be a single long take of a man, a woman and a dog crossing a snowy field (Fig. 6.37), though actually there are three dissolves used to cover the breaks between camera rolls. On the sound track over this ''shot'' is a portion of Robert Grosseteste's ''On Light: Or the Ingression of Forms'' read by six alternating female voices at the arbitrary rate of one word per second. This medieval mystical text, though somewhat difficult to follow because of its choppy presentation, reprises some of the basic themes of the film. It is about the nature of light, whose role in the cinematic process is almost too obvious to miss, and whose centrality has been asserted by filmmakers and film critics from Josef von Sternberg to Tony Conrad. More importantly, though, it asserts that a small set of mathematical ratios is fundamental to the composition of the universe. This comes close to summarizing *Zorn's Lemma* itself, where Frampton has composed as many elements as he could in multiples of twenty-four. From the number of frames per second of sound film projection, to the number of frames each image in the second part of the film is projected, to the (adjusted) number of letters in the alphabet, the entire film seems to be guided by the same set of numerical relations.

The initial cycle of hypothesis generation and confirmation engendered by part two of *Zorn's Lemma* is quite short in comparison with *Print Generation*, where very many confirming instances were needed to infer the structure of the film. Several factors account for *Zorn's Lemma*'s abbreviation of the generation/confirmation cycle. In a study of the comprehension of sequential patterns, H. A. Simon and K. Kotovsky (1963, 541) identified three factors that impeded subjects' apprehension of patterns: unfamiliarity with the units of the pattern; an insufficiently wide repertoire of relations to test between these units; and inadequate means for organizing the discovered relations. *Zorn's Lemma* avoids all these difficulties. The alphabetical schema is not only familiar to every literate person who can speak English, but is highly overlearned and therefore easily accessible from memory. The relationship between units of part two of *Zorn's Lemma* is simple progression. And, since simple progression is the only relationship between these units, the storage and organization demands on the viewer are minimal.

Still other factors ensure the ease with which the structure of part two of *Zorn's Lemma* is correctly hypothesized. Not only is the schema of the alphabet familiar to speakers of English, but by the time part two begins it has already been suggested by the explanatory articulation of part one. At the conclusion of the reading of the alphabetical poem, the alphabetical schema is explicitly represented in the first cycle that presents the letters of the alphabet against the black background. And finally, once generated, the hypothesis that the words in part two of *Zorn's Lemma* will be presented in alphabetical order within cycles meets with only confirming instances.

A work with few schemata that provides quick and continuous confirmation does not make a very interesting perceptual object.

Boredom is the inevitable result of continuous confirmation of a simple schema. In order to prevent (or at least reduce) this, Frampton has provided hierarchies of schemata, and each one can trigger a cycle of hypothesis generation and confirmation.

Zorn's Lemma seems at first to be controlled by one or two schemata that meet with quick and continued confirmation. There is the use of the alphabetical order of the words, and then their replacement by images. As even casual reviews of the film have pointed out—which leads me to believe it is rather apparent even on a single viewing—the images replace the least common letters first. This provides the general outline of part two of the film, but at least one reviewer sensed that there might be more to the film's organization:

> As I mentioned, images are substituted for words during the film at irregular intervals in the second and longest section and I suspect that if you could count the intervals, or the number of times certain letters appear, you would come up with some pattern that would spell out some statement like "by Hollis Frampton," "how to win a war," "how to stop pollution," or "new sex techniques." (anonymous review, Frampton file, Museum of Modern Art)

As far as I know, there are no secretly encoded messages in *Zorn's Lemma*, but there are more patterns in the film. This reviewer sensed what Gombrich calls *graded complication*, a tendency he finds in decorative art to provide the viewer with hierarchies of pattern so that when one level is fully apprehended there is another, fresh pattern waiting to be noticed (1979, 12–13). In *Zorn's Lemma* one such fresh pattern is that not only are the words presented alphabetically in each cycle (action, baron, car, delta), the words presented for each letter are alphabetical, too (action, active, addict).

The replacement images provide another set of numerical schemata. The alphabet schema allows viewers to anticipate the local details of each cycle and the end of each cycle, but since the number of cycles can be indeterminate, it does not allow viewers to anticipate the end of the film itself. Some of the replacement images, however, do allow this kind of anticipation. N is replaced with a shot of a glass tank slowly filling with dried beans; B is replaced with a shot of an egg frying; K is replaced with a shot of a man painting a wall. Each of these actions suggests a rather definitive point of completion. Though the alphabetical images could conceivably repeat indefinitely, these actions allow the viewer to predict the end of part two.

The schemata operating *within* the replacement images are clear enough, but whatever principles determine the relationships *between* them are less apparent. According to Frampton, the replacement images begin with morning (an egg frying for B) and continue to night (a tracking shot of the city at night for W). "I did try to take a little care," Frampton explained, "not quite Joycean care but a little care—to keep the depicted events in the part of the hourly cycle where they would not seem too outrageous, to present things at appropriate times of day in relation to the frying of the egg and the journey through the night" (MacDonald 1979b, 30). However Frampton thought he was using the daily cycle as a principle of construction, it is of little use to viewers: it is unlikely that they would hypothesize this schema, and the film provides almost no confirmation if they do. The egg and the streets at night are the only shots that definitively identify themselves as part of a daily cycle. Most others may not be "outrageously" placed, that is, they are not directly disconfirming, but are irrelevant to the daily cycle. The egg and the street at night are the only replacement images that could lead the viewer to hypothesize such an order, but the streets at night shot only appears as the eleventh of twenty-four replacement images, and the egg is the twenty-first. By the time the viewer even has the chance to hypothesize such a schema, there has been a wealth of schema-irrelevant instances, and some of the earliest replacement images—a stand of cat-tails for Y, and waves breaking for Z—provide directly contradictory instances since they are daytime shots, positioned "later" in the alphabet than the shot of the streets at night.

Other hypotheses suggested by Frampton would also meet with disconfirmation. For example, a couple of dozen words in the film stand out because they are not filmed in the urban environment, but are words superimposed over other shots. Since they stand out from the hundreds of other word-images, one might expect some pattern to emerge from them. Not so, according to Frampton, who said that the film incorporates a number of deliberate errors (what I would call unschematized elements). The superimposed words are just words he later decided to add. Similarly, he decided that twenty-four shots should violate the norm of twenty-four-frame shots established in the film. So, twelve shots are twenty-three frames, and twelve are twenty-five. Their locations were determined by chance.

Complex Permutations

Many of Frampton's "progressively complex *a priori* schemes" exceed the capacity of the human perceptual system. The difference between a twenty-three- or a twenty-five-frame shot and a twenty-four-frame shot is imperceptible. His notion of *Zorn's Lemma*'s spatial form is also a bit far-fetched. He suggests that rather than the single-dimension spatial form of most films, this film is two-dimensional, with the 109 cycles forming rows, and the twenty-four cycles forming columns. But the relationships "down the columns" are scarcely memorable, even though viewers actually see the words in this order; those along the so-called rows of the array demand an unthinkably large memory.

Frampton's ambitions for progressively complex *a priori* schemes raise an important question: at what point does graded complication exceed the perceptual and cognitive capacities of viewers? This is one of the central theoretical issues posed by serial music, which I suggested earlier in this chapter was an important influence on the simple schematic artwork. Leonard Meyer (1967, 284–93), for example, suggests that serial music tends to exceed the capacities of the listener, especially in its later forms in which *all* musical parameters are serialized (duration, loudness, timbre and attack as well as pitch). Meyer's critique has four elements. First, he argues that serial music is insufficiently redundant, so that subtle differences between elements cannot readily be detected. Second, because serial music rejects traditional musical forms, listeners lack familiar schemata that they can match to the structure of the serial work. Third, serial music cuts against the grain of human perception: patterns of pitch and duration are more easily perceived than patterns of timbre and attack, but total serialism requires that listeners notice the patterning of all parameters. And finally, serialism requires listeners to attend to too many details at once, and the listener's limited "channel capacity" just cannot cope with complex information streaming in from multiple sources at the same time.

Perhaps the most spectacular application of the serial aesthetic to the avant-garde film (as well as the most vivid demonstration of how a "serialized" film overloads the viewer) is Frampton's *Palindrome* (1969). As Frampton said,

> At the time I made *Palindrome* I was, as I periodically do, giving thought to serial music. Procedurally, the film is flatfootedly Webernian. One of Webern's mature procedures was to make a *generative* row—often it was a hexachord, in which the last six notes are the retrograde inversion of the first six—and then to manipulate that row rigorously (though I don't think Webern was averse to "cheating" here and there). (quoted in MacDonald 1980, 123)

Whether Frampton's description of Webern's compositional strategies is precisely accurate is not as important as the fact that he self-consciously modelled the film on something close to Webern's serial procedures. As far as our interest in *Palindrome* is concerned, Webern's later compositions have two important features. First, Webern's degenerative[12] tone row is roughly palindromic, in that the row's first six notes are similar to the second six. Since the serial tone row cannot actually repeat notes (see pp. 97–98), Webern's row cannot be an exact palindrome, but the pitch relations between the first six notes are symmetrical to the pitch relations in the last six. Second, the palindromic form of the small-scale row is repeated by the large-scale structures of the composition. For example, the third movement of his *Concerto, Op. 24* (1934) has five parts that are also roughly palindromic; parts one and five are similar, as are two and four.[13]

The complexity of *Palindrome*'s structure rivals that of Webern's late work. The film's imagery is completely abstract. Frampton collected the discarded ends of rolls of processed film from the garbage at the processing laboratory where he was working.[14] The roll ends were incompletely developed because the clips that held the film during development prevented the chemicals from evenly developing all areas of the emulsion. The images Frampton selected have generally biomorphic forms and sometimes evoke three dimensional space, but there are no recognizable objects. From these found images, Frampton assembled a series of four-second "cells." Each cell consists of twenty-four frames of a single found image; a flurry of twenty-four frames of twenty-four different found images; twenty-four frames of another found image; and twenty-four frames of black. These four-second cells were then printed in various permutations: the original color version; color negative; black-and-white; black-and-white negative. Frampton then created further permutations by using superimposition. Each of the original cells was printed on top of itself, so that one layer ran forward, and the other ran backward. (Note that layering a cell onto a reversed version of itself makes a small-scale palindrome, roughly equivalent to Webern's degenerative row.) These superimpositions were also printed in color positive, color negative, black-and-white positive and black-and-white negative versions. Finally, Frampton also superimposed permutations from the black-and-white versions. In one set he printed one layer through a yellow filter and the other layer through blue. In the other, he printed one layer through magenta and the other through green.[15]

Even with only a single viewing, it is clear enough that the film is built up of small-scale cells consisting of an image, a flurry of images, another image and a segment of black. But it is practically impossible to identify the basic cells and the various permutations, even on an editing bench, because the images are so totally abstract. Unlike *Artificial Light*, *Palindrome* does not begin with several cycles of the cells in simplified form, but begins rather complex permutations from the beginning. According to Frampton's description in the Filmmakers' Co-op catalog, the film has twelve permutations of forty "phrases." But this cannot be right, because the film would have to have a total of 480 cells in various permutations, which would make it thirty-two minutes long.[16] Actually, the film has 320 total cells and is twenty-one minutes and twenty-four seconds long, exclusive of the titles.[17] My educated guess is that there are sixteen basic cells with ten permutations, with each permutation appearing twice, once in the first half, once in the second.

Identifying the basic cells and permutations is hard enough, but it is child's play compared to discovering the large-scale structure of *Palindrome*. The large-scale structure has two elements: the systematic repetition of the basic cells and the systematic variation of the permutations. Since some of the images are somewhat memorable, it is possible to discern the basic idea behind the systematic repetition of the basic cells. The large-scale structure is a palindrome, but modified: every eighth cell is switched with the one next to it. Thus, assuming that each letter stands for a four-second cell, in the center of the film we see:

ABCDEFGH | HGFDECBA

This pattern is repeated throughout, so that the arrangement of the cells in the second half of the film is the reverse of the first half, except that every eight cells, two cells switch position. I suspect that some modified palindrome also structures the variation of the printing permutations, but I have been unable to discover it. Since the images are so abstract, even if we identify a repeated image or cell, we often cannot tell whether the version we see is the original or some permuted version of it. And this makes tracking the various permutations across the whole film virtually impossible without literally spatializing the film by cutting it to pieces and comparing the cells side-by-side.[18]

Palindrome is a fascinating and problematic film. Its "flatfootedly Webernian" form seems to support Meyer's argument that a totally serialized structure exceeds the listener/viewer's perceptual and cognitive capacities. The film also dramatizes the problems of transposing Webern's musical ideas into visual form. Most generally, we might consider to what extent the perception of certain kinds of formal structure is dependent on sense modality. Can the perception of rhythm, for example, be simply transposed from sound to image? *Palindrome* is not especially challenging in this regard: the film has a simple and rigorously consistent rhythm, the pulse of the four-second cells, whereas most any piece of music (serial or otherwise) would have a more complex rhythm. A second issue concerns the relationships between small-scale elements. The notes in the musical tone row are part of a numerical schema: they can be ranked in a progressive series, and they can be positioned from low to high in "musical space." So not only do we perceive the individual notes, the *relationships between the pitches* has a coherent, perceptible form. But the abstract images in *Palindrome* are members of an artificially constructed permutational set and cannot be so ranked. Like musical sounds, the images are abstract; but unlike musical notes, they are "unconnected," in the sense that the relationships between them cannot be spatialized. Thus, instead of hearing or seeing a coherent "tone row," the viewer sees only a collection of unrelated images. In this way, the relationship between the cells in *Palindrome* is formless, even though in other ways the film is perfectly patterned.

It might be tempting to simply dismiss attempts to transpose serial form into film as mere experiments that inevitably escape comprehension. But Karen Holmes's *Saving the Proof* (1979) uses serial techniques to create a permutational schematic film whose structure is more readily comprehensible.

Saving the Proof subjects a relatively small number of representational images to a set of permutations. The images are primarily of a woman in black walking through mostly deserted urban spaces; toward the end of the film, a few show the spaces without the walking woman. After the titles, the film lays out three sets of three images that form its basic permutational set. The first three images show a woman walking by a chain-link fence, a set of glass doors, and the reflective windows of an office building (Figs. 6.38, 6.39, 6.40). The next three shots repeat this first set with slight variations (Figs. 6.41, 6.42, 6.43). The next set of three shots lays out three more images from the basic permutational set (Figs. 6.44, 6.45, 6.46). Again, these are repeated with slight variation. Then the final set of images is set out (Figs. 6.47, 6.48, 6.49), and repeated with slight variations.

The rest of the film repeats these images in increasingly complex variants. The order of the images is generally preserved, though it is sometimes systematically varied. For example, the first eighteen

Fig. 6.38. A

Fig. 6.39. B

Fig. 6.40. C

Fig. 6.41. A′

Fig. 6.42. B′

Fig. 6.43. C′

shots (the basic nine images and their initial variants) could be diagrammed:

A B C | A′B′C′ | D E F | D′E′F′ | G H I | G′H′I′

The next cycle permutes the order slightly:

B C A | B C D | E F D | E F G | H I G | H I C

Subsequent permutations also introduce complex variants in the transitions between shots. The film uses short dissolves between shots until about one-third through the film, when it switches to the use of a complex optical transition. A silhouette of the walking woman is used as a matte that "wipes" from one image to the next, but maintains the appropriate order of the images (Figs. 6.50, 6.51, 6.52, 6.53). In the last third of the film, the permutations grow even more complex. Superimpositions are used to layer the basic images onto their variants, making the subtle differences, such as the direction of figure and camera movement, more apparent. (Notice, for example, that image D [Fig. 6.44] and image G [Fig. 6.47] are very similar, except for the direction of the woman's movement and a slight difference in shot scale.) Near the end, we see a few new images and some spaces and surfaces without the walking woman, and the film challenges us to integrate these new variations into the structure established by the first part of the film.

I do not suggest that *Saving the Proof*'s structure is apparent on a single viewing. I offer it as an example of a permutational schema of intermediate complexity—more compelling than the simple theme-and-variations of *Artificial Light*, and more comprehensible than the

Fig. 6.44. D   Fig. 6.45. E   Fig. 6.46. F

Fig. 6.47. G   Fig. 6.48. H   Fig. 6.49. I

byzantine permutations of *Palindrome*. This structure of intermediate complexity represents Holmes's adaptation of serialized film form in consideration of the limits of the viewers' perceptual and cognitive capacities.

The Limits of the Simple Schema

The simple schematic film represents a substantial subset of Structural film, but it would be a misconstruction of my argument to suggest that the concept captures the entire domain of Structural film. It would be a grosser misconstruction of my intentions to suggest that every simple schematic film could be exhaustively analyzed with the approach I have suggested here. Many films with simple schemata also use other compositional strategies that demand quite different processing. Nonetheless, even in combination with other kinds of organization, the simple schema is still a significant aspect of the viewer's experience.

Take, for example, Michael Snow's *Wavelength*, a film historically important to the formulation of the concept Structural film. If *Wavelength* actually were a continuous zoom across a loft, as it is too often described, then it would be an ideal example of the simple numerical schema (though it might be too simple to warrant much interest or analysis). *Wavelength*, of course, is no more accurately described as a continuous zoom than Hitchcock's *Rope* (1948) is accurately described as a single long take. *Wavelength* is an expressive mixture of printing effects and semi-narrative incidents; its restricted camera position is only one of its features, but for various reasons it

Fig. 6.50. D/E

Fig. 6.51. E/F

Fig. 6.52. F/G

Fig. 6.53. G/H

is this feature that has been most memorable to a number of critics. In 1967, mechanical camerawork that so insistently ignored the narrative action was relatively novel, especially in the avant-garde where hand-held cameras moving freely around the actors and environment were the norm. Also, because there *are* hints of narrative, toward which the camera makes no concession, at times even denying our view of them, the camerawork moves from its normal subordinate position to perceptual prominence. And finally, the camerawork is memorable because it is highly structured, as other elements of the film are not, even if it is not a perfectly continuous zoom. Thus, the film as a whole has been under-analyzed and misrepresented in favor of its one simple numerical schema.

Though *Wavelength* cannot be reduced to this schematic structure, within a much more complex structure, its simple numerical schema does function as a way of spatializing the form of the work. At any point during the film, viewers can calculate their progress and hypothesize about the ultimate extent of the zoom; and, once a hypothesis has been selected, viewers can anticipate the film's approaching closure. The sound track also aids the spatialization of the film by functioning as an analogue to the zoom: it consists of an electronically generated tone that gradually increases in pitch from fifty cycles per second to 12,000 cycles per second. Again, like the image track, the sound track is not perfectly schematic (it includes other sounds), but the electronic tone builds anticipation about the conclusion of the film. It bears repeating, though, that the processes of spatialization, memory and anticipation with respect to the zoom explain far less about *Wavelength* than spatialization, memory and anticipation explain about *Zorn's Lemma*.

Paul Sharits's work falls into the same class as *Wavelength*. *n:o:t:h:i:n:g* and T,O,U,C,H,I,N,G (both 1968) contain simple numerical schemata, but these schemata are responsible for a relatively small portion of the viewer's experience. The gradual spelling out of the titles by the periodic appearance of letters on the screen does permit the viewer to hypothesize and anticipate certain features of the films. In *n:o:t:h:i:n:g* Sharits uses other markers of the passage of time as well: a bulb-shape is gradually drained of fluid; a series of beeps gradually grow further and further apart. But, as Sitney puts it, other aspects "overpower" these schemata (1979, 389). Sharits's works, like other examples of the flicker film, overpower the processing of these schemata with bottom-up stimulation, and a neurological explanation better accounts for these effects. Of course, the suggestion that our response to Sharits's work is exclusively physiological or photochemical is another reduction. I mean only to suggest that this work has significant aspects that derive their effects from relatively low-level processes.

Simple schemata can also be used at the local level for rhythmic effects, without the processing benefits of global template schemata. I hesitate to call this a bottom-up device, since music theorists generally agree that rhythm inheres not in the stimulus itself but in the perceiver's anticipation of coming beats (Meyer 1956, 104–08; Davies 1978, 176). Given the language of these theorists, who use terms like inference, knowledge and information, it seems that a problem-solving approach might be perfectly appropriate to the analysis of rhythm, too. Nonetheless, even if rhythm is hypothesis-driven, it operates on a much smaller scale than the hypothesis generation and testing cycle that solves for the overall structure of a film. Since it works on such an atomistic level, rhythm warrants a separate, even if brief, discussion.

Ernie Gehr's *Serene Velocity* (1970), for example, is patterned by incremental changes of the focal length of a zoom lens. At the beginning of the film, the focal length shifts between 50mm and 55mm every four frames. After a while, the zoom shifts between 45mm and 60mm, still every four frames. As the film progresses, the periodic shifts grow more dramatic, though the basic four-frame pulse is maintained.[19] Since the jumps from one focal length setting to another occur regularly and at very small intervals (fractions of a second) the experience of the rhythm is more immediate, if not more direct, than the gradual comprehension of the form of the work. Actually, *Serene Velocity* has a simple numerical schema for this overall structure, too. At first the focal length of the zoom jumps between slightly different, nearly normal focal lengths. As the film progresses, the focal lengths used are more telephoto and wide angle, in effect, traversing the space of the hallway much as *Wavelength* was rumored to traverse the space of the loft. Frampton's film *Critical Mass* (1971) creates a rhythmic pattern by using a small-scale permutational schema in the progressive loop printing of footage of an argument. In the only film in which he used actors, Frampton staged a nasty, pointless argument between a man and a woman in front of a plain white background. As if it were not repetitive enough, Frampton printed the film in small sections about one second long. The second section repeats about half of the first; the third, half of the second; and so on, so that due to the overlap, we actually hear the argument twice. Again, since the units of the pattern are so small, it is experienced as rhythm and does not involve an extended hypothesis generation and testing cycle to detect it. Its exact structure takes some time to decipher, though, especially if the viewer tries to follow the argument at the same time. (Like many other simple schematic films, *Critical Mass* also deviates from its schematic structure. Toward the end of the film, the image of the actors gives way to a sequence of increasingly abstract patterns.)

Another relative of the simple schematic film does not use familiar and highly overlearned schemata but borrows schemata from other sources. I have already mentioned John Knecht's *The Primary Concerns of Roy G. Biv* (1978), which uses the relatively familiar schema of the order of colors in the spectrum. Sometimes, however, these borrowed schemata are very obscure. In his film *Grand Opera* (1979), for example, James Benning re-edited ten shots from his earlier *One-Way Boogie Woogie* (1977) by assigning each shot a number between zero and nine. He then arranged the shots, in twenty-frame lengths, to the first 527 digits of pi. Since most people do not know more than a few digits of pi, this schema has no processing benefits.

Michael Snow's *So Is This* (1982) is a relatively late Structural film. Like Frampton's *Poetic Justice* (1972), it represents a side of Structural film that was less concerned with the physical materials of the film process than the relationship between visual representation and language. It anticipates the "New Talkie," a genre of avant-garde filmmaking in which writing and speech become increasingly prominent. *So Is This* is not a simple schematic film. I cite it here because it lays bare the viewer's cycle of hypothesis generation and testing which I have been discussing, and thereby demonstrates another way in which a film might "insist on its shape."

So Is This consists entirely of words presented on a mostly black screen. In the film, Snow makes constant and explicit reference to what will happen in the film itself, so that *So Is This* functions by seizing control of the hypothesis generation phase of our processing of the film. "The rest of the film will look like this," reads its second sentence. "The film will consist of single words presented one after another to construct sentences and hopefully (this is where you come in) to convey meanings," it continues, thereby providing explicit answers to what we would normally hypothesize and gradually confirm. We are made conscious of this procedure a little later when we read: "This film will be about 2 hours long. Does that seem like a frightening prospect? Well look at it this way: how do you know this isn't lying?" At this point, we become fully aware of the difficulty of our position as hypothesis generators and testers. The form of the film is not only novel, it suggests no global template schemata. We are obliged to form our hypotheses solely on the basis of what Snow tells us on the screen, and we now must consider that these words are likely to be erratic and whimsical, if not downright dishonest.

So Is This does move into other areas of discussion (though not without reminding us that we are probably wondering if it will): censorship, the use of the written word in other films, and our ability to understand writing. As the film ends, we are once again reminded of the dilemma that arises from the lack of global schemata. The film's last sentence is "This film will seem to stop." Even after a minute without a word on the screen, as the projectionist lets the tail of the film run through the projector in accordance with Snow's projection instructions, we are so unsure what will happen next that we are likely to remain in our seats until the house lights come on. Whether we react with humor or anxiety, what we respond to is the overt and self-conscious frustration of our viewing strategies for the minimal strain of the American avant-garde film.

In an important sense Snow's project in *So Is This* is the same as my project here: to make explicit the processes of spectatorship of a kind of avant-garde artwork. In addressing this issue, I have proposed another category, the simple schematic artwork, that is in a way broader than Structural film, the super-genre it was meant to refine. But although my category extends widely across different media, it is from the beginning rooted in the set of common perceptual and cognitive processes it demands of the viewer. Snow has chosen to dramatize these processes; I have tried to provide a vocabulary and a set of concepts that allow us to speak sensibly about aspects of the experience of these works that the Modernist interpretive schemata approach to the minimal strain has for too long led us to pass over in silence.

7

The Usual Suspects
Still at Large:
The Interpretive Schemata
of the Assemblage Strain

The assemblage strain of the American avant-garde cinema is a fugitive genre: practiced by many filmmakers, but until recently never openly acknowledged as a coherent body of work programmatically exploring a set of aesthetic problems. The assemblage strain was far from invisible, for it was found in the work of some major American avant-garde filmmakers: in the found-footage films of Bruce Conner, Chick Strand, and Al Razutis, and in the collage films of Harry Smith, Robert Breer, Stan Vanderbeek and Larry Jordan. But the idea that the avant-garde film's appropriation of the imagery of popular culture might constitute a cohesive aesthetic program was not a particularly compelling notion for the critics of the 1960s and 1970s.[1] This, of course, is especially peculiar considering the role Pop artist Andy Warhol played in the American avant-garde cinema.

Warhol's film career was brief, but prolific. He made more than 100 films between 1963, the year of his dramatic introduction to the avant-garde film, and 1968, the year a nearly successful assassination attempt halted his active involvement in film production. In 1969, P. Adams Sitney singled him out as the most important precursor to the Structural film, the style that would dominate the avant-garde for most of the next decade. But in spite of Warhol's long-running influence, there was little concern over the impact of the aesthetics of Pop Art on the avant-garde film. In fact, by the mid-1970s, not even Warhol's films were seen in the light of Pop Art. To begin to understand why, we must understand the treatment that Pop Art itself received in the world of the visual arts. As we will see, by the end of the 1960s, Pop Art was generally interpreted in ways that suggested its similarity to Minimalism, thereby incorporating Pop Art part into the Modernist project.

Pop Art's Interpretive Schemata

Most major art critics were antagonistic to Pop Art when it was first exhibited in the very early 1960s.[2] Abstract Expressionism had won their acclaim and gained international prestige for the American visual arts. When Pop Art repudiated the aesthetics of Abstract Expressionism it was not just a rejection of the taste of established critics but a challenge to the critical principles used to explain advanced art. According to Harold Rosenberg (1960), an Action Painting was evidence of the artist's spontaneous and sincere gesture; the careful finish of a Pop painting could only be the product of careful labor. Clement Greenberg had valorized the Abstract Expressionists' "atmospheric" space, created by building up layers of color; Pop Art was as mechanical and flat as the commercial art that served as its subject matter. Pop challenged not just the interpretive schemata for Abstract Expressionism but many fundamental notions about art in general. Critics complained that Pop was artless because the painters did not transform their subject matter but slavishly copied it. And the subject matter itself was often considered unworthy of artistic treatment: Modernism was founded on the distinction between high art and mass art, they argued, and Pop was indistinguishable from advertising.

Unlike most advanced art after World War II, Pop paintings were pictures of recognizable objects. Accordingly, critics often tried to interpret them *topically*—that is, as though they were actually about the subject matter they represented. But for two reasons the topical approach was difficult with Pop Art.

First, such a topical reading would suggest that Pop was out of step with advanced art of the twentieth century. During the ascendancy of Abstract Expressionism, representational art had collected a number of unattractive associations. One of these was with socialist art. This certainly made it unattractive to conservatives, and after the American Left's disillusionment with the Soviets in the late 1930s, Socialist Realism lost its appeal for the Left as well. Representational art also smacked of the provincialism of 1930s American art, which after the international prestige of Abstract Expressionism seemed very backward. To suggest that Pop was "about" some topical aspect of current life would be to suggest that while it rejected Abstract Expressionism, it did so by resuscitating a retrograde and unsophisticated aesthetics.

The second difficulty for critics attempting topical interpretations was that the paintings were highly ambivalent toward the subjects they represented. Was Lichtenstein's work, for example, a celebration of the comic strip or a critique of the culture that produced it? It was neither, according to Ivan Karp, and this was one of its virtues: "Sensitivity is a bore. Common Image painting [another early term for Pop] is an art of calm, profound observation and humorous wonderment without sensibility. It does not criticize. It only records" (1963, 27). But Pop's neutrality disgusted Hilton Kramer:

> Pop Art does not tell us what it feels like to be living through the present moment of civilization—it is merely part of the evidence of that

Fig. 7.1.
James Rosenquist, *F-111*, 1965.
Oil on canvas with aluminum,
10′ x 86′. © 1993 James
Rosenquist/Licensed by VAGA,
New York, NY.

civilization. Its social effect is simply to reconcile us to a world of commodities, banalities and vulgarities—which is to say, an effect indistinguishable from advertising art. This is a reconciliation that must—now more than ever—be refused, if art—and life itself—is to be defended against the dishonesties of contrived public symbols and pretentious commerce. (Selz 1963, 38–39)

Even among those who sincerely believed that Pop had something to say about the current state of the human condition, there was still confusion about Pop's attitude toward mass culture. John Russell argued that it was an oversimplification to reduce Pop to a critique of mass culture: "Pop is not, as many people have supposed, a satirical art: it is an affirmative art, and affection plays a great part in it" (Russell and Gablik 1969, 22). But in the eyes of Mary Josephson, Pop was not at all "affectionate," it was decidedly critical of the society from which it drew its iconography: "The hoax of Pop being in love with popular culture or mass advertising (which contemporary advertising used to promote Pop and its own self-parody) is now untenable. As Pop becomes an episode in the history of the sixties, its hostility toward the culture from which it appropriated its images begins to appear" (1971, 43).

Statements by the artists could not or did not resolve the issue. Occasionally a Pop artist did take a stand for or against mass culture. Claes Oldenberg phrased it rather poetically:

I am for Kool-art, 7-UP art, Pepsi-art, Sunshine art, 39 cents art, 15 cents art, Vatronol art, Dro-bomb art, Vam art, Menthol art, L & M art, Ex-lax art, Venida art, Heaven Hill art, Pamryl art, San-o-med art, Rx art, 9.99 art. Now art, New art, How art, Fire sale art, Last Chance art, Only art, Diamond art, Tomorrow art, Franks art, Ducks art, Meat-o-rama art. (1967, 98)

James Rosenquist said he hoped his *F-111* mural (1965, Fig. 7.1) would be an antidote to the inhuman side of advanced technology, but he stopped well short of condemning *all* mass culture. He hated the F-111 and the lie-detector, but in general, he found machines "exciting" (Swenson 1965, 109). Typically, though, the Pop artists were more circumspect about the moral position of their work. Lichtenstein, for example, claimed he used comic strips "as visual objects, as paintings—not as critical commentaries about the world" (Coplans 1963a, 31). Similarly, Rosenquist was more apt to talk about the colors of the objects he painted than about their functions in the world.

Of all the Pop artists, Warhol was the most stubbornly ambivalent about the subject matter of his work, and this makes topical interpretations of his work particularly difficult. In a painting like Rosenquist's *F-111* it is apparent that the artist is suggesting parallels between a variety of consumer goods and modern American armaments. For example, the chrome-plated hair drier on the child's head evokes the shape of the nose of the fighter plane that runs the length of the mural. Thus, however obliquely, American consumer culture is implicated in the violence in Vietnam. But when Warhol presents one hundred soup cans in a single canvas, it is impossible to determine his attitude toward his subject matter (Fig. 7.2). In interviews, Warhol invariably disavowed any intentional social criticism, but no one would take seriously Warhol's claims that he loved modern culture, because Warhol invariably exaggerated. To G. R. Swenson's inquiry as to why he began to paint soup cans, Warhol responded: "Because I used to drink it. I used to have the same lunch every day, for twenty years, I guess, the same thing over and over again" (117). When he went so far as to suggest that he wanted to be a machine, and to acknowledge openly that he could produce startlingly high numbers of paintings because he emulated the means of mass production, critics took it as a put-on, whose level of irony was impossible to judge.

Pop Art's ambivalence toward mass culture posed a serious problem for critics who hoped to understand it in terms of the Modernist project. Max Kozloff articulated this problem with remarkable clarity in an early essay critical of Pop (1962). If Pop was a celebration of mass culture, it offended one of the most deeply held convictions of the partisans of Modernism, the distinction between high art and popular culture. As articulated by Clement Greenberg in "The Avantgarde and Kitsch" (1939), this view held that mass culture was a celebration of the basest instincts of modern society, and that the true artist must transcend this wide-spread depravity. The art thus produced would be unacceptably strange to the culture at large, and the serious artist would be perpetually alienated from the society whose values he or she could not share. If Pop celebrated these values, Kozloff argued, it was a sign of moral sickness and cowardice. If, on the other hand, Pop artists cited aspects of mass culture in order to criticize it, then they were tedious: any thinking member of American culture in the 1960s already held the views they were espousing.

Topical interpretation of Pop Art remained problematic. But soon after Pop's appearance in the New York art world, critics de-

Fig. 7.2. Andy Warhol, *One Hundred Cans*, 1962. Synthetic polymer paint on canvas, 6′ × 52″. © 1993 the Andy Warhol Foundation for the Visual Arts, Inc.

veloped a set of interpretive schemata meant to show that while Pop did reject the aesthetics of Abstract Expressionism, it nevertheless had a place in the Modernist tradition. The earliest of these was the Dadaist interpretation.

The Dadaist interpretation of Pop was predominant during Pop's earliest days. In fact, before the term ''Pop'' stuck to the style, one of several terms for it was ''neo-Dada.'' According to this view, the Pop painting was a pictorial equivalent of a Marcel Duchamp ready-made: just as Duchamp presented everyday objects as sculpture, the Pop artists presented everyday images as painting. And, as was the case with Duchamp's Dadaist gestures, the Pop painting's import was a function of its offensiveness. At first, shock value was sometimes Pop's primary virtue. In 1963, an early exhibitor of Pop reveled in its unacceptability:

> The greatest art is unfriendly to begin with. Common Image Art is downright hostile. Its characters and objects are unabashedly egotis-

tical and self-reliant. They do not invite contemplation. The style is happily retrograde and thrillingly insensitive (a curious advance). Red, Yellow, and Blue have been seen before for all they are worth. In Common Image Art they are seen once again. It is too much to endure, like a steel fist pressing in the face. (Karp 1963, 26)

For John Coplans, another early Pop partisan, Pop was not quite so violent, but its value still came from its fierce rejection of past art:

Seen from this point of view the painters of the soup can, the dollar bill, the comic strip, have in common not some moral attitude toward their subject matter that some say is positive and others say is negative, *but a series of painting devices which derive their force in good measure from the fact that they have virtually no association with a European tradition.* (Emphasis in original; 1963b, 28)

Before long, the simple Dadaist reading of Pop evolved into a Cagean affirmation of artistic freedom. Pop's rejection of past art was still crucial, but this rejection was interpreted in terms of the art-process schema that would be so important to the Structural film: instead of just shocking the viewer, Pop emphasized the conventional nature of aesthetic concepts by demonstrating that the most mundane materials and working methods could have aesthetic value. As Suzi Gablik put it, the point of this demonstration was to secure "a greater mobility and flexibility toward art in general, whereby every art situation is more total and inclusive of the simultaneous levels which occur in actual experience" (Russell and Gablik 1969, 14).

The reception of Warhol's painting fits this general pattern: initially seen as Dadaist provocation, later seen as a meditation on the artistic process. Like Roy Lichtenstein, whose work was also initially seen as an affront to the fine arts, Warhol made more or less faithful copies of images from popular culture sources. But while Lichtenstein used the relatively "lofty" comic strips, Warhol "copied" even "lower" images: the Campbell's soup can, Brillo boxes, S & H Green Stamps and perhaps lowest of all, money itself. In interviews, Lichtenstein invariably took pains to explain how carefully he transformed his sources (Swenson 1963, 93; Coplans 1963, 31). To questions about *his* style, Warhol responded with flippant dicta like "I think everybody should be a machine" (Swenson 1963, 116). And when Warhol began to use commercial reproduction techniques like the silkscreen, there was almost no avoiding the conclusion that his work was meant as a challenge to accepted notions of art. But critics soon translated Warhol's wisecracks into the serious tones of the art-process schema. In the catalog of a 1965 exhibition of Warhol's work, Samuel Adams Green argued that Warhol's "mechanical" look was meant to rid us of a narrow-minded view of the art object:

Warhol will often accompany an image painting with a canvas, blank, extending the idea of making useless replicas of packages into the realm of art. In doing so he plays within the gap between art and life, setting up an often humorous exchange between the two, interchanging their roles as they imitate each other. He asks us to take both our art and our individuality a little less seriously. His personality-purged work makes

> the Abstract Expressionist's subconscious searching seem indulgent. By using the silk screen to make paintings exactly alike, he challenges the prejudice that a work of art must be unique. (1965, 231)

Such art-process interpretations were crucial to critics' efforts to make sense of Pop Art and its rejection of the aesthetics of Abstract Expressionism.

The lowly subject matter of Pop Art led some critics to conclude that Pop Art had completely abandoned proper ''aesthetic'' concerns. Early on, Pop painting was defended in art-process terms, but no one would have suggested that it could be defended on formal grounds. Since one of the points of the art-process interpretation of Pop was that the artist had begun to relinquish control over aspects of his or her work, the notion that one of these Pop paintings was actually a carefully composed picture was far from most critics' minds. In 1964 even a favorably disposed critic wrote of ''the dismal failure of Pop Art—its inability to engage an observer on an aesthetic level'' (Leider 1964, 47).

As the 1960s wore on, however, critics began to compare Pop to current trends in abstract art, and the gulf between the ''Dadaist'' Pop and geometric abstraction began to narrow as critics began to analyze Pop with concepts that had previously been applied to contemporary abstract art.[3] For example, in a forward-looking essay in 1964, Robert Rosenblum wrote:

> Already the gulf between Pop and abstract art is far from unbridgeable, and it has become easy to admire simultaneously, without shifting visual or qualitative gears, the finest abstract artists, like Stella and Noland, and the finest Pop artists, like Lichtenstein. The development of some of the Pop artists themselves indicates that this boundary between Pop and abstract art is an illusory one. (1964, 56)

Two years later, Peter Plagens advanced the same argument in *Art-forum* in more specifically Greenbergian terms:

> The critical establishment has largely overlooked the formal contribution of Pop; in the rush to assure that history does not again make a fool of journalism, the impact-innovations (imagery, literary content and the role of the artist) have been proclaimed, and the underlayers of color, space, structure, scale and surface have been left unattended. (1966, 36)

In his analysis, Plagens tried to demonstrate that among other things, Pop had developed yet another stage in the Greenbergian evolution of the picture plane. Instead of the atmospheric space the Abstract Expressionists built up with overlapping planes of color, the Pop artists ''suffocated'' the space by bringing color planes into collision.

In 1968 Suzi Gablik and John Russell mounted an exhibition of Pop Art for the expressed purpose of reinterpreting Pop Art by linking it to Minimalism. In the introduction to *Pop Art Redefined*, the book they published to accompany the exhibition, Gablik and Russell explained that their book, like their exhibition, ''aims to redefine the areas in which Pop made a unique contribution; and it sees Pop in terms of formal ideas and not in terms of the jokey, gregarious, eupeptic and loosely organized phenomenon which was seized upon with such relish by the mass media in the early 1960s'' (1969, 7). In his introductory essay, Russell makes this point through a comparison of Warhol with Noland:

> When Warhol first showed pictures like the green Coke-bottle painting . . . people could not get beyond the triviality, as they saw it, of the basic motif. But the fact is that any common object, if looked at hard enough and long enough, will lose its temporal identity and become an abstract form. . . . [The] bottle on Warhol's canvas is not a description of something: it *is* something, as absolutely as the chevrons on a Noland of some years back. In the one case, as in the other, what is being asserted [is] the autonomy of the picture: the two artists are like men who set off in opposite directions and yet arrive at the same destination. (Russell and Gablik 1969, 38)

I do not want to overstate the case: formal analyses of Pop painting were increasingly common after the late 1960s, but such formal analyses of Warhol's work are more rare. Warhol's painting generally proved more difficult to justify on the basis of its painterly or compositional qualities than that of any other major Pop artist.

Warhol was the only Pop artist who did not defend his work against charges of artlessness. On the contrary, Warhol readily confessed. And as if to corroborate his confession, the paintings themselves seem to resist close analysis. His compositions come in two varieties: an image positioned centrally on a solid background, and a repeated image arranged in orderly rows and columns. Of course his work was never quite as machine-like as Warhol made it seem. As many critics have pointed out, even while using the silkscreen process, Warhol could vary the image by varying the pressure on the squeegee or the amount of ink applied to the screen, as he did in *Disaster* (1963). Sometimes Warhol would depart from the neat grid arrangement of the soup can paintings and position the repeated images in less orderly fashion as he did in *Optical Car Crash* (1963, Fig. 7.3). Analyses of Warhol's work in terms of its composition are certainly not unheard of, but Warhol's art projects an air of indifference and hasty execution that encourages art-process interpretations of the choices Warhol did or did not make, and discourages analysis of his exploration of the essential features of the medium. Thus, the art-process schema continued to play a significant role in the interpretation of Warhol's work, even as critics saw Pop as a whole in increasingly formal terms.

By the late 1960s, the novelty of Pop Art had worn off, and with it had gone much of its value as Dadaist provocation. Supporters of Pop who wished to maintain its timeliness and relevance increasingly interpreted Pop as part of the same exploration of the picture plane that was so important to Minimalism. It was at this time that Sitney wrote ''Structural Film.'' The prevalence of formalist views of Pop in the late 1960s partly explains why Pop *per se* plays no role in the aesthetics of Structural film even though Warhol was its most important precursor. But this explanation is incomplete: if Warhol, of all the Pop

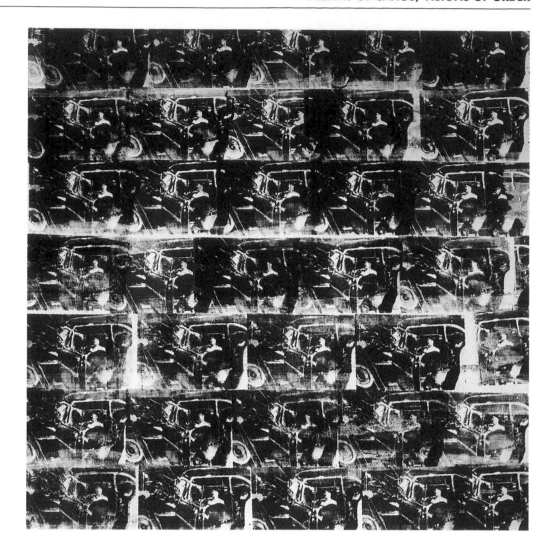

Fig. 7.3. Andy Warhol, *Optical Car Crash*, 1963. Silkscreen ink on synthetic polymer paint on canvas, 6′ 9 7/8″ × 6′ 10″. © 1993 the Andy Warhol Foundation for the Visual Arts, Inc.

artists, resisted formalist and anti-illusion interpretation, why was Dada not the first cause of the Structural film? The answer to this question involves the interpretation of Warhol's films. His paintings may have resisted Greenbergian readings, but critics of the avant-garde saw Warhol's films in formalist, self-critical terms from the very beginning.

The Minimalization of Warhol's Films

Warhol's films were infamous for two reasons. His early films were notoriously boring: they combined mind-boggling length with little on-screen action. And second, though there was a sexual undercurrent to almost all his films, his films became more sexually explicit as his career wore on. It was the silent films of his early career that had the formal innovations that endeared him to the partisans of the avant-garde: the fixed camera position; the roll-long takes without cutting; and the improvised and minimal "action." For several of these early films, he was awarded *Film Culture*'s Independent Film Award. When he abandoned the static, frontal style of the early films for the scripted plots and editing of narrative films later in his career, many writers on the avant-garde film dismissed him. As Sitney put it in *Visionary Film*, Warhol's exit from the avant-garde film was as abrupt as his entry in 1963: "He immediately began to produce major cinema. For years he sustained that production with undiminished intensity, creating in that time as many major films as any of his contemporaries had in a lifetime; then, after completing *The Chelsea Girls* (1966), he quickly faded as a significant film-maker" (371).

But for writers who looked at Warhol's career as a whole, as Stephen Koch did in *Stargazer* (1973), stylistic innovation played a smaller role; the focus was on Warhol's voyeuristic obsession with fame, and more importantly, with sex. Since the sexual themes were given prominence over stylistic innovation, Koch did not dismiss the later films because of their more traditional style. Instead, Koch looked for the key to the whole career, which he discovered in Warhol's narcissistic personality. From this perspective, *Blow Job* (1963) is more important for what it says about sex than for the outlandish conceit of the immobile camera showing only the actor's face for twenty-five minutes. Thus, for Koch, the undercurrent of sexuality linked *Blow Job*, *Kiss* (1963), and *Sleep* (1963) to the later films of his "superstars"—the drag queens, male hustlers and bored kids who were tacky versions of Hollywood sex symbols. From Koch's perspective, then, even the novel formal devices of Warhol's films are manifestations of his personality. The fixed camera position of his early films, for example, is a symptom of his inability to sincerely interact with others.

Koch made a convincing argument for the importance of the exploration of sexuality to Warhol's career as a whole. But if one looks almost exclusively at the first half of his career, as most writers on the avant-garde film did, the sexual themes are not as thoroughly developed, and Warhol's static style assumes much greater prominence. Koch explained the style as an outgrowth of the filmmaker's personality; it was sometimes attributed to Warhol's inexperience, technical incompetence or indifference. David Bourdon (1971, 48) argued that it was a conscious attempt to apply the minimalist aesthetic that was emerging in the visual arts. But whatever the motivation for it, Warhol's decidedly minimal style was more prominent in his early films than in his later narrative films. Thus, by dismissing his later work, the world of the avant-garde film saw Warhol as an artist carefully exploring novel stylistic devices.

The de-emphasis of the Pop aspects of Warhol's films is not due solely to the avant-garde critics' concentration on the early portion of his career. After all, the style of his early films was no more restrained than much New York Pop, which was only gradually interpreted from a Greenbergian perspective. But while Warhol's paintings resisted formalist interpretation, critics immediately interpreted his early films with the anti-illusion schema.

This is not to say that there was not a strong Dada flavor to Warhol's early films. Quite the contrary; few avant-garde films are as provocative as Warhol's early silents. The irony and outrage of Warhol's early work was not lost on Sitney in his "Structural Film" essay, where he saw the work partly as a Duchampian gesture aimed at the avant-garde itself: "On one level at least—and that is the only level of importance to us—Warhol turned his genius for parody and reduction against the American avant-garde film itself. The first film that he seriously engaged himself in was a monumental inversion of the dream tradition within the avant-garde film" (371). There is no doubt that there is a Dadaist element in *Sleep*, but it is doubtful that Warhol aimed to satirize the avant-garde film specifically. Interpreting *Sleep* as a "monumental inversion" of the dream tradition implies that Warhol was interested in the history of the avant-garde film; nothing else in his work or public statements would support such an assertion. And, critics at the time did not see his works as parodies of anything; generally, they interpreted his work in deadly earnest.

The earliest coverage of Warhol in *Film Culture* consisted largely of reports of what was happening at the Warhol Factory; these were written by people who were themselves involved with Warhol. A number of Warhol associates published poems about his films.[4] Ronald Tavel (1966), Warhol's early scriptwriter, published a long piece on the production of the early sound film *Harlot* (1964). And two of Warhol's friends from the established art world published more traditional critical essays: Henry Geldzahler (1964), a curator at the Museum of Modern Art, wrote on *Sleep*, and art critic Gregory Battcock wrote three essays on early Warhol films (1965a, 1965b, 1966).

Stories of *audiences* outraged by Warhol's early films abound, but the critical treatment of these films was much more restrained and respectful. Even when Dada was invoked, it was in the deadly serious Cagean terms that would become so familiar in criticism of the Structural film. According to Battcock, *Screen Test*'s provocation of the viewer was no prank, but served an important social function:

> Warhol will challenge the existing order on all levels, using his own terms, even though they will be unacceptable to most people and delay acceptance of his art. Quick acceptance of a statement which attempts to subvert within the conditions and restrictions of the status quo and according to its lexicon is to be expected even though that statement must ultimately be false. (1965b, 62–63)

The object of *Screen Test*'s challenge is the false depiction of sexuality in the commercial narrative cinema. Just as we saw with the interpretation of the minimal strain, the art-process schema interprets the artwork as a comment on the shortcomings of the reigning norm, the Hollywood film.

But while the Dada element in Warhol's films was not completely ignored, Dada readings of the films were never as prominent as Dada readings of Warhol's painting. Jonas Mekas saw Warhol as a relative of cinéma verité, and described his work—with complete seriousness—as a superior brand of realism. In 1964, in his *Village Voice* column he valorized Richard Leacock, Don Pennebaker and the Maysles; then he turned to Warhol:

> It is the work of Andy Warhol, however, that is the last word in the Direct Cinema. It is hard to imagine anything more pure, less staged, and less directed than Andy Warhol's *Eat*, *Empire*, *Sleep*, *Haircut* movies. . . . He is opening to filmmakers a completely new and inexhaustible field of cinema reality. . . . What to some still looks like actionless nonsense, with the shift of our consciousness which is taking place will become an endless variety and an endless excitement of seeing similar subjects or the same subject done differently by different artists. Instead of asking for Elephant Size Excitement we'll be able to find aesthetic enjoyment in the subtle play of nuances. (Reprinted in Mekas 1972, 154)

Like Mekas, Battcock saw Warhol as strongly motivated by realist goals. In *Screen Test*, an actor remains on screen for the entire seventy minutes of the film; Battcock argued that during this time the actor reveals his personality in spite of the blatantly artificial aspects of the production: "Mario's totally convincing performance is heightened by the rather sloppily applied make-up and wig, which speak of Genet and Greenwich Avenue in a startlingly real and at the same time cruel manner" (1965b, 62). Likewise, in his essay on *Blow Job*, Battcock saw the "inadequacies" of the production as its realist virtues:

> Like the protagonist of other Warhol films, he is left to his own devices and since he is obviously either incapable of or un-interested in coping with the situation he finds himself in a fairly ludicrous position. In this sense the actor becomes an element or tool used in such a way never before considered in the film. This is another example of Warhol's formidable ability to extend and redefine reality—a preoccupation intrinsic to art. (1965a, 20)

Battcock and Geldzahler referred to Warhol's "realism" as well as to Cagean interpretations of Warhol's films, but the main point of their articles was to introduce the Greenbergian perspective that would be so important to critics of Warhol's films later in the decade. Geldzahler, as an assistant curator at the Museum of Modern Art, was in a unique position to connect Warhol's early films to current work in the visual arts. In the first *Film Culture* issue to carry a piece on Warhol, Geldzahler already explicitly interpreted it from a Greenbergian perspective:

> In painting in the past fifty years we have become increasingly aware of the limitations and special qualities of the medium: texture, two dimensionality, brushstroke, etc. And Warhol's film, in which we are constantly aware of the filmic process, sometimes even seeing the frames that end the reels, frames that any sophisticated movie maker would edit out, makes us aware of exactly the limitations and qualities of film itself. (1964, 13)

In 1966, Battcock made a more extended Greenbergian analysis of *Empire*. (Though it was still only two pages long; the articles on

Warhol, like the rest of the articles in *Film Culture*, were generally very brief at this time.) Battcock argued that every aspect of the film was designed to demonstrate the essential properties of the film medium:

> Clearly, Warhol has dismissed the idea that "movement" is an essential characteristic of movies. Movement can after all, be presented and experienced in other media—the dance, theater, and sculpture—so it is not dealt with in this film essay on the reidentification of the essential message of the cinematic medium. (1966, 39)

Battcock concludes that the passage of time is the defining quality of the film medium:

> The subject of *Empire* is, then, an investigation of the presence and character of film—a legitimate if not a requisite concern for the artist. And the terms established for this investigation are the black and white of film technology and the obvious yet frequently denied limitation of time. (1966, 40)

From its very first discussion in the pages of *Film Culture*, Warhol's style was seen as a reduction of the artwork to the essential features of its medium. Mekas saw Warhol's essentialism as a "purification" of cinema (1964b); Battcock, like most other critics, interpreted it as Greenbergian self-criticism.

In 1969, Sitney initiated the avant-garde's second wave of interest in Warhol when he named Warhol as the "major precursor" to the Structural film. It was not Warhol's genius for parody that motivated his link to Structural film; Sitney's use of Warhol depended on a formalist reading of his work, and in the debate that followed Sitney's essay, the anti-illusion schema became the standard view of Andy Warhol in the realm of the avant-garde film.

In Sitney's original "Structural Film" (1969), his association of Warhol with the aesthetics of Minimalism was somewhat equivocal. On the one hand, he argued that "Warhol is one of the two major inspirations of the structuralists" (1969, 2). On the other hand, he tried to distinguish Warhol's Pop aesthetics from the aesthetics of the Structural film:

> Yet Warhol, as a pop artist, is spiritually at the opposite pole from the structuralists. His fixed camera was at first an outrage, later an irony, until his content became too compelling and he abandoned the fixed image for a kind of in-the-camera editing. . . . In fact, the antithesis of the structural film to the pop film (basically Warhol) is precisely the difference between Pop and Minimal painting or sculpture, where the latter grows out of and against the former. Here the analogy must end, because the major psychologies of structural cinema and minimal art are not usually comparable. (1969, 2)

Sitney's attempt to have it both ways—Warhol is the precursor to Structural film while he is "spiritually" opposed to it—was somewhat muddled since he did not explain what he thought was the difference between Pop and Minimalism. Nor did he explain the difference between the "psychologies" of Minimalism and Structural film.[5]

Sitney's finessing of these distinctions can be seen as an effort to remain faithful to the general direction of Warhol's career even though he was primarily interested in only part of it, the often-mentioned early silents. In the most recent version of "Structural Film," in *Visionary Film*'s second edition (1979), Sitney tried to give readers a sense of this career by liberally citing Koch's work on Warhol. From Koch's perspective, the formal devices of Warhol's films are manifestations of features of his personality. Where Sitney, for example, saw the fixed camera position as an attack on the Romanticism of the avant-garde film, for Koch it indicated Warhol's passivity and voyeurism.[6] Koch also suggested that there is an element of self-consciousness in Warhol that gives his early work a reflexive twist. *Haircut*, like the other silents, "is about the hypnotic nature of the gaze itself, about the power of the artist over it" (1973, 55). Sitney seized this particular passage, which he used to fit Warhol into the Romantic trajectory of the American avant-garde film: the attempt to reproduce the human mind. As Sitney put it: "Warhol must have inspired, by opening up and leaving unclaimed so much ontological territory, a cinema actively engaged in generating metaphors for the viewing, or rather the perceiving experience" (1978, 373). For Sitney, Warhol's most important contribution to the avant-garde film was the concern for the temporal aspect of film perception: "The great challenge, then, of the structural film became how to orchestrate duration; how to permit the wandering attention that triggered ontological awareness while watching Warhol films and at the same time guide that awareness to a goal" (1978, 374). Sitney's emphasis on Warhol's contribution to the Structural film did not stop him from addressing the other aspects of Warhol's work, if only by citing Koch. But after Sitney's 1969 essay, the Greenbergian view of Warhol's cinema was increasingly common, especially in treatments of his early films.

Peter Gidal's 1971 book on Warhol is not nearly as programmatic as Sitney's attempt to incorporate Warhol into the Romantic trajectory of the avant-garde. Gidal's critical perspective shifts constantly. His analysis is vaguely psychoanalytic when he suggests that part of Warhol's value lies in his ability to enact fantasies that we normally repress (12). He also sees Warhol's film work in Cagean metacritical terms: it is a critique of the narrowness of the Hollywood cinema (112). And like many others, he sees Warhol as a realist: Warhol's films offer a realistic (or at least an honest) depiction of sexuality (124–26) and American politics (134). Gidal's treatment of Warhol is an idiosyncratic mixture of many critical views; he argues that the subjective and impressionistic quality of his analysis is one of its virtues (17). But actually, when Gidal addresses Warhol's early silents, he relies heavily on the Greenbergian terms that were becoming the party line on that phase of Warhol's career: "A film such as *Empire*'s (eight-hour) emphasis is on the nature of film reality, the gradation of shades from black to white on film, the nature of time's (forward) movement" (1971, 90). The Dadaist aspects of Warhol's early silents are not ignored, but Gidal places far greater emphasis on

Warhol's exploration of the properties of the film medium—especially duration.

Like Gidal, Malcolm Le Grice emphasized Warhol's exploration of duration at the expense of the Dadaist side of Warhol's work. In 1977, Le Grice published *Abstract Film and Beyond*, a response to Sitney's "Structural Film" aimed at securing equal coverage for European filmmakers. Le Grice began his discussion of Warhol's contribution to the "new formal film" with a suspicious acknowledgment of the Dadaist aspects of Warhol's work:

> Warhol has always been more concerned with impact than form—formal innovation being a by-product of impact. He is essentially a neo-Dadaist attempting to provoke response, and using his media, including film, primarily to propagate attitudes. (1977, 93)

But Le Grice wasted no time in rereading Warhol's work in terms of the history of the avant-garde as *he* saw it, the development of a materialist, anti-illusionist film practice. As in Sitney's essay, duration is at the heart of Warhol's contribution. "The main basis of illusion in cinema," Le Grice's argument began, "stems from the manipulation of time and space relationships between shots" (93). According to Le Grice, although Warhol may not have been aware of it, his early films were decidedly anti-illusionist in that they refused to compress time through editing:

> Whatever Warhol's intention (and the suspicion remains that he was more concerned with provocation than the refinement of durational sensibility), his contribution in this area goes beyond simple provocative exposure to long periods of minimal change, as in *Empire* (1964), an 8-hour film of the Empire State Building from a fixed position. This kind of exposure inevitably results in a breakdown of involvement in the film. Attention unavoidably moves "out" of the film to awareness of its physical context and the current time and space of its presentation—a functional boredom.
>
> But in Warhol we also discover the value of a new cinematic concept, that of representational equivalence in duration. . . . In a form of cinema based on confrontation with the material aspects of the medium this unbroken, durational equivalence provides the only counteract to illusion in the representation of time. (1977, 94)

Not only did Le Grice read the "neo-Dadaist" Warhol as an anti-illusionist artist, he did it in a specifically Greenbergian way:

> This new awareness of film's primary dimension, that of time, can be seen as equivalent to the abandonment of deep, illusory perspective in painting, in favour of a shallow picture space, directly relatable to the material nature of the actual canvas surface. Early Warhol films establish a "shallow" time which permits a credible relationship between the time of interior action and the physical experience of the film as a material presentation. This is Warhol's most significant innovation. (1977, 95)

What Koch saw as an outgrowth of Warhol's personality and Sitney saw as parody of the Romantic avant-garde, Le Grice saw as an anti-illusionist assertion of the true nature of cinema. But all of them at least mentioned Warhol's connection to Pop Art.

When Paul Arthur wrote "Structural Film: Revisions, New Versions, and the Artifact" a year after Le Grice's *Abstract Film and Beyond*, he did not need to mention Dada, Duchamp or Pop Art. He summarized the importance of Warhol's work strictly in the anti-illusion terms associated with Structural film:

> holistic shape, duration as the real-time equivalent of projection time, the foregrounding of material substrate (namely the frame, the continuous nature of the strip, its grain, and the flatness of the support) are posed as strategies which dissolve the self-inclusiveness and "transparency" of the projected object and trigger the viewers' self-conscious responses to the production of meaning. (1978, 6)

In the realm of the avant-garde film, Warhol had gradually been divested of the aesthetics of Pop which he incarnated in the world of the visual arts. But while his Pop background had been almost completely forgotten, Warhol's place as the founder of the Minimalist aesthetic in the American avant-garde cinema was secured.

Bruce Conner and the Absurd Mosaic

Besides Warhol there is, of course, another avant-garde filmmaker who is consistently associated with Pop Art and images appropriated from popular culture: Bruce Conner. In some ways, their careers are similar. Like Warhol, Conner had an established career as a visual artist before he turned to film, and his involvement with film led to involvement with multi-media artworks. Just as Warhol became involved in the music scene (with the Velvet Underground), Conner began to produce light shows in California in the mid-1960s. But whatever the similarities between their careers, the criticism of their film work could hardly be more different. The criticism of Warhol's films was highly programmatic: they were increasingly included in the Structural paradigm as reflexive statements about the material of film. The criticism of Conner's films, like the assemblage strain in general, has been more ad hoc.

A few critics have suggested that Conner is concerned with the reflexive investigation of the film medium. According to Le Grice, Conner, "in spite of his associative montage construction, contributed to the concept of films as physical material" (95). In 1981, Warren Bass listed the "reflexive examination of the film medium itself" among Conner's principal aesthetic concerns (15). But the critical articles on Conner's work conduct no detailed analysis of reflexivity. The most one finds—and this is rare enough—is a mention of how "Conner reminds the viewer of the artificiality of the medium by projecting words or numbers onto the screen" (Beltz 1967, 57).

Instead of being seen as a self-conscious analyst of the film medium, Conner has been seen as the avant-garde's great humanist. William Moritz and Beverly O'Neill argue that works with traditional subject matter were dismissed as irrelevant or unimportant during the

1960s and early 1970s. Only after the dominance of Greenbergian formalism had subsided could Conner's work be properly appraised. As Moritz and O'Neill put it in their survey of Conner's work: "Today, a careful scrutiny of his total output—especially the films—reveals Conner, the humanist. His work functions as a warning system, sensitizing us through his brilliant use of manipulated found footage, to the nature of public media's entropic vision" (1978, 39). But even in formalist art's heyday, Conner generally evaded Greenbergian interpretations. In the first *Film Culture* issue to include coverage of Conner, Carl Beltz concluded:

> Conner stands as a kind of twentieth century Peter Breughel. For like the great Flemish master he distorts the visible world in order to penetrate a reality of being rather than appearances; his vision is cosmic in breadth; he deals with some of the most provocative issues, both artistic and otherwise, of his time; and finally, with an evocative ambiguity and painful irony he touches something which we sometimes call the human experience. (1967, 59)

Even stylistic devices in Conner's work are interpreted as part of the humanist theme. In discussing *Cosmic Ray* (1960–62), Moritz and O'Neill point out a contrast between the "raw, informal vigor" of Conner's original footage of a nude dancer and the "kiss of death" apparent in the static found footage. This contrast reprises the theme of the film as a whole: "Thus, on a purely formal level, Conner has achieved an antithesis between vitality and morbidity, and the vital trend definitely rises triumphant in the end" (1978, 40).

In fact, the thematic reading of Conner's work went so far as to include the very same formal devices that formed the basis of anti-illusion readings of the minimal strain. In Conner's work, however, these devices are not interpreted as having much anti-illusion value. Le Grice, for example, cites the use of loop printing—part of Sitney's original definition of the Structural film—in *Report* (1965), but dismisses it as "not part of the development of loop or repetition as a central basis of form" (110), even though it precedes *all* the films he does cite as precedents to the "materialist" use of loop printing. The most dramatic example of the thematic interpretation of formal devices involves a rather long passage of flicker footage in the middle of *Report*. According to Conner himself, this was inserted to emphasize the fact that *Report* is a movie and to shift attention to the specific viewing situation (Bass 1981, 16). But in interpretations of the film, the flicker passage invariably is read thematically. According to Moritz and O'Neill, the irritating flicker involves us in the shock of the Kennedy assassination (41). Sometimes it is read narratively: Bass (1981, 16) and Moritz and O'Neill (1978, 41) suggest that it is a metaphor for Kennedy's fading heartbeat. One critic even interprets it as a mystical power:

> This is the influence of invisible forces, objectively registered in the flicker as electrical anarchy, suggested throughout the film's imagery as the workings of hidden power. In the flicker something goes wrong in the power structure, the image disappears, while in the film as a

whole some inexplicit force has caused the destruction of the hero. (Kelman, 242)

Why, if they used loop printing and flicker effects, are Conner's films not interpreted through the use of the art-process and anti-illusion schemata that were so widely applied during the 1960s and 1970s? Part of the answer lies in when and where he produced his work. Conner released only one film (*Marilyn Times Five*, 1969–73) between 1969 and 1976. Thus, during the years of burgeoning academic interest in film, Conner kept a low profile. Other than a half-page review of *Marilyn* (Shedlin 1974), there were no new articles published on Conner's work between 1968 and 1976, when the art-process and anti-illusion schemata saw their widest application. Second, as a California filmmaker, he was easier to ignore than New York filmmakers. *Film Culture* had always given the most extended coverage to New York filmmakers, and in the era of Structural film this was especially true. Furthermore, *Artforum* had also moved to New York in the mid-1960s. *Artforum* was founded in Los Angeles with the intent of covering the growing California art scene, and in its early years, Conner's artwork appeared on its pages quite regularly. But by the time Conner's reputation as a filmmaker had surpassed his reputation as a visual artist, *Artforum*'s focus was on New York art.

Probably the most important reason Conner was not interpreted with the art-process and anti-illusion schemata is that he was not seen as part of a general movement. Interpretive schemata are usually a means of generalizing about the concerns of a group of films or filmmakers, typically by linking them to broader concerns in the art world, like ''the anti-illusion project'' that exercised critics like Le Grice and Annette Michelson. Conner's association with Pop Art was not enough to link him to these broad concerns, again partly because of the New York emphasis of avant-garde film criticism. Conner's brand of Pop was distinctly West Coast; the most prominent Pop artists worked in New York, and the prototypical New York style was the flat, frontal style of Warhol and Lichtenstein. Thus, if one wished to associate Conner with Pop, one would have to make the connection not to the well-documented New York Pop, but to the less-known California assemblage scene.

Critics who do see Conner's work in the context of assemblage and collage pose the issues raised by his films—and the rest of the assemblage strain—with remarkable clarity. To put it simply, the central issue is the tension between order and chaos. Some writers emphasize the tendency toward disunity. As Beltz puts it:

First viewings give the impression that a number of pre-existing clips have simply been thrown together in almost random fashion, or that the work has somehow grown organically. Within any one work, whether film or object, the various parts intersect one another and rupture the separate identities of individual elements. But these apparently brutal combinations and juxtapositions also enable Conner to liberate any single item from an existence on only one level, whether formal or contextual. The result is a highly fluid work to which additional parts could seemingly be grafted or even eliminated. Conner's art contains no straight lines and nothing predictable in the sense of self-conscious "good design." The works seem always to be in the state of becoming, or growing bigger and more powerful. (1967, 57)

This strongly suggests that the exact organization of the images in Conner's films is not terribly important—except insofar as it projects an air of indifference. For Brian O'Doherty, this kind of fluid organization makes Conner's work similar to Robert Rauschenberg's combine paintings, in which objects are attached to the canvas:

> For the film clips of reality are used as object—not as objects prompting surrealist associations, but as objects from real life loudly claiming attention while being forced into a relationship to contribute to the movie. The movie is split open again and again by real life hurting through it. This is remarkably like the effect Robert Rauschenberg gets in his latest paintings. (1964, 196)

For critics like Beltz and O'Doherty, the interest in assemblage films lies in the ways they challenge conventional ideas about the unity and autonomy of the artwork.

But other writers try to establish the way Conner's films do cohere, in spite of their apparent disunity. Many of Conner's films do not have highly structured global schemata. Thus, like many films of the poetic strain, Conner's work is often thought to be a cinema of primarily local effects. To account for Conner's films' overall organization critics often appeal to what we called atmospheric unity, by suggesting that his films are organized around a particular mood or tone. For example, some critics simply find his films "nostalgic" because he uses old footage. Moritz and O'Neill interpret Conner's work as "hopeful" and "transcendent" because they find that though many of his films are filled with images of disaster, the films tend to end on lighter notes. In addressing the overall organization of his work, critics often employ structural analogies, such as the quasi-musical form viewers sometimes find in the poetic avant-garde. Anthony Reveaux, for example, suggests that Conner's films are "chamber music of the mind" (1981, 12). But often Conner's films do not fit even quasi-musical schemata, and critics appeal to more bizarre analogies. One critic finds Conner's work an "intellectual cinematic puzzle" (Alexander 1967, 73); another finds it "a Zen puzzle" and "an absurd mosaic" (Anderson 1978, 35–36).

These odd metaphors are especially suggestive of the problem facing the viewer aiming to make sense of the assemblage strain of the American avant-garde film. And how viewers test for and impose order on these "Zen puzzles" and "absurd mosaics" is the subject of the next chapter.

8

The Logic of the Absurd:
The Assemblage Strain

Any assemblage, in any medium, maintains a tension between its incorporated elements and the new composition that comprises them. This rudimentary observation has an important implication: assemblage is not a single, unitary aesthetic form. Because of the wide range of forms it may take, the concept of assemblage has been mobilized by artists and critics of every stripe. Many Modernists, for example, view assemblage as a means of galvanizing the flatness of the picture plane. In their view, the prior life of the assemblage material is overshadowed by the new composition whose flattened picture plane makes the flatness of the incorporated element its only (or most) important feature. Critics of a Postmodern bent are more likely to emphasize the eclecticism of the assemblage work and to view the incorporated elements as synecdoches for the contexts from which they were drawn. From this perspective, the new whole is a provisional, unstable combination of elements, and to a significant degree these elements maintain their autonomy.[1]

My aim is not to advocate either a Modern or a Postmodern view of assemblage. But the tension between the Modern and Postmodern perspectives dramatizes the tension between unity and disunity implicit in any assemblage. This chapter lays out the implicit viewing procedures with which viewers negotiate this tension in the films of the assemblage strain of the avant-garde cinema.

The first point to make about avant-garde assemblage is that it shares many of its principles of construction with the heavily edited film poem, such as those made by Stan Brakhage, Bruce Baillie or Marie Menken. At the local level of shot-to-shot connections, the assemblage filmmaker, like the film poet, juxtaposes shots on the basis of a wide range of associations—metaphors, implied causality, and graphic and scenographic matches. At the global level of overall organization, again like the film poem, the assemblage ranges from very open-ended to highly structured. There are some dramatic exceptions, but the assemblage film also shares the film poem's emphasis on local effects at the expense of large-scale structure.

The assemblage strain includes two styles of filmmaking: what I call *collage animation* and *compilation*. Collage animators create images by pasting together parts cut from other pictures, especially those in magazines and newspapers. Avant-garde compilation re-edits fragments of found footage from old movies, television commercials, and educational and industrial films. Each of these styles uses particular strategies of composition, and each triggers particular perceptual and cognitive processes on the part of the viewer.

Collage Animation

Avant-garde collage animation developed in the 1950s in the work of Robert Breer, Harry Smith and Stan Vanderbeek. Breer's earliest films include animated collage segments among a range of animation styles. But after *Jamestown Baloos* (1957), Breer's collage imagery is no longer animated, but appears in one-frame flashes, mixed in with his own drawings and paintings.

Smith's films are hard to date with precision, but he made a handful of collage films in the 1950s, after a decade and a half of working with other forms of animation. His most ambitious collage animation, some would say *the* major example of the style, is *No. 12* (also known as *Heaven and Earth Magic* or *The Magic Feature*). It circulates now in a sixty-six-minute black-and-white version. Originally, however, Smith conceived *No. 12* as a performance lasting several hours: the black-and-white collage animation was to be projected through a series of masks and color filters, which would be selected by the response of the audience. The film's images are collages of late nineteenth century engravings. The engravings are generally shot against a black background, and movement within the individual collages is generally simple. Roughly speaking, the film is a narrative about a woman's ascent to heaven (on a dentist's chair, no less) and her return to earth. But *No. 12* is so filled with detail and is so densely allusive, that the outline of the story, let alone its meaning, is hard to figure out without extra-textual guidance. After one more collage animation, *No. 13*, Smith turned to live-action cinema and painting in the early 1960s.

Vanderbeek produced more collage animations than either Breer or Smith. From 1957 when he made his first film until 1965 when he turned to performance art and multi-media presentations, Vanderbeek made more than a dozen collage animations. Whereas Smith's collage animations seemed timeless and dream-like, largely due to his choice of sources, Vanderbeek used contemporary imagery to satirize modern life. His collages are typically rough assemblages of magazine pictures that never quite coalesce into spatially coherent scenes, and comic exaggeration seems to be the primary mode of these films.

Larry Jordan began making collage animations in the early 1960s, just about the time Vanderbeek quit. Since then, Jordan has been considered the preeminent collage animator in the avant-garde. His meticulous style is just the opposite of Vanderbeek's. The source images are usually cut from black-and-white Victorian engravings and are carefully assembled into coherent spaces that usually give a strong impression of three dimensions.

It would be fair to say that collage animation was not at the top of the avant-garde cinema agenda during the 1970s and 1980s, but a number of less widely known filmmakers have continued to develop the form in some remarkable films: Frank Mouris's *Frank Film* (1973), Doug Haynes's *Common Loss* (1979), and Lewis Klahr's series of super-8 films, *Tales of the Forgotten Future*.[2]

I have suggested that all assemblage exploits the tension between the individual identity of the interpolated image and the new whole that comprises it. But these collage animations are complex instances of assemblage, because they exploit this tension on several levels: the construction of the individual images, the local juxtaposition of these images, and the overall structure of the film. We cannot simply classify these films as unified or disunified. The viewer must negotiate unity or disunity at each level, and at each level unity has several components. There is a potentially endless variety of styles of collage animation, but it is possible to make some generalizations about how the viewer makes sense of these films. Because the materials of the collage animator present a unique set of constraints and opportunities, and the manipulation of these materials is particularly evident to viewers, one productive way of making sense of these films is to consider collage as a *craft*.

I begin my examination of the craft of collage by drawing on the work of a perceptive art theorist named Annette, who, incidentally, is nine years old.[3] Annette was asked, "If you were in charge of a museum, and had to buy paintings for it, and you had a whole bunch to choose from, how would you decide what to buy?" She responded: "Well, I would get up very close to them, and look at them with my magnifying glass, and if I found any mistakes I wouldn't buy them." I would also like to draw on the work of an anonymous theorist, also nine years old, who addresses the avant-garde:

> Question: How can you tell if a painting is good or not?
> Answer: Well, some of them are sloppy and they go all over the place.
> Q: What if the artist meant them to be sloppy?
> A: Well, I wouldn't know about that.
> Q: So, if it's sloppy, you don't think its a good painting?
> A: Right.

What these kids say strikes us as funny because they have what we have come to think of as an unsophisticated notion of art, which they naively confuse with craftsmanship.[4] This cuts against the grain of our usual thought about art, particularly within the avant-garde cinema. Yet Annette and her friend's sensitivity to craft can help explain the use of collage in these avant-garde animations.

Twentieth-century thought on the arts has generally held craft in low regard. Even if at one time the distinction between art and craft might have suggested only that true art needed skill *plus* something more, it now more commonly suggests a radical opposition between art and craft. In fact, today the terms "art" and "craft" generally refer to two entirely distinct sets of institutions. The radical separation of art and craft can be traced to Benedetto Croce and R. G. Collingwood, who argued that art proper lies in imaginative effort, not in the execution of a material form. Croce and Collingwood did not believe there was anything wrong with craftsmanship—many great artists were also craftspersons—but craft just was not what made a real work of art. On their view, craft was irrelevant to art, and the level of craftsmanship did not affect the artistic value of a work one way or the other.

For many Modernists, the separation of art and craft has become an active deprecation of craftsmanship. One manifestation of this is the notion we could call the respect-for-materials approach to craft: materials are not to be mastered and transformed, but respected and honestly displayed. "Timber should look like timber and stone like stone," as E. H. Gombrich paraphrases this idea (1979, 65). But as Gombrich points out, as reasonable as the respect-for-materials idea seems, this approach to artistic material became widespread in Western art only when industry invented cheap substitutes for expensive materials. Traditionally, the relationship between artist and material was an adversarial one: artisans demonstrated their skill by shaping material into patterns and structures it seemed to resist.

Within the realm of the avant-garde film, the deprecation of craft is especially acute. Since the avant-garde is supposed to be an oppositional film practice, and what it opposes is highly crafted, the *un*masterful use of material should proudly be displayed as a mark of that opposition. This notion is most common with regard to those avant-garde films that borrow most from the narrative conventions of Hollywood, such as Warhol's films and those of the Kuchars, as well as many "underground" films.[5] In addition, the avant-garde sees craft in the sense of "crafty," that is to say, as a kind of deception. This, of course, leads to what is sometimes installed as *the* Modernist stance toward the materials of art: the artist ought not to master material, but openly display it, or even better, analyze it, lest he or she be accused of illusionist deception. The rhetoric surrounding Structural film is shot through with this notion.

This currently unfashionable notion of craft as the mastery of recalcitrant material can help us understand assemblage in general, and avant-garde collage animation in particular. I am not arguing that this notion of adversarial craft is universally valid to all modes of art; I am arguing that it is particularly appropriate to the collage form where the material is particularly recalcitrant. The formal qualities and the intertextual references of the collage element can be controlled by the collagist only to a relatively modest degree. Because the collagist's materials always bear some traces of their previous lives, as viewers we are always aware of the filmmaker's effort at reintegrating these materials. In the context of the avant-garde collage animation, the level of craft refers to the degree to which the collagist minimizes the autonomy of the elements and maximizes the coherence of the collage.

Here I have to part company with Annette. For her, the artwork's level of craft was a prescriptive criterion of evaluation. I use it descriptively, as a means of mapping out the range of options available to the avant-garde collage animator. As I think my examples will show, this range is not a simple continuum or set of definite categories. Nevertheless, there are two basic approaches: what I call the *highly crafted* approach, and the *bricolage* approach. Let me now turn to the films, looking first at the local level of the individual image, and then at higher levels of organization.

The Craft of the Image

Within the individual image, the craft of the collage animation is a matter of three things: consistency of source imagery, coherence of space, and precision of assembly. At the level of the image, Larry Jordan's work is a model of the highly crafted approach in all three regards. His collages are constructed almost exclusively of Victorian engravings and are therefore quite consistent in style. But even given this restriction, the fund of engravings at his disposal is large enough to provide images that fit together into a coherent space. Jordan usually starts with a wide view of an architectural space or a landscape and layers objects on top of this background. With appropriately sized images of objects, rendered from the appropriate point of view, Jordan can fill these spaces while maintaining consistent depth cues, thereby giving an impression of a palpable, three-dimensional space. And the precision of the assembly is flawless. The images are cut out with extraordinary accuracy and they are held perfectly flat during photography so that wrinkles do not draw attention to the edges of the cut-out images. Taken all together, these factors explain why we do not sense that Jordan's images have been ripped out of another context and provisionally grouped into a new composition.

The level of craft of the image in collage animation is not an all-or-nothing proposition. Jordan's images are highly crafted in all three respects, but it is possible for filmmakers to create collages that are highly crafted in one regard but not others. Given that creating a spatially coherent collage requires a sizable fund of source material, spatially coherent collages may well be constructed out of images with very diverse styles. Such is the case in Haynes's *Common Loss* (Figs. 8.13–8.24). The spatial perspectives of the individual source images are compatible, but the variety in the style of the images makes it quite apparent that the collages are an assemblage of diverse sources.

In bricolage films, on the other hand, consistency of style and compatibility of perspective are not concerns. Vanderbeek's *Science Friction* (1959) assembles images from diverse sources utterly without regard for the relative sizes of the objects or the perspectives from which they are rendered. The bizarre juxtaposition of incompatible sizes and perspectives is itself a source of humor in the film. A muscle-bound man fits under a microscope. A wrench spans a man's head and twists it. This happy disregard of spatial and stylistic consistency also gives the bricolage filmmaker complete freedom in the

Fig. 8.1

Fig. 8.2

objects and events he or she represents. If, as in *Science Friction*, Vanderbeek needs a shot of a man in a surgeon's mask looking to the right, he simply pastes the rightward-looking eyes onto the photo of the surgeon. One consequence of this freedom is that bricolage films can openly satirize any public figure who appears in the popular press. In *Science Friction*, Eisenhower is shown starting a nuclear war. In Breer's *Un Miracle* (1954), the Pope juggles first a set of balls and then his own head.

Movement introduces a new set of problems for the collage animator, beginning with rendering the movement itself. Not surprisingly, Jordan's highly crafted work is very fluid and smooth—motion is recorded in one-frame increments. On the other hand, bricolages tend to be jumpier. In fact, in Lewis Klahr's work, some motion is not really animated at all. In *For the Rest of Your Natural Life*, Klahr affixes images to sticks that extend outside the frame and moves them puppet-style across the background (Fig. 8.1). Because of the herky-jerky movements of the images, and because we can see the separation of the paper cut-out on the stick and the background, Klahr's pseudo-animation exaggerates the disparity among the collage elements to the point of parody. Even when Klahr does animate his collages, he will do so in twelve- or twenty-four-frame increments. The result is a kind of strobe effect in which we see key points along the movement of an object, but not all the points in between. Again, the bricolage approach gives the filmmaker greater freedom in the movements he or she can represent. If Vanderbeek needs to have Eisenhower reach for the button that launches a nuclear attack, he just picks out an arm, puts it on a picture of Ike and shoots its movement a few frames at a time. But insofar as the highly crafted approach aims to maintain consistent and three-dimensional spatial relationships, the kinds of movement that can be represented are more limited. It is extremely difficult to make it seem like an object is really moving on a surface that recedes into depth, such as a person moving across a floor. Consequently the objects in the highly crafted collage animation tend to float around the space of the picture. And this makes it likely that the highly crafted film will seem somewhat dream-like, a quality often associated with Jordan's work, as in the second part of *Duo Concertates* (1964), *Patricia Gives Birth to a Dream by the Door* (Fig. 8.2).

The interaction of movement and space creates a second movement problem. Even with a well-developed sense of depth in the background, movement tends to make the figures seem vehemently flat. There are several reasons for this. First, the most common collage animation technique—sliding the figure across the ground—produces only lateral movement parallel to the picture plane. Animated movement in depth is extremely rare, since it requires a series of incrementally larger or smaller images of the object to be moved toward or away from the camera. The second reason movement flattens the collage animation is that objects moving through the field of vision afford to us slightly different angles of view as they move. In other words, any lateral movement shows more than one view of an object. Since the cut-out figure affords only one view, its movement em-

phasizes its flatness. Thus, even in the highly crafted collage animation, the effect is of a flat image inextricably welded to a foreground
plane, sliding side-to-side in front of a fully rounded, three-dimensional space.

Both the highly crafted collage and the bricolage often inject
depth into their animation, though with quite different results. The
highly crafted film can diminish the feeling of flatness, but only to a
degree. In *Masquerade* (1981), Jordan lets smoke drift in front of the
image, a scene of the aftermath of duel (Fig. 8.3). In *Orb* (1973),
Jordan uses a kind of multi-plane technique. The foreground is phys-
ically separated from the background and kept in shadow (Fig. 8.4).
As the camera smoothly zooms out, the lighting shifts to illuminate
the object in the foreground (Fig. 8.5). The multi-plane technique
creates a sensation of real depth between the planes. Jordan also uses
superimposition to break down our sense of the distinct planes of
space. This technique gives films like *Our Lady of the Sphere* (1969)
and *Moonlight Sonata* (1979, Fig. 8.6) a space that is not fragmented
into distinct foreground and background planes, but that no longer
gives the sense of solid objects.

In bricolage, the same depth-rendering techniques inevitably
seem jokey and parodic. In *In the Month of Crickets*, Klahr blows
smoke across a raggedly cut out picture of a bridge from which a
murder victim's body is dropped (Fig. 8.7). In the same film, Klahr
renders an optical point-of-view shot: using the cut-out-on-a-stick
technique, Klahr raises a picture of a cocktail glass toward the camera.
But the awkwardness of these techniques—unlike an actual cocktail
glass, the picture of the cocktail glass is completely opaque—makes
Klahr's renderings of the stylistic devices of the crime drama a parody
of film noir.

Attempts to render depth in bricolage inevitably seem a bit like
jokes; but highly crafted collage affords the opportunity for more
sophisticated play with the distinction between surface and depth. For
example, Jordan creates ambiguity through contradictory spatial cues.
In *Moonlight Sonata*, Jordan has an acrobat walk along the horizon
line as if it were a tightrope (Fig. 8.8). But the horizon is not actually
a line upon which one could walk; moving the character along the
horizon line in the picture as if it were accentuates the contradiction
between the flatness of the collage and its apparent depth.

Inter-shot Relations and Overall Coherence

At the local level of the individual image, collage animation presents
a set of unique problems for the filmmaker. But between shots, we find
in collage animation many of the same types of relationships created
by the poetic strain of the avant-garde film, particularly graphic
matches and metaphors. For the most part, in collage animation these
intershot relationships function as they do in the poetic strain. Collage
animation, however, sometimes makes specialized use of metaphor.

As part of what I called the avant-garde's radicalized rhetoric,
metaphor represented a significant challenge to the viewer's com-

Fig. 8.3

Fig. 8.4

Fig. 8.5

Fig. 8.6

Fig. 8.7   Fig. 8.8   Fig. 8.9

prehension of the poetic strain. Because it shows only the metaphoric replacement (the vehicle, and not the tenor), radical metaphor limits redundancy and puts great demands on the viewer. In bricolage animation, however, radical metaphors are usually replaced with conventional and redundant metaphors that are more easily comprehended.

Consider, for example, Vanderbeek's *Science Friction*. Few films, in or out of the avant-garde, are as obvious as *Science Friction*. The film begins with a series of images that show people being abused by tools and technology. A man in a hospital bed is hit on the head with a hammer; a muscle-bound man is viewed through a microscope—he, too, is struck by a hammer; the head of a man in a business suit is twisted with a wrench. These opening images, with the title, establish the film's basic theme: advanced technology is dangerous and inhumane. After these opening images, the bulk of *Science Friction* is narrative. The last three-quarters of the film is a story of nuclear war between the Soviet Union and the United States that expands to involve the French and the Italians. This war is introduced by images of Eisenhower looking through a telescope at Kruschev, of Eisenhower pushing a red button, and of missiles taking off (Fig. 8.9). But after these introductory images, the war is represented primarily through a series of bizarre metaphors. For example, about halfway through the film, a variety of objects—a fork and a cigarette lighter, for example—move vertically out of the frame.

Research in the comprehension of metaphors suggests that metaphors used in unambiguous contexts are no more difficult to process than literal discourse. Traditional "deviation" theories of metaphor hold that the replacement of one item (the tenor) with another (the vehicle) requires a conscious search for the ground of similarity between them. According to the "schema" theory of metaphor, no such conscious search is required. An unambiguous context primes a number of schemata, and some of the vehicle's features fit those schemata with no more effort than it would take to account for the features of the tenor.[6] The US-Soviet war in *Science Friction* provides a context that makes the processing of the film's many metaphors very easy. By the time the flying fork metaphor appears in *Science Friction*, viewers are already thinking of missiles because they have already seen images of them. And part of the missile schema is the information that missiles are elongated objects moving vertically through space. In this context, with the US-Soviet war schema primed, we are prepared to see any elongated object moving vertically as a metaphor for a nuclear missile. The viewer's comprehension of the metaphors in *Science Friction* is aided not only by the explicit narrative context but by the high redundancy of the film. In the passage with the flying fork, for example, at least a dozen objects are turned into flying missiles, including a fireman, a cigarette lighter, a painting of the Virgin and Christ (Fig. 8.10), and automobiles (Fig. 8.11).

Fig. 8.10

This might account for the basic comprehension of metaphors in collage animation, but to stop here would miss the point of collage animation's use of the iconography of popular culture. The schema theory of metaphor explains why Vanderbeek's incongruous images are so easy to comprehend, but it has us looking at these images through the wrong end of the telescope. Even if Vanderbeek's peculiar metaphors are not bone-rattling disruptions, why tell the story in such an unusual, even if obvious, way? *Science Friction* is not just a cautionary tale that makes reference to a hypothetical nuclear war. It is a humorous treatment of such a war, and one with further thematic implications. The schema theory can explain how we understand the *communicative* function of metaphors, but it cannot explain their use as aesthetic devices. For this, we must again adopt a pragmatic perspective.

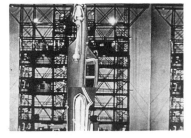

Fig. 8.11

Metaphors are comparisons, and they suggest that the compared items share features. However, psycholinguistic research shows that comparison statements are not symmetrical.[7] The simile ''A is like B'' is not equivalent to ''B is like A,'' though both suggest that A and B share features. The asymmetry of comparisons is of crucial importance to the comprehension of metaphors in collage animation. Andrew Ortony's research on the comprehension of metaphors (1985) shows that metaphors tend to be interpreted as suggesting that the tenor has the salient features of the vehicle. In our schematic form, the metaphor ''A is a B'' means A has B's most salient features, and reversing the order of the terms changes the metaphor's meaning. For example, the metaphor ''my surgeon is a butcher'' suggests that my surgeon has the salient features of butchers; that is, he or she cuts dead flesh into coarse chunks. On the other hand, the metaphor ''my butcher is a surgeon'' suggests that my butcher cuts meat with the skill and finesse that are salient features of surgeons. In film metaphors, the tenor role is played by the item that is part of the established context. In the film *Strike* (1925), for example, the workers, part of the established narrative context, play the role of the tenor, and the metaphor suggests that the workers have the salient properties of the bull: they are powerless, innocent, and dispassionately killed to serve the interests of others.

But in collage animations, metaphors often do not fit the canonical form wherein the salient features of the vehicle are applied to the tenor. In *Science Friction*, the context establishes the launching of rockets as the tenor, so the metaphor should suggest that the rockets have the salient features of the interpolated material. But the metaphors are actually based on the shapes and movements in the inter-

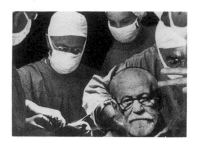

Fig. 8.12

polated material. For example, the salient features of the Statue of Liberty—usually a symbol of American generosity and freedom—cannot be applied directly to nuclear weapons. Since the vehicle's salient features are incompatible with the context, the comparison between the Statue of Liberty and a nuclear missile is an apparent violation of the principle of relevance for which the viewer must account.

In *Science Friction*, the missile metaphor is repeated with various oblong shapes more than a dozen times, and the repetition makes a thematic point. The film explicitly shows national leaders, especially Eisenhower, as infatuated with weapons. But by repeating the rocket metaphors, the film also suggests that this infatuation is a pervasive social attitude, since not only rockets but buildings, kitchen implements, automobiles and soft drink containers look and behave like phallic projectiles. Blatantly sexual symbols are prevalent in the American avant-garde, and Vanderbeek encourages a specifically Freudian interpretation of these items by including an image of Freud in the film's opening sequence (Fig. 8.12). Quite clearly, then, the repeated metaphors are used to make the point that everything in our culture is a manifestation of the same destructive drive.

These metaphors are reversals of the canonic form. In these reversed metaphors, the vehicles—the interpolated images—are no longer a means of commenting on the tenor by emphasizing certain of its features. Reappraising the vehicle is the point of the metaphor. This reappraisal tends to make the interpolated image look silly or even sinister, and in this way bricolage animation tends to take a critical stance toward the culture that provides its imagery.

Reversed metaphors are one manifestation of a key difference between bricolage and highly crafted animation. Highly crafted animation—particularly if it uses "anonymous" images whose sources are unrecognizable—might be considered "centripetal": the pull of the "centering" new composition is stronger than the pull of the diverse intertextual references. Bricolage, on the other hand, tends to be "centrifugal": the centering pull is weaker than the outward pull of the intertextual references. As *Science Friction* demonstrates, the point of the bricolage's collection of such diverse material is not so much to craft a coherent new whole as it is to analyze, reappraise or ridicule the sources of the interpolated material.

At the overall level, collage animation uses the same types of global schemata used by the poetic strain of the avant-garde film. There is, however, one modest surprise: filmmakers using the bricolage approach, which at the local level seems least unified, tend to provide more coherence at the global level.

Some collage animations do not have a highly structured global schema, and their overall organization is, to use the terms we set out in our discussion of the poetic strain, either atmospheric or quasimusical. This is true of many of Jordan's films, where images evoke particular moods without suggesting a clear narrative development. Collage animation might also have an overall structure based on the graphic or scenographic structures of the images. Jordan's *Orb* develops just such a global graphic structure with its very limited color palette of pale magenta and blue and very prominent repeated shape, the orb of the film's title.

Narrative schemata provide a high degree of global coherence to many bricolage films. As we saw in *Science Friction*, these narratives tend to be rather bare-boned affairs that are neither very complicated nor very compelling. The point of bricolage animation is not to tell a good story, but to marshal very disparate material into some coherent structure. We can look at this, too, as a kind of craft. The bricoleur, having temporarily yielded to the material at the local level by using it "raw," ultimately masters the material by incorporating it into a story.

Bricolage stories are sometimes comprehensible partly *because* of the raggedness of their assembly. Klahr's *In the Month of Crickets* is a rendering of a noirish murder mystery through particularly crude bricolage animation. The bricolage radically destabilizes events and characters. For example, the protagonist, a detective, is represented by images of so many different men that it is difficult for the viewer to recognize the character from scene to scene. The events are vaguely familiar, yet obscure: someone is seduced, money changes hands, there is a killing. The film as a whole forms a narrative only because we recognize the fragments of the familiar form of the murder mystery. *In the Month of Crickets*, like *Science Friction*, is highly centrifugal: its global coherence derives from its refusal to fully incorporate the interpolated images into a new whole. In its haphazard grouping of collage elements, intertextual references to the original contexts of the source images are especially salient. And it is these references to the detective genre that allow us to piece together a coherent narrative.

Fig. 8.13

A Final Example: Common Loss

With its loose narrative framework embroidered with an evocative and metaphorical montage, Doug Haynes's *Common Loss* recalls the poetic strain of the avant-garde. The film marshals thousands of individual pictures, each of which is meticulously cut out and painstakingly animated, into an allegory about growing up.

Fig. 8.14

The film uses a number of spatial constructions, most of which give a strong impression of three-dimensional space. Sometimes this space is rendered rather schematically, as in Figure 8.13. Typically, though, the space is more thoroughly developed. Haynes often uses the technique we saw in Jordan's work: a single image of a landscape or interior space serves as the background, and pictures of objects are layered on top of it. In *Common Loss*, however, these spaces are made dream-like (even more than in Jordan's work) by the juxtaposition of incongruous objects and settings and gross discrepancies of scale. For example, Figure 8.14 shows a collage using an upside-down image of the interior of a piano as a background. In the context of the film, this background suggests the exterior of a space ship. Figure 8.15 shows a surrealistic landscape in which watches fly through a tube held in

Fig. 8.15

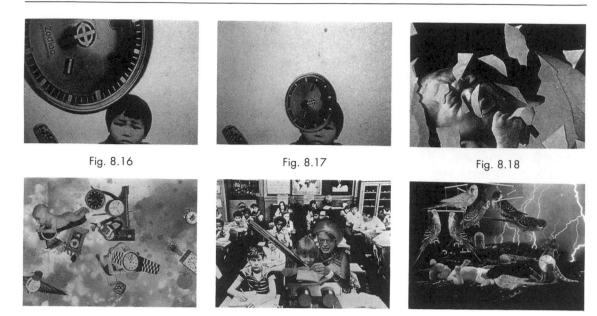

Fig. 8.16   Fig. 8.17   Fig. 8.18

Fig. 8.19   Fig. 8.20   Fig. 8.21

an oversize hand. But in spite of such incongruities and discrepancies, perspectival relationships are consistent, so the collages present a hallucinatory, but still palpable space.

As a rule, movement in collage animation tends to flatten space. In many sequences in *Common Loss*, movement is restricted to the typical lateral sliding across the foreground plane. But on the whole, the film's movements are relatively sophisticated, and many accentuate the sense of depth. For example, in one early sequence, as foreground objects move to the left, the background also moves to the left, but more slowly. This compound movement creates a strong sense of depth by mimicking camera movement: the camera seems to track right along a row of objects in front of a slightly more distant, stationary background. In another instance, an object actually moves along the camera axis toward a stationary figure: a clock comes from out of frame behind the camera, moves into the space of the picture and hits a child on the head (Figs. 8.16, 8.17).

The largest segment of the film is framed as a loosely structured dream, but *Common Loss* is narrative in overall form. The film begins with images of the filmmaker preparing to work at the animation stand. Soon the images which he is cutting begin to move on their own, creating an allegory about growing up. An egg tumbles through outer space toward earth, where it is caught by a grandfather clock with human arms (Fig. 8.13). The clock hurls the egg to the floor, it breaks open and a human baby is inside (Fig. 8.18). A voice (presumably from the grandfather clock) commands "you must learn to count, what counts most, and how to become accountable." A large hand sends the infant flying through space, to be pursued by a pack of flying watches and clocks (Fig. 8.19). As we hear a grating collage of sounds, we see collages of images of children, infants, toys and cartoon characters. A few moments later, a clock flies through several landscapes. The clock knocks the head off the Venus de Milo, and knocks a child to the ground. Most of the rest of the film is apparently the fallen child's dream.

The dream itself is rather loosely organized, playfully elaborating motifs introduced in the framing story, especially birds, butterflies and clocks. The dream at first seems to be a child's pleasant fantasy, filled with brightly colored flowers and balloons. But the film grows increasingly nightmarish. One collage shows children at school (Fig. 8.20). As a girl writes with an outsized pen, a woman's voice instructs, "Fill in the blank, children." She repeats the phrase several times, but changes the intonation so that it suggests her goal is to fill in the "blank children." Later, in a particularly frightening scene, we see a baby lying on a rocky landscape, beneath a mobile of colorful, moving birds (Fig. 8.21). As lightening flashes in the background, a dinosaur with a clock for a torso rips the heads off the birds, and drops their lifeless bodies to the ground.

The dream ends with a grating crescendo of alarm clocks ringing as we see an array of dozens of vibrating watches and clocks. The film playfully returns to the framing situation as the filmmaker's hands reach into the frame and crumple the collage of the watches and clocks (Fig. 8.22). After a few images of the animator and his work place, the film concludes with live-action footage of butterflies, one of the key motifs of the collage segments. The film's final image, of thousands of butterflies in a tree (Fig. 8.23), recalls one of the most beautiful collages in the film (Fig. 8.24).

In its use of polyvalent montage within a loose narrative framework, *Common Loss* adapts the craft of collage animation to the norms of the poetic strain. But the links between Haynes's film and the poetic strain are not just matters of style and structure. The film also dramatizes a central tenet of Brakhage's aesthetics: in mourning the loss of the innocence of childhood, *Common Loss* is an elegy for the untutored eye that inspired Brakhage's cinema.

Fig. 8.22

Fig. 8.23

Fig. 8.24

Avant-garde Compilation

Just as avant-garde collage animation is associated with Smith, Vanderbeek and Jordan, the avant-garde compilation is traditionally associated with the work of Bruce Conner. Conner came to the avant-garde film with an established reputation as an assemblage artist. His first film, *A Movie* (1958), was originally conceived as part of a work of sculpture, though it is now shown as an independent work. This film is probably the most widely known example of the assemblage aesthetic in the avant-garde cinema, but found footage appears in countless avant-garde films. Recently William Wees compiled a list that includes almost 150 avant-garde filmmakers who have used found footage in their work.[8]

The development of the found-footage compilation was shaped by the assemblage aesthetic, which was already well developed in San Francisco when Conner moved there from Kansas in the 1950s. Assemblage sculpture had been exhibited in the Bay area as early as 1951 (Factor 1964, 38). One of these early San Francisco assemblagists, Wallace Berman, is credited with being a major influence on the development of the burgeoning California assemblage scene, though his own assemblages are now lost. According to John Coplans, it was Berman who influenced Conner to move from collages to three-dimensional sculpture and suggested what became Conner's early stylistic trademark: nylon stockings filled with unpleasant found objects like hypodermic needles, sink stoppers and dolls' heads (Coplans 1964, 27). Conner's sculptures and films shared not only the working methods but also the themes of Berman's work; both artists' work is somber and preoccupied with death and sexuality. Berman was particularly stubborn about this aspect of his work. Warned that one of the works in his only show of sculptures (1957) was potentially obscene, he refused to remove it and was arrested and convicted of inciting lewd and lascivious passions (Coplans 1964, 27).[9] By the early 1960s, Robert Rauschenberg's "combine" work had achieved remarkable success on the New York art scene, and assemblage painters and sculptors were recognized as a distinct and important school of American visual art. And as West Coast art began to grow in prominence, Conner's sculptures made him one of its leading exponents.

The influence of assemblage art on the found-footage film was mediated by existing norms of avant-garde filmmaking. One such norm was the minimal strain of avant-garde filmmaking. Films that subject a single image, or a small set of images, to the kind of systematic permutations typical of Structural film regularly draw their images from found footage. For example, *Film in which there appear sprocket holes, edge lettering, dirt particles, etc.* (George Landow, 1965–66), *Variations on a Cellophane Wrapper* (David Rimmer, 1970), and *Eureka* (Ernie Gehr, 1972–79) are minimalist films that use found footage.

My concern in this section is with the use of found footage in compilation films, heavily edited collections of footage drawn from disparate sources. Such compilations of found footage are common in the avant-garde after the mid-1960s, and they have become especially prevalent since the heyday of the minimalist strain. Craig Baldwin, Abigail Child, Standish Lawder, Al Razutis, and Chick Strand have all produced bodies of compilation work that explore the form developed by Conner.

The avant-garde compilation of found footage is a synthesis of assemblage art and the norms of the poetic strain of the avant-garde cinema. Like film poets, at the local level compilation filmmakers use polyvalent montage to link shots through various associative pathways. Like the poetic film and the collage animation, at the global level the compilation can be structured by global schemata that range from highly structured to very open-ended.

As a form of assemblage, avant-garde compilations maintain a tension between the individual identity of the incorporated elements and the new whole created by the filmmaker. And like the collage animator, the compilation filmmaker may choose to accentuate or minimize the coherence of the new work. Conner, for example, tries to reduce the disjunction between disparate materials. Having collected a large mass of material, he tries to use only footage with the bland visual style he finds in institutional or educational films. As a result, his view of directorial expression in the commercial film is ironic for a "personal" filmmaker: "After the '60s, commercial filmmakers were influenced by independents and decided to let their personalities show in the camerawork and direction. Generally, I find that useless for my purposes" (MacDonald 1982, 21). In *Valse Triste* (1976) and *Take the 5:10 to Dreamland* (1977), both of which I will discuss in more detail later in this section, Conner takes the additional step of toning the films sepia, not only accentuating the nostalgia generated by the old footage but also encouraging the viewer to see the footage as representing a more consistent "world." By avoiding color he can create a single "character" from several figures from different sources. As he explained:

> In black and white you can imply that a figure walking down a road is the same person who walks through the door of a house, even though the scenes may be from two different films—you're not distracted by the color. Your attention moves in the direction of the action. If somebody's wearing a dark jacket in one image and a dark sweater in the next, it's easier to disguise the difference and convey a continuity. But if in one image it's a dark blue jacket and in the next it's a maroon sweater, the disparity is emphasized. I try to make separate things become one. (MacDonald 1982, 21)

The organizational problem posed by the use of disparate sources is not simply a matter of reducing or exploiting the disjunction between different visual styles. More fundamentally, the problem is to provide a framework for the *comprehension* of the images. One strategy used at a rather local level is to reduce the spatial inconsistencies through the use of classical continuity editing devices, especially the eyeline match. *A Movie* has a particularly dramatic and well-known example of this technique. Conner shows a naval officer looking through a periscope; cut to a shot of a semi-nude woman; then to a shot of the officer giving an order; finally to a shot of a torpedo being fired. This short sequence suggests that the officer sees the woman and fires a torpedo at her, even though the images are obviously drawn from different sources. By eliding the spatial incongruity by using the eye-line match (or the periscope-line match), Conner makes the spatial relationship comprehensible. (Though not completely coherent: after all, periscopes view exterior spaces, and the woman is in an interior.) But even more important, since our understanding of causal relationships depends on our understanding of spatial relationships, when spatial relationships between objects are specified, causal relationships can often be inferred. In *A Movie*, we

Fig. 8.25

Fig. 8.26

Fig. 8.27

Fig. 8.28

infer not only that the woman is in a location that can be seen by the officer, we infer that his behavior is affected by what he sees. It is our inference of his intent to fire the torpedo at the woman that gives the sequence its aggressively sexual character.

As this example might suggest, the kinds of shot-to-shot connections found in the avant-garde compilation are generally of the same types as those found in the poetic strain. But such connections may have particular effects in the compilation film.

Inter-shot connections in the compilation film are not always loaded with thematic meaning. The import of such links often derives from the simple fact that wildly diverse materials have been meaningfully linked. Such juxtapositions often have a comic edge. William Farley's *Made for Television* (1981) is actually made *from* television: it is a barrage of shots taken from a variety of television commercials. One sequence begins with a woman sneezing into a tissue (Fig. 8.25), and through a series of implied causal links it amplifies the effects of her sneeze. Farley cuts from the sneeze to a shot of trees blown by a storm (Fig. 8.26); to a breeze blowing a table cloth (Fig. 8.27); and finally to a man being knocked over (Fig. 8.28). A good part of the fun of these films is that such coherence is wrought from such disparate material.

But even with these coherent inter-shot connections, avant-garde compilations, like bricolage animation, may be of the centrifugal type—the point of the interpolation of diverse material is not to construct an internally coherent new whole, but to reappraise the source of the interpolated material. For example, Conner's *Mongoloid* (1978) assembles images from educational films and television commercials as a means of illustrating the eponymous Devo song about the mindlessness of bourgeois behavior. Conner includes a shot of a man being enfolded in a giant suitcase. The image was originally meant to demonstrate the effectiveness of a sinus medication—using it is like sending your sinuses to dry, healthy Arizona. But in the context of the song about bourgeois behavior, the salient features of the shot—a man shut up in a piece of luggage like a pair of socks— make the commercial itself seem to be an unflattering demonstration of bourgeois mindlessness.

Kenneth Anger's *Scorpio Rising* (1963) has a more extended example of centrifugal interpolation in the form of a series of metaphors using images of Christ. Anger cuts from a scene in which the biker, Scorpio, admires pictures of James Dean and Marlon Brando to shots of Christ. The pop song ''I Will Follow Him'' on the sound track focuses the metaphor by articulating its possible ground: the biker's allegiance to his gang and his admiration of Dean and Brando are like the Christian's devotion to Christ. But the biker's allegiances are made to look silly or even sick; Anger also includes shots of Nazi troops and shots of motorcycle gang members submitting to sexual torture. The suggestion that this is something like Christian devotion prompts the viewer to see Christ as similar to the other ''heroes'' of the film: a cult figure with a death wish. In a later segment, Anger inserts a very short shot of a biker's unzipped jeans into a scene in which a man kneels before Christ. This juxtaposition makes it seem that the man has kneeled, not out of respect, but to perform fellatio. Images of Christ are interpolated into *Scorpio Rising* not to make the representation of Scorpio more vivid, but to make the viewer see Christ in a new, ironic light.

Fig. 8.29

Open-ended Schemata

Turning to more global levels of organization, we find that many compilation films use open-ended global schemata, similar to those we found in the avant-garde's poetic strain. For example, as David Bordwell and Kristin Thompson (1993, 131–39) argue, the overall organization of Conner's *A Movie* is best understood as quasi-musical. The film is filled with a wide variety of local connections. But at the overall level, coherence derives from the film's shifts in mood and pace, which are matched to the three segments of Respighi's *The Pines of Rome* that comprise the soundtrack. Another open-ended schema results from using the compilation form to explore various facets of a particular topic. For example, Ron Finne's *Keep Off the Grass* (1968) explores Texas culture during the Vietnam War. Mary Filippo's *Who Do You Think You Are* (1987) examines the meaning of cigarette smoking in affluent, industrialized cultures.

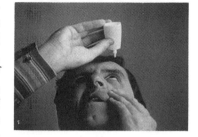

Fig. 8.30

    Viewers cannot easily anticipate the overall shape of these topically structured films, but the general topic suggests a range of concepts that are likely to be explored. Alfonso Alvarez's *Film For . . .* (1989) is a biting commentary on the situation of women during the Reagan years. Much of the film's sound track is drawn from an old (1950s or 1960s) panel discussion among conservatives about the changing role of women in society. The film inserts a range of diverse source material—cartoons, television news, educational films—into this discussion, thereby satirizing the conservatives' views. For example, when one of the women on the panel says she does not want to go into the military or do heavy physical labor, we see three weightless male astronauts clowning inside a spacecraft (Fig. 8.29), which undermines the implication that ''men's work'' is too strenuous or dangerous for women. The film's overall organization is not as highly structured as, for example, a narrative, but viewers can anticipate that the film will address certain subjects related to the central topic, such as romantic love, housework, and women in the workplace.

    If viewers are unable to discover even a topical or quasi-musical schema at the global level of a film, they can still make a general appraisal of its overall mood or atmosphere. In such films, meaning is built up gradually through the connotations of the images, and their order is not especially important. As in the poetic strain, appealing to atmospheric coherence alone provides a kind of global schema of last resort. Viewers can always establish some coherence by labeling the film's mood: Conner's *Crossroads* (1976) is ''eerie,'' Chick Strand's *Cartoon Le Mousse* (1979) is ''sad,'' Brakhage's *Aftermath* (1981) is ''chaotic'' or ''random.''

    Avant-garde compilations have strategies for using these atmospheric global schemata in ways unlike the film poem or the collage

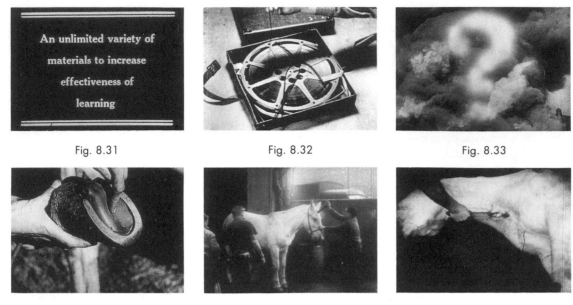

Fig. 8.31   Fig. 8.32   Fig. 8.33

Fig. 8.34   Fig. 8.35   Fig. 8.36

animation. The first of these atmospheric strategies is to structure the compilation as an obviously random collection of a large number of media images. The very looseness of this format helps make its point: popular culture is represented as a bombardment of disconnected and meaningless discourse. Brakhage's *Aftermath* and Lenny Lipton's *Cornucopia* (1968) reinforce this point by degrading the images through superimposition and heavy color filters to make the images less legible and less attractive. Farley's *Made for Television* is a rapid-fire barrage of images from TV commercials. Its final shot recapitulates the point already made by its loose structure with a final metaphor: a man using eye drops as if in response to the "irritation" of the television commercials (Fig. 8.30).

A second approach to the atmospheric global schema in the compilation film is what we might call the "explicit enigma" form. These films have open-ended structures, and their titles cue viewers that their overall schemata may be obscure or arbitrary: for example, Standish Lawder's *Construction Job* (n.d.), Dirk Kortz's *Temporary Arrangements* (n.d.), David Rimmer's *Bricolage* (1984) and Louis Brigante's *Assemblage* (1967).

One of the most intriguing of these explicit enigma films is Chick Strand's *Loose Ends* (1979). The film reiterates the enigma notion introduced by its title with an intertitle (Fig. 8.31), an image of a pile of film fragments (Fig. 8.32), and later on, a question mark superimposed over an image of smoke (Fig. 8.33). But unlike *Construction Job*, which quite openly refuses overall coherence, *Loose Ends* teases the viewer with suggestions of coherent narratives and political commentary.

Our sense of the film's coherence derives in part from the relatively small number of sources that provide the film's images and sounds. Because this film uses more material from each source (rather than drawing a tiny fragment from each of many sources), more of the images are topically similar. There are many images of agriculture and food, of animals, of violence, and of cinematic and photographic images and equipment. These are the film's major themes, and at the global level the film can partly be understood as a set of variations on them.

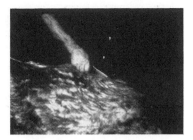

Fig. 8.37

In broad terms, the film has three major movements. The first movement is dominated by images of cinema and cinema apparatus, many of which are drawn from an educational film about the invention of the cinema. Voice-overs at the beginning frame the film as a children's story, the "Let's Pretend Story of Beauty and the Beast." Also in the first movement, we see various images of animals, including the slaughter of a horse from *Blood of the Beasts* (1949), George Franju's documentary about a French slaughterhouse. The second movement is more explicitly narrative. It begins with several minutes taken from a teacher-training film about a troubled female student, and continues with a surrealistic story (in voice-over) about a young woman who becomes possessed by the personality of her first love. The third movement begins with documentary images of desperately poor WWII refugees, followed by images of agriculture and bountiful crops. After a sequence in which it appears that a child is shot and a house catches fire, the third movement concludes with images of the most abject third world poverty and starvation.

Fig. 8.38

Though the three major movements are largely independent, which makes the overall meaning rather obscure, the film is a *tour de force* of polyvalent montage: virtually every shot develops the context established by its neighbors. Consider this sequence from the first movement. We see re-creations of pre-cinema studies of animal and human locomotion. One of the experiments shown uses rubber bulbs attached to the bottom of a horse's hooves. We see a hoof in close-up as someone pokes the bulb. Cut to a stylus moving in response to the compression of the bulb. We then see a white horse being led to a building. After another close-up of the bulb (Fig. 8.34), we see the horse again. Then the sequence suddenly turns somber. As it turns out, the white horse is from *Blood of the Beasts*, and the horse is killed (Fig. 8.35)—with a poking movement not unlike that seen in the close-up of the hoof. The horse's throat is slit (Fig. 8.36), and its hide is cut away from the carcass (Fig. 8.37). But then the film shifts mood again: cut to a close-up of a hand stroking the fur of white dog (Fig. 8.38), an image which matches the lighting, texture and movement of the shot of the skinning of the horse. Strand's editing is so startling because it conceptually and graphically matches images that shift so radically in mood.

Fig. 8.39

Fig. 8.40

Such sudden shifts of mood also help explain the film's enigmatic overall structure, whose innocent beginning contrasts with the horror of its end. *Loose Ends* concludes with a series of profoundly disturbing images, including mass graves (Fig. 8.39) and starving

Fig. 8.41   Fig. 8.42   Fig. 8.43

Fig. 8.44   Fig. 8.45   Fig. 8.46

children fighting over meager scraps of food (Fig. 8.40). Over these images we hear the concluding voice-over from *Last Year At Marienbad* (1961). Its English translation appears in subtitles: "From this intricate frieze of grotesque boughs and wreaths, like ancient foliage, the whole story has come to an end. In a few moments it will harden forever in a marble past buried in a frozen garden of soothing formality, with clipped shrubs and ordered paths." In the context of *Loose Ends*, the "soothing formality" of the "frozen garden" becomes a metaphor for cinematic representation: it suggests that historical images will inevitably lose the power to move us. But among these images is a shot of children in a movie theater, recalling the framing situation suggested by the opening of the film. Its finely crafted montage has brought us from the "Let's Pretend Story of Beauty and the Beast" to some of the worst catastrophes of the twentieth century. And the suggestion that children have been watching them renews the horrifying power of images that had been in danger of becoming documentary film clichés.

Many avant-garde films use the graphic qualities of the image to link shots at local levels. Because the two-dimensional array of shapes in an image is remembered so briefly, such associations are generally apparent only between adjacent shots. In the discussion of the poetic strain of the avant-garde, I suggested that graphic qualities of the images can link shots at more global levels, if such a graphic structure is the most prominent global structure in the film. Global graphic structures are most apparent in films whose overall organization is what I have been calling atmospheric. One such found-footage compilation is Conner's *Take the 5:10 to Dreamland*.

Take the 5:10 to Dreamland is structured as a theme-and-variations on ascending and descending movements with three major segments. The first segment begins with a shot of water dripping into a pool in a woods (Fig. 8.41) followed by a shot of a cloudy sky, and consists of more shots whose movements are predominantly downward. Shots in the next segment move upward, and in the final segment they move downward again. When the predominantly downward direction of the first segment is reversed, the transition is marked by a shot of a girl bouncing a ball (Fig. 8.42). The up and down pattern of the film is compressed into this image of the bouncing action. After a series of graphic matches between shots of rising objects (Figs. 8.43, 8.44), the direction of the movement reverses again. The transition to this third segment is marked by a shot of a girl who looks at herself in a mirror, then turns and moves away (Fig. 8.45). Both her turning and the image in the mirror are again representations of the film's global structure concentrated at the local level of a single shot. And, the girl in the mirror holds a ball, recalling the shot that served as the transition between the first and second segments. The third segment consists of a series of shots of downward movements, ending in a shot of a clouded sky followed by the film's final shot of rain falling onto the surface of a pond (Fig. 8.46). The final shot is not only part of the third downward movement, but with the penultimate shot of the clouds, it mirrors the opening of the film.

In view of our propensity to forget surface detail, we would expect the graphic relationships between adjacent shots to be more salient than the graphic relationships between separated shots. But *Take the 5:10 to Dreamland* de-emphasizes local graphic relationships. Conner has separated many of the shots with long fades, thus inhibiting our response to the graphic match. *Take the 5:10 to Dreamland* is all the more remarkable because it builds a global graphic structure while undermining our apprehension of local graphic connections.

Compilation Narratives

In chapter 3, I argued that narrative plays an important role even in films not considered primarily narrative. This is true in the found-footage compilation, too.

Some found-footage compilations have narratives that are quite evident, even at first glance. Charles Levine's *Horse Opera* (1970), for example, condenses about a dozen films into a single archetypal cowboy story. Craig Baldwin's ROCKETKITCONGOKIT (1986) uses the found-footage compilation to document the story of the imperialist exploitation of Zaire, and to parody the treatment of political history in such widely known compilation documentaries as *Victory at Sea* (1952–53) and *Air Power* (1956–57).

Richard Beveridge's *Turn to Your ~~Gods~~ Dogs* (1977) demonstrates how a single over-arching narrative can provide a highly structured context for a diverse array of found footage. *Turn to Your ~~Gods~~ Dogs* uses footage of three main types: a promotional film encouraging families to attend movies regularly; documentary footage

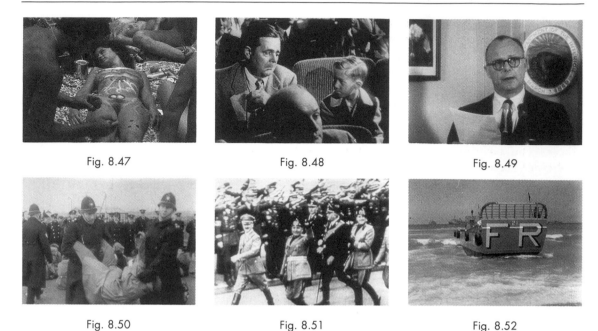

Fig. 8.47   Fig. 8.48   Fig. 8.49

Fig. 8.50   Fig. 8.51   Fig. 8.52

of a nudists' festival on a beach; and a variety of images of government officials, the military and the police. Some of the footage establishes a framing story—a family goes to a movie theater. What they ''see'' is a mixture of the nude beach footage and the shots of government officials and military action. Beveridge periodically cuts back to the family in the theater so that they seem to be reacting to the other found footage. For example, when the first images of the nudists appear (Fig. 8.47), the father and son exchange knowing, approving glances (Fig. 8.48). Thus, one of the primary means of establishing coherence within the overall narrative is to encourage viewers to impute causal relationships between disparate images.

The embedded story, what we presume is a newsreel viewed by the family, uses the radical metaphor strategy to incorporate footage from wildly disparate sources. Early in the ''newsreel,'' Beveridge cross-cuts between images of the nudists and a United States Department of the Interior official declaiming about an intolerable threat to the social order (Fig. 8.49). This cross-cutting evokes a conflict between a peaceful counter-culture and a repressive state, and this context makes a very wide array of images comprehensible. It is easy to understand the images of British police breaking up an anti-nuclear protest as an example of the same kind of repression (Fig. 8.50). But Beveridge also includes shots of Hitler (Fig. 8.51), Mussolini, nuclear explosions and even American football games, which we interpret as metaphors for, and manifestations of, the repressiveness of the state and mainstream culture. And though we never actually see a confrontation with the nudists, it is metaphorically represented by images of marines landing on a beach (Fig. 8.52), charging soldiers, speeding covered wagons (Fig. 8.53) and stampeding elephants, from which the nudists seem to be retreating (Fig. 8.54).

Fig. 8.53

Turn to Your ~~Gods~~ Dogs marks the limits of the highly coherent compilation narrative. But in compilation narratives that make heavier use of both ellipses and metaphor, narrative comprehension is a more complex affair than it is in *Turn to Your ~~Gods~~ Dogs* or *Science Friction*. The structure of a narrative with an ellipsis, or an instance of metonymy (such as the representation of the murder of the little girl in *M* (1931), which I discussed in chapter 3) could be represented:

1 [ ] 3 4 5 6 7 8 9

indicating that the viewer must infer one of the major events. Using the same notational system, we could represent the use of metaphor, such as the one for the killing of the workers in *Strike*, like this:

Fig. 8.54

*
1 2 3 4 5 6 7 8 [ ]

indicating that one image has been drawn from outside the diegesis. The construction of a hypothetical film that deploys the metaphor and ellipsis strategies together can be illustrated like this:

[ ] [ ] [ ] [ ] [ ] * [ ] [ ] [ ]
[ ] [ ] [ ] * [ ] [ ] [ ] * [ ]
[ ] * [ ] [ ] * [ ] [ ] [ ] [ ]
1 [ ] 3 [ ] [ ] [ ] [ ] [ ] 9

It is within such a conceptual space that the narrative structure of the compilation narrative may be understood. Each column represents the set of images that share some semantic feature with the event in the ''baseline'' of the narrative and could therefore replace it. Those images that are close to the baseline share many semantic features with the base event; those higher up are more incongruous and share fewer of the base event's features. The compilation narrative draws relatively little from the baseline that would be so liberally represented in classical narratives and pulls a great deal of material from the columns of metaphorical replacements. And the replacements, drawn from the upper reaches of the metaphor columns, are likely to be very incongruous, thus requiring greater effort to comprehend. At the same time, the compilation narrative relies heavily on our ability to infer the causal and spatial links between represented events, again demanding more processing effort.

My use of the terms ''metaphor'' and ''metonymy'' and my two-dimensional diagram of their interaction points up the similarity between my account of the compilation narrative and other accounts of symbolic communication, such as Roman Jakobson's ([1958] 1972). But there are important differences, the most crucial of which is scope. Jakobson's notion of the syntagmatic and paradigmatic structures of language was offered as a theory of features that are fundamental to all linguistic communication. In fact, it has been extended to all symbolic communication, linguistic or not. Similarly, his essay

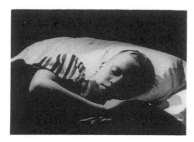

Fig. 8.55

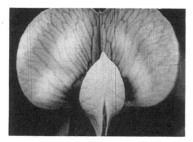

Fig. 8.56

Fig. 8.57

Fig. 8.58

on speech disorders (1956) suggested that metaphor and metonymy were umbrella concepts for *the* two types of mental organization. And more recently, Christian Metz (1982) argued that the metaphor/ metonymy distinction was a reflection in language of the basic distinction between the Freudian processes of condensation and displacement. These theories reduce complex phenomena to binary oppositions that often lack discriminatory power. As Schofer and Rice demonstrate in their study of figurative representation (1977), the metaphor/metonymy distinction cannot even be coherently applied to the figures of classical rhetoric, the field that supplied the terms in the first place.

The analysis of avant-garde compilation is a much more modest and therefore more defensible goal. Avant-garde compilation is a specific filmmaking style that requires specific viewing strategies. Since these films are highly elliptical, the viewer must be more prepared than usual to make bold inferences about spatial and causal relationships of the sort demanded by the rhetorical figure of metonymy. Since metaphors are so prevalent, viewers must look for even very tenuous conceptual links between images. This is the strategy the viewer must adopt in comprehending narrative in the avant-garde compilation: to readily infer metonymic replacements along the story line, and search for often wildly exotic metaphors.

Since metaphor and metonymy are so heavily used in the compilation narrative, they begin to carry primary responsibility for the representation of the basic story events rather than just commenting on them as is the case with more traditional narrative metaphors. This makes the system very flexible. Given any random collection of images, there is undoubtedly a combination of metaphoric and metonymic readings that would allow inventive viewers to find some sort of narrative in them.[10] But the compilation narrative, as loosely structured as it is likely to be, still identifies its baseline by the early introduction of characters. For example, *Valse Triste* clearly identifies its primary character, and this identification occurs at the very beginning of the film when the viewers are assembling the schemata they will use to comprehend the film. Viewers will test the images for relevance to some context; this context must be established early. If characters appeared only late in the film, the viewers would have no reason to believe that those characters formed part of the narrative baseline and would treat them as images on the same level as any of the other images in the film.

Conner's *Valse Triste* does identify a "protagonist" early in the film, but the narrative that follows is not especially obvious. Why insist on a narrative interpretation? The specifically *causal* relationships between the images in *Valse Triste* are fundamental to understanding the thematic coherence of the film. Without these causal relationships, that is, without this narrative armature, even the theme begins to dissolve. Not every shot in the film is part of this armature, but its key elements are distributed widely throughout the film. After the shot of the boy going to bed (Fig. 8.55) and a few shots of rural family life, Conner cuts from a woman's hands folding satin sheets

(Fig. 8.56) to a time-lapse close-up of a flower opening (Fig. 8.57) and then to a model at a fashion show opening her coat to show her close-fitting dress (Fig. 8.58). The graphic matches on the opening fabric and flowers have clear sexual overtones, though these images are not yet linked to the boy. But this sexual theme soon is reiterated in an image closer to the baseline of the story: girls, about the same age as the boy, perform a group exercise in which they lie down and wave their legs in the air (Fig. 8.59). This obliquely represented erotic encounter or fantasy triggers a male sexual response, represented through an obvious metaphor—a squirting hose falls to the pavement (Fig. 8.60). This response causes guilt, metaphorically represented through an eye-line match suggesting that a family standing in front of a farm house is about to be crushed by a phallic log sliding toward them (Figs. 8.61, 8.62). The film concludes with an image that extrapolates the images of guilt by expanding the water imagery from the shots of the hose and the log into an image of disaster: a string of black cars moves slowly though a flooded town (Fig. 8.63).

Fig. 8.59

Fig. 8.60

Lest this interpretation seem far-fetched, I will point out that it uses only the most blatant sexual metaphors like opening flowers and squirting hoses. The sexual symbols in avant-garde compilation provide more than sophomoric humor. Since the narrative is represented in a way that is so difficult to process, these easily interpreted symbols give viewers important cues to the events. In *Valse Triste* a change in the mood of the music (Sibelius's ''Valse Triste'') reinforces the sexual encounter interpretation by suggesting a specific emotional response to the images. When the music changes from lively and cheerful to mournful just as Conner cuts to the spraying hose, it suggests that the sexual response will have negative consequences. Without the reconstruction of the causal relationships between the images of the erotic fantasy, the ''orgasm,'' and the imagined threat to the family, the theme of sexual anxiety is considerably weakened.

The question remains, if these metaphors are in fact so blatant, why is the film's narrative so hard to see? Simply put, such heavy use of metaphor and metonymy and the inclusion of material that cannot easily be assimilated to the narrative places extraordinary demands on the viewer's cognitive powers.

Given the difficulty in the processing of their stories, it is clear that these films are not thinly veiled classical narratives, and the stories in them do not completely unify the films. On the contrary, these narratives are often very slender, without many events; and, as the example of *Valse Triste* shows, they can be not only trite but downright silly, even though they do play a real role in the viewer's comprehension of the films. But a narrative whose few, uninteresting events are difficult to comprehend apparently violates the principle of optimal relevance. Consequently, we demand a reward for our extra effort, and we attempt to reprocess the film in hopes that we can understand why the story was represented in such an oblique way. In *Valse Triste*, this ''second look'' is motivated not just by the apparent violation of optimal relevance, but by the omission of the second half of the framing situation. This encourages the viewer to entertain the

Fig. 8.61

Fig. 8.62

Fig. 8.63

idea that the film is *not* a dream and to test it for other organizing structures, such as the string of graphic matches between the sheets, the opening coat of the model and the opening flower.

A Final Example: The Great Blondino

The assemblage aesthetic was still prominent in San Francisco art when Robert Nelson and painter William Wiley made *The Great Blondino* (1967). Nelson has often cited Conner's work as being a major influence (MacDonald 1983, 39), but the influence of assemblage art on *The Great Blondino* is even more pervasive than this suggests. Like earlier California assemblage, Wiley's paintings and collages were still preoccupied with sex, but they were generally lighter in mood than the gloomy, apocalyptic tone that characterized Conner's sculpture and Christopher Maclaine's films. For example, Wiley's sets for the San Francisco Mime Troupe's 1963 production of Alfred Jarry's *Ubu Roi* turn everything into sex organs: costumes are equipped with oversize breasts, tongues and testicles; and keys, scepters and even the food look more or less like genitalia.[11] This grotesquely humorous approach to sexuality permeates *The Great Blondino* and accounts for much of its iconography.

But the film interests us here not only because of its ties to West Coast art. With its fragmentary narrative, its hyperdeveloped dream sequences and its prominent graphic structure, *The Great Blondino* nicely demonstrates how assemblage was adapted to established norms of avant-garde filmmaking.

The Great Blondino is roughly based on the story of Harry Blondin, a nineteenth century acrobat whom Wiley had used as the subject of a number of paintings. Blondin's most remarkable feat was pushing a wheelbarrow across a tightrope over Niagara Falls. Of course, most viewers are not familiar with Blondin, so his story does not suggest any specific narrative development. But it does supply the film with its protagonist, Blondino. Dressed in a gray and white comic-book-hero outfit, he spends the film dreaming, fantasizing and wandering about observed by an ever-present, though not very intimidating, plainclothes policeman, identified in the credits as ''the Cop'' (Fig. 8.64).

The Great Blondino began as an improvised narrative, but ultimately the story of Blondino serves as an armature supporting a diverse array of found footage. Uninterested in following a script or a tightly planned production schedule, Nelson and Wiley shot the film on weekends over an extended period, using whoever was available and whatever story ideas came to mind at the time. At the end of shooting, they had a chaotic mass of disjointed footage. As Nelson said later:

> It was almost a year before I finally edited it. I had no idea what to do. I kept knowing I would get to it, and finally, still without knowing what to do, I just dove in and started mixing the footage with TV outs and other material. As I was working on it, I could see a kind of story evolving, so I went with that. After a while it seemed to be making itself, telling a story in some crude, episodic way. (MacDonald 1983, 42)

Fig. 8.64

Thus, even though *The Great Blondino* includes a significant amount of original footage, the film has much in common with other films constructed purely of found footage.

Even a cursory look shows that the film is an assemblage of materials that are only partially integrated into a new whole. Unlike Conner's films, in which the collected footage is made stylistically uniform, *The Great Blondino* exploits the disjunction between the various sources. Rather than printing all the footage on monochrome stock, Nelson and Wiley mix different film stocks and visual styles. In fact, even within the footage they shot themselves, the filmmakers introduce such shifts, alternating unpredictably between the color original and a black-and-white print. But such shifting also is part of a strategy to blur the distinction between their own footage and the primarily black-and-white found footage. Many of the color shots are contrasty and harshly lit, thereby reducing the apparent color. Skin tones in the color footage are often so pale that the image looks black and white anyway, and the bleached-out sky in many of the shots heightens the effect. The Cop wears a suit so dark that it photographs as black, and Blondino is nearly colorless as well. His costume's gray stars and stripes against a white background, and the gray tights, combined with actor Chuck Wiley's pale complexion and dark hair, would make Blondino a black-and-white character even on Technicolor film.

This partial integration is also apparent at higher levels of organization. The film's narrative is very loosely structured: the bulk of the film consists of Blondino's dreams and fantasies which seem only peripherally related to his tightrope act. But given that Blondino is introduced by the film's first scene, and that he appears throughout the film, we test the rest of the film for its relevance to this character. Between Blondino's many dreams lie the primary events that form the core of the film's simple, episodic story.

Other than being observed by the Cop, Blondino's interactions with other characters are limited to three incidents. Near the beginning of the film, the Cop hands him a blindfold that he wears intermittently throughout the film. Later, in the course of his wanderings, he encounters an attractive blonde woman, ''the Trollop'' (as she is iden-

Fig. 8.65

Fig. 8.66

Fig. 8.67

Fig. 8.68

tified in the credits). As usual, the Cop observes. The Trollop lures Blondino with her sexy walk, but when Blondino tries to touch her, a dissolve turns her into a red painter's easel, and Blondino has another crazy fantasy. The third interaction comes in the final segments of the film, where the Cop openly antagonizes Blondino. Blondino walks with his wheelbarrow, stopping near a brick wall where a shiny, penis-like protuberance pierces it. Blondino rubs the protuberance as if he were masturbating, and it grows dramatically, as if aroused. But the brick wall disappears, showing that the phallus is held by the Cop. They struggle and the Cop socks Blondino in the jaw, knocking him unconscious. Once again, Blondino dreams.

In the film's last "episode," Blondino attempts a tightrope walk, seen in movie theaters and on television, only to fall onto seaside rocks. In colorfully distorted images, Blondino seems to have survived as he gets up, recovers his wheelbarrow and continues to walk. The Cop, observing as always, is shocked, and the film ends with Blondino walking along a hill on the horizon beneath a blue sky.

The Great Blondino poses two problems for the viewer guided by the principle of relevance. The first involves the primary episodes themselves: there is no explicit causal connection between any of the eight segments of the film. Although the primary segments do contain the same characters, it is not clear how each episode contributes to the context established by the previous ones. Second, the subjective sequences are terrifically prominent but do not contain the characters from the primary level. How, then, are they relevant to Blondino and the primary narrative?

One way in which the subjective sequences are relevant to the primary events is that they provide information about Blondino's personality. This information is important if we are to infer anything about his goals since his actions in the primary sequences are very enigmatic. If his longest dream is any indication, Blondino is preoccupied with sex, but his preoccupation is neither particularly healthy nor guilt-free. This dream segment's recurring image is Blondino napping on a leopard skin rug, while in the top half of the frame a half-dozen pink-skinned male and female nudes frolic with ropes and gauze (Fig. 8.65). The appealing pleasantness of these shots, however, is upset by several images that associate sex with violence and disease. Following the playful nudes, images of a female acrobat who strips while hanging by her teeth links her partial nudity with her physical discomfort (Fig. 8.66). The fleshiness that was so inviting in the shots of the nudes is even more dramatically twisted in the series of seven short shots of diseased eyes, copied in living color from a medical book. Recurrent shots of a man sawing a log are used, most evidently, as a humorous translation of the verbal cliche of "sawing wood" meaning "sleeping" (Fig. 8.67). But the sawing of the log obliquely suggests castration, and if this sexual meaning is not obvious at first, castration is literally and explicitly brought to the screen in several shots showing the gelding of a horse (Fig. 8.68). Since the relationship between the dream images and the other elements of the film is never explicitly drawn, it is difficult to fix the meaning of the dreams with precision. Nevertheless, through the dreams, the viewer learns that Blondino has his share of sexual desire, even though he feels a significant amount of anxiety about it. And this information about Blondino's sexuality is relevant to the interactions of the characters. Twice Blondino's sexual desire leads him into traps set by the Cop.

Our inferences about the goals of the characters are also supported by *The Great Blondino*'s use of archetypal characters: the detective and the femme fatale. In very general terms, we understand that Blondino's relationship to the openly sexual Trollop will not be in his interest in the long run; we might suspect that the Cop has hired her to pump him for information or to encourage him to attempt the dangerous tightrope walk. None of these hypotheses are specifically confirmed, but the incident with the Trollop suggests a range of hypotheses that could account for the relevance of the sequence.

The role of the Cop is also somewhat mysterious. When the Cop finally explains his role in segment seven, it is only in the most general terms: "When the committee first heard about this fellow, we were quite sure that his operations, if you can call them that, were not in the national interest." Later: "We have investigated practically every single part of the operation." And finally: "We feel that this man is going to cause serious harm." The Cop's explanations do not really tell the viewer anything new, except that the Cop represents some "committee," and not his individual interest. Exactly what this committee is, and what sort of danger Blondino represents to it, remains a mystery. Of course the implication of the Cop's depiction as vaguely McCarthyite is clear enough: the Cop's investigation of Blondino evokes the use of "national security" as an excuse for government suppression of dissent.

The Great Blondino's heavy use of metaphors contributes to the viewer's difficulty in reconstructing the narrative. We have already seen that well-developed contexts—such as those in *Strike* or *Science Friction*—make metaphors easy to process. Similarly, some metaphors in *The Great Blondino* are easily fit into its narrative. For example, during Blondino's tightrope walk, Nelson and Wiley cut to shots of performing animals: a horse walks down the street, a bull pulls a cart at a rodeo, and one elephant leaps over another at a circus. These animals, who perform what look like dangerous stunts, are metaphorical substitutes for Blondino much in the way that the bull substituted for Eisenstein's workers. Since these animal images are being placed in an already developed context, we tend to interpret them as suggesting that Blondino has the salient qualities of these animals: he is innocent or naive, he is controlled by others, and he will not benefit much from his performance. Once again, these metaphors are easy to process because, given the context of Blondino's experiences with the Cop, the salient features of the images of the animals fit easily into our schema for Blondino's exploitation.

In *The Great Blondino* some metaphors do more than comment on the action—the action itself is conveyed through them. These metaphors, like those in *Valse Triste*, are more difficult to process because they do not immediately fit an established context. For ex-

Fig. 8.69

Fig. 8.70

ample, after Blondino falls from the tightrope, we see a large mechanical octopus pulling a man from a shore into a body of water. The salient qualities of the image of the malevolent octopus do not seem relevant to Blondino's fall, which appears to be accidental. However, superimposed over this image is the title, "The eight sucker-bearing arms of the agency." This title suggests a metaphoric link between the octopus and the Cop's "committee"—both are dangerous and hard to evade. With the octopus linked to the Cop's committee, we hypothesize that the Cop caused Blondino's death just as the octopus caused the death of the man on the shore. Though this metaphor is comprehensible in a fairly specific way, it is difficult to process for two reasons. First, it is actually two metaphors. The viewer must understand the metaphorical link between the Cop's committee and the octopus in order to understand the metaphorical link between the octopus' attack and Blondino's fall. Second, the metaphor does not confirm an already obvious assumption. Blondino's fall appears to be accidental, so the image of the malevolent octopus is the only representation of the Cop's involvement in Blondino's fall.

The Great Blondino also makes use of what we have been calling centrifugal interpolation. For example, at the beginning of *The Great Blondino*, the white knight from an Ajax detergent commercial charges down a city street, aims his lance at a woman whose dress has been soiled (Fig. 8.69) and changes her into Blondino (Fig. 8.70). The most salient features of the footage—the knight's costume and his magic power—demand our attention without contributing to our understanding of Blondino's character or the events of the story. The magical power ascribed to the detergent by the original commercial is prominent but unmotivated and made to look all the more ridiculous.

Many images that at first seem to be violations of the principle of relevance can be explained by relating them to Blondino's personality or to the action of the primary narrative. But some still seem irrelevant. In *The Great Blondino* the pattern of the graphic qualities of the images is not only highly organized but also highly redundant, so that when the semantic structure fails to account for the relevance of the images, the surface organization is extremely salient.

By repeating certain compositions throughout the film, Nelson and Wiley use the graphic space to organize the film as a whole, composing it as a set of variations on a set of compositional themes. Part of the reason for this might be financial. Consider their use of matte shots, a relatively costly and time-consuming procedure of combining two images by photographically "cutting out" an area of one image and replacing it with a portion of another. Early in the film, when the Cop gives Blondino the blindfold, Blondino is shot in close-up in the center of the frame. At the same time, Blondino also appears in a smaller, rectangular frame superimposed in the upper left corner of the frame. Later, this framed image will return, precisely fit onto the movie screen in an airplane while Blondino makes his tightrope walk. Having made a matte to fit the screen in a shot of the interior of an airliner, Nelson and Wiley can use it to generate similar compositions at other points in the film even when the matte is not motivated by the need for a precise fit between two images.

Nelson and Wiley use a central circular image in a similar way, but this composition is so prevalent that the economic explanation can only partially account for it. Throughout the film they show a strong taste for compositions dominated by a central circle, often linking several images by repeating this compositional pattern. For example, in segment four a series of graphic matches links shots of a golf ball driven at the camera, a woman's gloved hand holding a round makeup case, and a man picking up a tire. Later in the same segment, a similar series links shots of computer tape reels, an oscilloscope screen, and a white circle. The circular image plays its most important role in the form of a round image of a face against a dark background, as in the shot of Blondino's blindfolding by the Cop. This composition is repeated obsessively. We see Blondino's laughing face through the barrel of a gun. A small, bright circle dominates the frame in the second half of Blondino's longest dream, and in it we see several images, including one of a man with a moustache. The moustached man returns in the same composition later in the film. The use of the composition culminates in the scenes of the Cop and the mysterious moustached man explaining their attitudes toward Blondino, in the only synchronized sound footage of the film. This circular composition provides a stable surface structure to passages whose semantic structure is rapidly shifting and not easily processed. Consequently, the graphic structure seems to motivate much of the incongruous found footage.

The dream sequences are also dominated by a set of recurring shapes that are used not only in the dream sequences but also as props in the primary narrative segments. For example, in one dream almost twenty shots repeat the same basic composition: over a long shot of a room is a superimposed, bright, central circle. With a snap zoom, the long shot changes to a close-up. In close-up, the superimposed circle no longer covers the contents of the room but instead falls completely inside the top part of the scroll shape now dominating the frame. At this point, the scroll shape is a meaningless graphic motif, but it is given more precise associations the next time it appears, in the scene in which Blondino encounters the Trollop. After Blondino reaches for the breasts of the Trollop (Fig. 8.71), she is replaced, through a dissolve, with an easel (Fig. 8.72). Part of the easel's decorative trim is a symmetrical scroll shape that Blondino fondles instead of the Trollop's breasts. Several shots later, the scroll shape returns. With a close-up of the scroll shape in the foreground and the easel in the background, the viewer recognizes the scroll as the top part of the easel (Fig. 8.73). The smooth, rounded shape of the scroll recalls the Trollop's round breasts, and this graphic similarity motivates the Trollop's replacement with the easel, which would otherwise seem quite arbitrary.

Horn shapes, such as the one used by the Cop to deceive Blondino, play a similar compositional role. After Blondino fondles the metal phallus held by the Cop (Fig. 8.74), the Cop knocks him

Fig. 8.71

Fig. 8.72

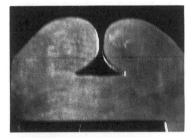

Fig. 8.73

Fig. 8.74

Fig. 8.75

Fig. 8.76

Fig. 8.77

Fig. 8.78

unconscious (Fig. 8.75). In the dream that follows, Blondino watches a horned rhinoceros pace at the zoo (Fig. 8.76). After this a triangular box equipped with a horn similar to the rhino's is pixilated around the same room where we earlier saw the scroll shape (Fig. 8.77). Finally, in a series of shots combining several key motifs, a painting of the triangular box, now covered with animal skins and still sporting a horn, is matted into a circle in the middle of another shot of the painting, so that three black horns seem to tickle each other. As in the dream following Blondino's encounter with the Trollop, his attempted erotic engagement is displaced in his dream onto inanimate objects that are associated with the objects of desire.

The graphic motifs of *The Great Blondino* are not subordinated to the narrative structure of the film, but neither do they form a completely autonomous structure. Through their consistent association with the events of the narrative, the graphic motifs acquire sexual overtones. Blondino's creation in the opening of the film, for example, is a humorous borrowing from popular culture with no direct causal relevance to the rest of the story, but the horn motif makes it part of a consistent sexual theme. Here, too, a real erotic encounter is displaced onto inanimate objects: the act of copulation, which normally creates a human being, is replaced by an interaction between the knight's lance and the woman's dress from the Ajax commercial.

The animal imagery is also tied to the sexual theme through the use of these graphic motifs. The link between the rhino and the phallus held by the Cop is clear because the image of the rhino immediately follows the incident between the Cop and Blondino, but the rhino images also motivate the shots of the hippos from the earlier long dream. The round, fleshy hippos drinking milk from the tub (Fig. 8.78) are themselves very sensual, but the inclusion of the rhino gives their meaning a particular sharpness: without the horn, the hippos are "feminized" versions of the rhino. Thus, each animal is an appropriate analog for the sexual focus of the dream in which it appears: the hippos replace the frolicking pink nudes, and the rhino replaces the Cop and the metal phallus. And, as the animals acquire sexual connotations, the human characters in *The Great Blondino* use animal skins to trigger erotic fantasies. Blondino sleeps on a leopard rug when he dreams about the pink nudes, and a series of ten shots pan over Blondino's face and upper body, emphasizing the leopard background. The Trollop is dressed in a zebra-patterned dress, and in the erotic fantasy following Blondino's encounter with her, the easel is photographed against a pixilated leopard skin background (Fig. 8.79). In its final appearance—as the covering for the horned box in segment six—the leopard skin is involved in the erotic image of the three horns tickling each other. The network of animals also includes the mechanical octopus. Just as the Cop used the metal phallus to deceive Blondino before knocking him out, the agency perverts sexually attractive animals into an animal-machine that destroys the man by pulling him into the dark water. The destructive power of the agency, finally made explicit by the Cop's explanation of the committee's work and by the villainy of the octopus, has sinister overtones that the skinny little Cop alone cannot convey.

This independence of the formal structure from the narrative is typical of avant-garde compilation. The careful patterning of the graphic qualities of the images is so prevalent and so prominent that it cannot be considered subordinate to the narrative structure, which itself is cliched and vaguely rendered.

If the narratives in these films have so little to recommend them, why have I made the story such a prominent feature of my analysis of the films? To put it simply, there are crucial differences between the viewer's cognitive processing of causally structured films and the processing of films that are structured only graphically or thematically. Our search for causal structure is so fundamental to our mental lives that it cannot be given up just because we are watching an avant-garde film. Conner and Nelson and Wiley have moved well beyond the bawdy Freudian juxtapositions of the California assemblage school by exploiting this drive for narrative comprehension; and when a causal structure is discovered in avant-garde compilation, as slender as it might be, it demands a major role in our comprehension of the film.

Fig. 8.79

My initial focus on the basic comprehension of the assemblage strain of the American avant-garde film led me to concentrate on the ways in which these films cohere. I have emphasized their narrative elements and the strategies viewers use to discover these narratives, while confessing all along that these stories are not the compelling sort that people like to pay money for. This emphasis on coherence is appropriate because we presume that human artifacts *do* cohere, though never perfectly, and the pragmatic perspective helps us chart the ways in which viewers are likely to handle the elements in these films that cohere in less obvious ways. This is not to say that the free-wheeling collections of images in collage animations and compilations are as controlled and relentless as the schematic films of the minimal strain. On the other hand, it demonstrates that the viewer's response to the "absurd mosaic" of the assemblage strain of the American avant-garde is nevertheless governed by the logic of human cognition.

AFTERWORD

THE AVANT-GARDE CINEMA IN THE AGE OF POSTMODERNISM

I began this book with the assumption that novice viewers find the films of the avant-garde generally difficult because they have not learned the avant-garde cinema's implicit viewing procedures. The overarching theme of my study of these viewing procedures is that the avant-garde film is *constructed* in two distinct but related ways.

I have argued, first of all, that viewers construct these films in the process of making sense of them. Basing my account of the viewer's activity on Constructivist cognitive theories of perception, language and reasoning, I suggested that comprehending avant-garde film requires matching the film's details to structures called template schemata. Each strain of the avant-garde film, the poetic, the minimal and the assemblage, suggests heuristics viewers can use to match a film's details to template schemata.

I have also suggested that the avant-garde film is constructed *for* viewers by critics who supply interpretive schemata for films whose basic comprehension is problematic. Unlike heuristics, which provide only loose rules-of-thumb for making sense of films, interpretive schemata propose specific meanings for specific elements of films. For example, the anti-illusion schema allows viewers to interpret any feature that emphasizes the flatness of the image as an assertion of the inherent qualities of the film medium.

Though I criticized the way a small set of interpretive schemata has been used to construct a Modernist image of the minimal strain, I want to make it clear that I do not think interpretive schemata are necessarily improper ways of making sense of films. Since they can be used to attribute meaning to a film even if the basic comprehension of the film is problematic, interpretive schemata are especially useful for novel films that frustrate established viewing heuristics, as the minimal strain did in the early 1960s. Nor are interpretive schemata solely the tools of critics. The avant-garde cinema admits no sharp distinction between the basic comprehension of "regular" viewers and the kinds of interpretation we normally expect from critics. As the story from chapter 1 recounting Hollis Frampton's irritable response to an impatient viewer indicates, the avant-garde cinema expects its viewers to be properly sensitized and educated. And tracking the way interpretive schemata contribute to this sensitizing and education is an important part of writing the history of the American avant-garde cinema.

It would be the subject for another book, but I sense that in the face of widespread dissatisfaction with Modernist interpretive schemata, we are currently witnessing the development of a set of Postmodern interpretive schemata. Whereas Modernist interpretation sought expressions of purity, such as unmediated views of subjectivity or open displays of the essential features of the medium, Postmodern interpretation tends to look for kinds of impurity, which it takes as symptomatic of Postmodern culture. Rather than the unified mainstream culture assumed by Modernists, Postmodern culture is seen as a cacophony of fragmented and decentered discourses. Rather than the unified "subject position" of the classic text, or the self-conscious subject position of the avant-garde text, the Postmodern text offers multiple, sometimes contradictory subject positions, which are often metaphorically described as "schizophrenic." Thus, a basic Postmodern interpretive schema might be: interpret any fragmentation, contradiction or disunity as a symbol for, and a manifestation of, the schizophrenia of Postmodern culture.

It might be argued that Postmodernism represents the newest major strain of avant-garde filmmaking. But Postmodernism—whether conceived as a style of art-making, a sociological change, a theory of culture or a style of cultural analysis—has not been attended by the institutional dislocations in the avant-garde cinema that the development of the minimal strain wrought. And the development of some new interpretive schemata notwithstanding, Postmodernism has not deranged the implicit viewing procedures for the avant-garde cinema the way the minimal strain did. What Postmodernism does represent for the avant-garde cinema is a dramatic shift in critical taste away from the restrained, non-narrative aesthetic of Structural film toward more narrative kinds of filmmaking. This "New Narrative" of the late 1970s and 1980s was not so much a coherent strain of avant-garde filmmaking as it was a confluence of diverse reactions to Structural film.[1]

Part of this reaction can be thought of as a sympathetic extension of the Structural film project along lines suggested by contemporary film theory. We noted in chapter 6 the felicitous similarity between the political concerns of the Structural film project and French-influenced film theory. Theoretician-filmmakers, such as Laura Mulvey and Peter Wollen, shared Structural film's interest in the materials and the nature of representation, but whereas the critique of illusionist filmmaking was largely implicit in Structural film, it was explicit in the "New Talkie," as these theory-influenced films were called. And since contemporary film theory was then generally pitched at commercial narrative filmmaking, rather than the avant-garde, New Talkies such as *Riddles of the Sphinx* (Mulvey and Wollen, 1977), *Thriller* (Sally Potter, 1979), and *Sigmund Freud's Dora: A Case of Mistaken Identity* (Anthony McCall, Claire Pajaczkowska, Andrew Tyndall, and Jane Weinstock, 1979) were more generally narrative than the Structural film.

Another pro-narrative reaction to Structural film was rooted in the desire of some avant-garde filmmakers to reach larger audiences, for reasons both personal and political. Many of these filmmakers shared Structural film's political aspirations—indeed, some had *made* Structural films—but they were no longer sympathetic to the austere and demanding aesthetics that limited the appeal of Structural film to relatively small circles of avant-garde film viewers. And the explicitly theoretical discourse that permeated the New Talkie was also a liability in this regard. Thus, although these filmmakers were certainly not uninterested in theory, films like Lizzie Borden's *Born in Flames* (1983) and Bette Gordon's *Variety* (1985) could be thought of as New Talkies without the theoretical talk.

Yet a third impetus behind the narrative orientation of avant-garde filmmaking after Structural film was the punk music scene. Primarily working in Super-8, and often screening their work in bars and clubs, Punk filmmakers such as Eric Mitchell, Vivienne Dick and Scott B and Beth B rejected both commercial filmmaking and the established avant-garde of Structural film. And though Punk film— like avant-garde cinema in general—is politically oriented, it was openly hostile to the academic political articulations of the New Talkie as well. Nevertheless, Punk films, like the New Talkies, were generally narratives, often modelled on low-budget Hollywood genre films. One basic prototype sends aimless amoral characters stumbling through inhospitable urban environments (*She Had Her Gun Already* [Dick, 1978]). Other films, such as Scott B and Beth B's *Black Box* (1978) and *Letters to Dad* (1979) and Richard Kern's *Manhattan Love Suicides* (1985) offer more sophisticated political allegories.

For a while, then, the widespread and intense disaffection from the aesthetics of Structural film seemed to portend the development of both a more popular narrative strain of avant-garde filmmaking, and a more arcane narrative strain, steeped in the convolutions of continental theory. But in one sense, the "featurization of the avant-garde," to use a phrase from Paul Arthur's suggestive analysis of the phenomenon (1986), was rather brief. A few filmmakers did make narrative features that circulated semi-commercially, beyond avant-garde film circles: Gordon's *Variety*, Borden's *Born in Flames* and Scott B and Beth B's *Vortex* (1982). But the aesthetic and economic problems of this version of the narrative avant-garde seem to have been insurmountable: the semi-commercial distribution of avant-garde film did not last much beyond the mid-1980s. With the important exception of the work of Yvonne Rainer, commercial distribution—even on a modest scale—has generally been open only insofar as filmmakers abandon avant-garde aesthetics. Witness Beth B's *Salvation* (1987), Borden's *Working Girls* (1987) or the difference between Jim Jarmusch's *Stranger Than Paradise* (1984) and his later work, such as *Down By Law* (1986).

In another sense, however, the feature-length avant-garde narrative is part of a long and continuing tradition—actually two traditions. The New Talkie's theoretically informed critique of representation is part of the legacy of the Modernist cinema of Jean Luc Godard

and Jean-Marie Straub and Danièle Huillet, as Peter Wollen's celebrated essay ''The Two Avant-gardes'' makes clear. Yvonne Rainer
is remarkable within the American avant-garde because the influence
of Modernist narrative filmmaking was already evident in her work
during the height of Structural film's prominence, and continued to be
evident long after the vitality of the New Talkie had faded. Thus, the
overtly theoretical New Talkie is not so much a novel strain of
avant-garde filmmaking as it is a moment when the interests of the
American avant-garde overlap those of the Modernist cinema.

The avant-garde feature narrative is also part of a tradition
within the American avant-garde. As I have argued, narrative has been
an important dimension of American avant-garde filmmaking, even in
films we do not think of as primarily narrative. And there are many
nearly feature-length narrative films in the poetic and assemblage
strains of the avant-garde that have lain practically unnoticed in the
shadow of Structural film.[2] *The Great Blondino*, which I discussed in
chapter 8, is one example, as are important but nearly ignored films
by Christopher Maclaine, Stanton Kaye and Richard Myers, among
many others. It seems to me that the newest narratives in the avant-
garde cinema (such as Leslie Thorton's *Peggy and Fred in Hell*
[1984–92] and Peg Awesh and Keith Sanborn's *The Deadman* [1989])
owe less to the Modernist tradition of Godard, Straub and Huillet or
even Rainer, than they owe to the underground tradition of Jack Smith,
Ron Rice and Andy Warhol. The political sensibilities of these films
might be rooted remotely in Godard's Dziga Vertov group, but their
junkyard ethos more directly evokes the collection of artists, hustlers
and hangers-on in Warhol's tinfoil-lined Factory.

The minimal strain was the trademark style of what Jim Hoberman called the ''authentically modernist'' avant-garde (1984, 64).
The assemblage strain's eclecticism may come to emblematize the
avant-garde in its ''Postmodern'' phase. And though it was largely
overlooked during the heyday of Structural film, the poetic strain has
remained a significant trend throughout. My point here is that these
three strains all are still viable traditions from which filmmakers
continue to draw. It might be argued that the New Narrative of the
1970s and 1980s represents yet another important strain of avant-
garde filmmaking. But I believe that the poetic, minimal and assemblage strains represent more durable and more cohesive tendencies,
and that together these three strains form the central tradition of the
American avant-garde cinema.

Looking back from what we like to consider a Postmodern
perspective, we see two alternative visions of avant-garde art. In one,
we see a heroic period of courageous experimentation and tireless
opposition. In the other, we see failure and the remains of an elitist
clique, cut off from the very culture it purported to change. I must
confess that I incline toward the heroic vision, but specifically with
regard to the American avant-garde cinema, there is more than a grain
of truth in both.

The struggles of the partisans of the avant-garde cinema in the
first two decades after World War II were nothing if not heroic. One

thinks particularly of exhibitors showing these strange films before the American avant-garde cinema existed: Maya Deren rented a theater for a one-night screening of her films; Amos Vogel screened virtually any kind of film available in 16mm—instructional, medical, poetic—at Cinema 16; at Jonas Mekas's Film-makers' Cinematheque any filmmaker could show a film (even if it were six hours long and showed only a man sleeping). And of course, the filmmakers themselves were heroic in those days when almost no one was paid to teach avant-garde filmmaking. Sometimes these heroic stories took the shape of tragedy. Christopher Maclaine lived practically as a street person, yet managed to beg and borrow enough to complete a few remarkable films in the 1950s; in 1975, he died alone and practically unknown after a decade in and out of mental hospitals.

The avant-garde cinema has had its elitist moments, too. One thinks of the rarefied limits of Structural film. Some of Hollis Frampton's work has structures and allusions so complex and dense that even the most committed critic can hardly untangle them on an editing machine. And there is Peter Gidal's steadfast refusal of practically anything we call pleasure in his Structural/Materialist films. Institutions played a role in this elitism, too. Anthology Film Archive's establishment of the ''Essential Cinema'' collection struck some as an elitist gesture, as did the design of Anthology's theater. In an attempt to create the perfect screening space for the avant-garde film, Peter Kubelka had each viewer seated in a chair with a high back and sides, a kind of cubby hole that isolated viewers and ensured that film viewing was an essentially private rather than collective experience. That these examples are in some sense elitist is hard to deny; whether they are failures I leave to the reader to decide.

Both have a measure of truth, but neither the heroic nor the elitist vision yields an adequate image of the American avant-garde cinema. We could cite appropriate counter-examples to either position. Making a living from the avant-garde film is no longer so heroic an effort for filmmakers who are tenured professors at major universities. Against impenetrable films, we could cite films of simplicity, beauty and humor (to be fair to Frampton's memory, some of these counter-examples could come from the body of his work, too). But this debate would miss the point, because both sides misconstrue the nature of the avant-garde cinema.

Both those who see the avant-garde as elitist and those who see it as heroic implicitly appeal to the same view of the avant-garde: it is defined by its rejection of the practices and values of more widely accepted art. Viewed sympathetically, this refusal is a fight against the commercialization and degradation of culture by the mass media. Viewed unsympathetically, this refusal is a sneering disregard for the tastes of the people, whose needs are more adequately met by popular art. But in either case, the avant-garde is defined negatively, in terms of what it does not do, as a kind of total liberation or rejection.

Viewed as an art of radical liberation, the avant-garde is the legacy of Romanticism, as writers from Poggioli to Sitney to Wees have made very clear. And although Romantic thought is usually taken to be opposed to the values of the Enlightenment, the emphasis on liberation in the avant-garde also evokes the legacy of classical liberalism,[3] in which society is itself defined negatively. In the classical liberal view, the social formation is rooted not in some positive conception of the "good," but in the protection of individual freedom. The liberal state's role is restricted to the negative one of preventing loss of "life, liberty and property," in Locke's phrase. The avant-garde is conceived in the image of this negativity, which it exaggerates. Because of this exaggeration, avant-garde artists are not always good citizens, even of liberal states—note, for example, André Breton's proposal that the ultimate Surrealist act would be to fire a revolver randomly into a crowd.

The classical liberal notion that society need not be based in a concept of the good has come under attack from a variety of positions that together have become known as communitarianism. Communitarianism holds that the liberal conception of society is inevitably rootless and disconnected, merely a confederation of free and equal strangers, whereas a legitimate, healthy society requires a positive articulation of communal values, which can be found in some traditional communities, such as the Catholic church.[4] One strand of the communitarian critique argues that classical liberalism, though it trumpets most loudly the ideal of freedom and the restricted power of the state, implicitly appeals to, or at least is compatible with, a conception of the good.[5] In *Another Liberalism*, for example, Nancy L. Rosenblum tries to reconcile the Romantic ideals of creativity, spontaneity, self-expression and community with a revised and nuanced notion of liberalism.

My approach to the avant-garde cinema is analogous to this communitarian reappraisal of classical liberalism. I have argued against a fundamentally negative conception, in which the American avant-garde film is simply another manifestation of a single, tra~ historical avant-garde, predicated solely on the rejectioi pressive tradition. I have argued that however radically indi other avant-gardes might be, the American avant-garde ci community that values novelty and experimentation, but that norms of film construction and comprehension that make n periments meaningful. In no way does such a move "de-po! the American avant-garde cinema. It suggests only that we ɛ the simplistic radicalism of avant-gardism for a more sut nuanced vision of the avant-garde's communal interests. I reaɫ this analogy may seem somewhat peculiar—the avant-garde cinema is certainly not the kind of community that communitarian theorists have in mind. Nevertheless, attention to the functioning of the avant-garde cinema as a community is a productive approach to understanding the political aspirations of avant-garde cinema, as well as to understanding the evolution of its formal conventions.

There are certainly precedents for "communitarian" views of the avant-garde. Dana Polan's *The Political Language of Film and the Avant-garde* argues that the avant-garde film is framed by a coherent political rhetoric (which Polan finds inadequate in certain key ways).

In *Points of Resistance*, Lauren Rabinowitz traces the evolution of a community of women filmmakers within the larger New York avant-garde film world. I would even include Sitney's *Visionary Film*: it is communitarian in that it is not concerned so much with the "avant-gardeness" of this cinema as it is with laying out some of its main thematic concerns and formal practices. *Dreams of Chaos, Visions of Order* is meant to extend this work by showing how the formal practices and critical rhetoric of the avant-garde cinema both exploit and are influenced by the cognitive capacities of its viewers.

While I certainly do not want to overstate the negativity of scholarship of the avant-garde cinema, I do not want to underestimate the importance or the longevity of the total liberation approach either. In chapter 1, I cited Sheldon Renan's 1967 definition of the avant-garde as an "explosion of cinematic styles, forms and directions." Two decades later, in the twentieth anniversary issue of *Millennium Film Journal* (1986), Fred Camper published a savage critique of contemporary avant-garde filmmaking, which is, he thinks, in a hopelessly derivative and lifeless "institutional" phase. But the genuine, "individual" avant-garde, according to Camper, is "fundamentally anarchic." Even more recently, William Wees's *Light Moving in Time* (1992) mounted a spirited and sophisticated defense of the liberation theory of avant-garde cinema. Wees makes Brakhage's "unruled eye" its central trope, and argues for its validity by appealing to the history of theories of vision and to contemporary research on perception. These metaphors of chaos and disorder—Renan's "explosion," Camper's "anarchy," Brakhage's "unruled eye"—are so durable because advocates and detractors alike think the avant-garde cinema is, in some fundamental way, uninhibited, unrestrained and uncontrolled.

In gloomy moods, I sometimes think the term "avant-garde" is spectacularly ill-chosen for this mode of filmmaking. For a cinema so concerned with opposition and liberation, it is ironic that of all its potential labels—independent, experimental, underground—it was the term with the cachet of aesthetic legitimacy and prestige that stuck. And as I suggested in chapter 1, the notion of the avant-garde as an aesthetic of rejection makes it particularly difficult to conceptualize the activity of the viewer. Nevertheless, the term avant-garde does properly link these films to strains of Modern art and to elements of Romanticism. The term also quite properly suggests that the *aspiration* to radical liberation—whether it takes the apparently chaotic form of Brakhage's work, or the exceedingly ordered form found in the work of Frampton—is part of the complex of values shared by this community of filmmakers.

Still, the term "avant-garde" has an inescapable danger, which I hope this book has done something to contain. "Avant-garde" is a military metaphor—it refers literally to a first wave of troops, who weaken the enemy for those that follow. Applied to aesthetics, the avant-garde metaphor suggests that art is a constant battle with a repressive tradition, and that revolt is the motor of historical change. As Jan Mukarovsky once put it, "the history of art is the history of revolt against reigning norms."

But this does not ring true for the American avant-garde cinema—at least not always. We like to think of Warhol's early films as overthrowing the norm of the poetic film as practiced by Brakhage, Baillie and others. But once minimal filmmaking was established as a significant strain of American avant-garde filmmaking, it was refined and elaborated for a decade. And when filmmakers revolted against the minimal strain, the revolt often took the shape of a return to older forms of avant-garde work, particularly the film poem and the assemblage strain. The American avant-garde community trumpets the ideal of aesthetic revolution, but lives a reality of refinement and revision. Thus, although the term ''avant-garde'' may be the product of a reasonable compromise, using it always risks misdescribing this cinema's history, which is sometimes better understood as a shared idiom of film language, or even as a craft passed from one generation of artists to the next.

These concluding comments should not be taken as another sign of the end of the avant-garde cinema—my aim has been to demonstrate its continuing vitality. My communitarian analogy is meant only to refine our conception of the cinema we have lately—for the last couple of decades—been calling avant-garde. We will want to preserve the notion that this is in some sense an oppositional cinema, and that these films are challenging in many ways. We can even continue to think of the avant-garde cinema as explosive, or anarchic, or unruled, so long as we recognize that this chaos has all along been bounded by norms of film construction and comprehension that make it meaningful.

NOTES

Chapter 1

1. For examples of the valorization of the avant-garde film because it requires an active viewer, see McCall and Tyndall (1978, 32), Cornwell (1972, 111), and Le Grice (1977, 90).
2. For examples, see Drummond (1979) and Hanhardt (1976).
3. Compare, for example, Renan's account of the Kuchars to MacDonald's in *A Critical Cinema*.
4. See especially Cornwell (1979b).
5. Examples could fill pages; one of the most notable exchanges occurred between Carroll and Stephen Heath in the pages of *October*. Carroll's side of the debate grew into *Mystifying Movies* (1988), an extended, detailed attack on psychoanalytic semiotics.
6. However, the assemblage strain may be growing in prominence: in the fall of 1992, the VIPER Film and Video Festival in Lucerne, Switzerland, mounted a four-part exhibition of avant-garde found-footage films. See the exhibition catalog, *Found Footage Film* (1992).

Chapter 2

1. For an account of the development of cognitive psychology and related fields, as well as an overview of some of its major issues, see Gardner (1985).
2. The most significant alternative to the Constructivist view of perception is the "ecological" approach advocated by J. J. Gibson. Gibson argues that the real world, as opposed to the artificially limited world of the laboratory, is so rich in perceptual information that the perceiver does not have to engage in such problem-solving procedures. However, following an argument suggested by Bordwell (1985), we are not actually concerned with perception in the real world, but with perception in the artificially limited world of the cinema. Particularly in the avant-garde, filmmakers can exploit the limitations of the film image for startling perceptual effects.

3. I am using "top-down" as John Anderson (1980, 43–44) and Irvin Rock (1983, 12) do. Processing is top-down to the extent that it is affected by memory, knowledge or context. Jerry Fodor uses the term in a slightly different sense. For Fodor (1983), bottom-up processing is mandatory, whereas top-down processing allows the perceiver some choice in how to process sense data. Thus Fodor would consider the perception of optical illusions (such as the illusory contour effect of figure 2.1) bottom-up processing because the visual system cannot help but perceive them. Rock would consider such processing to have a top-down component to the extent it relies on knowledge about physical objects in the world.
4. The perception of temperature is not always exclusively bottom-up, however, as a simple experiment suggests. The subject's hands are placed in separate buckets of water, one hot and the other cold. After a few moments, the subject's hands are moved to a single bucket of lukewarm water, which feels cold to one hand and hot to the other.
5. This research is reviewed in Glass and Holyoak (1986, 429–31).
6. Schemata and related concepts are reviewed in Tannen (1979, 137–44).
7. For an overview of research on discourse processing, see van Dijk and Kintsch (1983). For a brief introduction to discourse processing that concentrates specifically on literature, see van Dijk (1979). For additional surveys, and a number of essays on the processing of literary narratives, see *Poetics* 9 (1980), a special issue on story comprehension.
8. When speaking of discourse processing, since film is a kind of discourse, I ought to say "readers or viewers." For convenience the term "reader" will stand for both. When speaking specifically about films, I'll use the term "viewer."
9. Bordwell and Rick Altman have contested this point over the years. See especially Altman (1989).

10. For example, see Le Grice's treatment (1977, 78–80) of the Whitneys's work as a forebear of the self-conscious exploration of the film material.

11. The most thorough analysis of the image in the context of the avant-garde film is in Maureen Turim's *Abstraction in Avant-garde Films* (1985). For an analysis of the extent to which images in avant-garde films defy reading, see chapter 2, "Beyond Reading: Image, Imagination, Aesthetic Economies at Play." Gregory Taylor (1991) takes another fruitful approach to the analysis of abstraction in his analysis of Sidney Peterson's *The Lead Shoes*.

12. Husserl's phenomenological exploration of how the mind structures experience is more and more seen as an anticipation of contemporary cognitive science. The connection between Husserl and cognitive science is examined in the collection of essays in Dreyfus (1982). Chapter 6, "Husserl's Theory of Perception," makes clear the similarities between Husserl's work and constructivist theories of perception such as Niesser's.

13. See Sinnott (1989) on approaches to ill-formed problems. The ground-breaking works in practical problem solving are Johnson-Laird (1983) and Kahneman, Slovic and Tversky (1982).

14. Scott MacDonald (1988) cites this ideal, as does Bruce Conner in an interview with MacDonald (1982).

15. In *Radical Pragmatics* (Cole, 1981) this argument is advanced by both philosophers and linguists. For an extended treatment of such a view, see Sperber and Wilson (1986).

16. My rudimentary account of pragmatics is modelled on Leech (1983).

17. *Artforum* even published a five-page photo essay on filmmaker and assemblage artist Bruce Conner making a sandwich (Garver, 1967). Though the level of irony here is hard to judge, I suspect that the photo essay was largely meant to parody conceptual art and such interest in the everyday activities of artists.

18. David James nicely sums up the irony implicit in Gidal's work: "Despite its Puritan urgency, Gidal's position ultimately consumed itself, for even as it discredited all previous film production, it supplied the grounds for its own discrediting" (1989, 279).

Chapter 3

1. See, for example, Youngblood (1970).

2. My use of the term "mode" follows Bordwell, Staiger and Thompson (1985, xii–xiv) and Bordwell (1985, 150).

3. One notable exception is the 1964 Ford Foundation grants of $10,000 each to a dozen filmmakers, including Kenneth Anger, Jordan Belson, Bruce Conner, Ed Emshwiller and Stan Vanderbeek ("In the Year of Our Ford," 1964).

4. For an analysis of the institutions of the American avant-garde cinema see Ruoff (1991).

5. For an insightful analysis of the limits of Brakhage's engagement with the political realm, see James (1989, 49–57).

6. Though, like many, I find this argument less persuasive when it is applied to the avant-garde's Minimal strain.

7. For a more complete discussion of the tacit inferences demanded by editing, see Carroll (1979).

8. The concept of radical metonymy is an adaptation of Max Black's concept, radical metaphor.

9. Sitney interprets this image, along with a shot of the woman's fingers, as representing the woman's masturbation. This interpretation is certainly plausible. But my intention is not to arrive at a single correct reading, but to show that this radical metaphor forces metaphorical interpretations into play in *any* interpretation of the film.

10. Carroll (1981–82) suggests some refinements on this idea with regard to movement.

11. See the chapter titled "The Lyrical Film" in Sitney (1979, 136–72) and the discussion of associational form in Bordwell and Thompson (1993, 127–39).

12. This notion follows van Dijk's (1979) treatment of poetic discourse.

13. For an analysis of Warren Sonbert's *Rude Awakening* as "fuguelike," as well as a useful brief discussion of musical analogies to film, see Carroll (1981–82, 75).

Chapter 4

1. It would be useful to distinguish between two broad tendencies within Abstract Expressionism, what can be called "Action Painting" and "color field painting." The action painters—notably Jackson Pollock, Franz Kline, and Willem de Kooning—produce work that is more energetic, gestural and sometimes somewhat figurative. The work of the color field painters—for example, Mark Rothko and Barnet Newman—is more tranquil and more purely abstract. The Abstract Expressionists compared to Brakhage are almost always the Action Painters, though most critics of the avant-garde film do not distinguish between the two types of Abstract Expressionist work.

2. See Osborn (1966, 67). Osborn's honor role of "serious" filmmakers with the Film-makers' Co-op consisted of Lewis Jacobs, Kenneth Anger, Bruce Baillie,

Bruce Conner, Ed Emshwiller, Hilary Harris, Stan Vanderbeek and Jonas Mekas. Brakhage is conspicuously absent from the article.

3. See Mancia and Van Dyke on Len Lye (1966); and on the work of Robert Breer, Carmen D'Avino, Ed Emshwiller and Stan Vanderbeek (1967).

4. In *The Painted Word* (1975), Tom Wolfe makes this point rather smugly, as if he were the only one with the courage to say it. For a more thorough account of the early trials of the Abstract Expressionists, see Guilbaut (1983).

5. Rosenberg's notion was at once taken up and widely used, but both Hilton Kramer (1953) and Clement Greenberg (1962) attacked it.

6. Brakhage's working methods may have come a bit closer to those of the Abstract Expressionists in his hand-painted films of the late 1980s. In these films, such as *The Dante Quartet* (1987), Brakhage paints directly on the larger size 70mm and IMAX filmstock, instead of the 16mm film used in his earlier hand-painted work. Of course, even the 2-inch wide 70mm frame is still vastly smaller than the monumental scale of the Abstract Expressionist canvas, and therefore requires very different working methods. In parts of *The Dante Quartet*, Brakhage also uses optical printing to briefly hold some of the hand-painted frames on screen. Thus, instead of seeing the images flash by at the frenetic pace of twenty-four per second, the viewer can actually examine some of the beautifully painted frames for a moment. The space of *The Dante Quartet* is certainly closer to that of the Abstract Expressionists than any of his work of the 1950s or 1960s, but there remain such enormous differences in scale, working methods and presentational form that any such comparisons should be met with extreme skepticism.

Chapter 5

1. Warhol's entrance to the film scene was aided by Jonas Mekas, founder of the Film-makers' Co-op, impresario of the Film-makers' Cinematheque, and publisher of *Film Culture*, at that time the only journal devoting significant space to the avant-garde film. The screenings at the Film-makers' Cinematheque were open to anyone who wished to show his or her work, but Mekas gave Warhol special attention. He lauded Warhol's work in his column in the *Village Voice* and helped him with the technical details of cinematography.

In announcing the award in *Film Culture* (1964), Mekas discreetly did not mention *Blow Job* (1963), a thirty-minute close-up on a man's face while he is sexually serviced off-screen, but he nonetheless lauded Warhol's work as a new height in honesty and realism.

2. Of course, interest in film on the part of painters and sculptors was hardly unprecedented. See, for example, Standish Lawder's (1975) account of the film experiments of early Modernist painters.

3. The controversy surrounding "Structural Film" began shortly after the first version was published. George Maciunas's negative comments on the piece were printed in *Film Culture Reader* (1970, 349). The controversy continued for at least a decade and a half; as late as 1984, David Ehrenstein devoted considerable space to disputing Sitney in his *Film: The Frontline 1984* (1984).

4. "Structural Film" was revised and reprinted in *Film Culture Reader*, and revised yet again for Sitney's *Visionary Film: The American Avant-garde* (page references to "Structural Film" will be to *Visionary Film*, 2nd ed.). Sitney also discussed Structural film in "The Idea of Morphology" (1972) and in a lecture at the Museum of Modern Art in 1971, published as "The Idea of Abstraction" (1976).

5. Maciunas (1970) criticized Sitney for omitting the Fluxus artists, and Malcolm Le Grice (1977) emphasized the Europeans.

6. See Maciunas (1970); Cornwell (1972; 1979b); and Arthur (1978).

7. See especially Jenkins (1981, 9–14).

8. Having criticized Sitney's definition in 1979, Cornwell used it with only minor qualifications two years later in *Films by American Artists* (1981).

9. On Michelson's analysis of Eisenstein, see Taylor (1992); on her analysis of Brakhage, see Peterson (1986b, 66–72).

10. My pointing out Snow's contribution to Michelson's argument should in no way be construed as a criticism. I mean only to describe a feature of the avant-garde mode of cinema: filmmakers make their ideas available to critics, who give filmmakers' views of their own films a rather privileged position.

11. In "Toward Snow" (1971) Michelson recommends an essay Sitney wrote for an exhibition of Snow's films and artworks (collected in Snow 1970b). In *Visionary Film* Sitney cites Michelson's "Toward Snow."

12. Seeing the artwork as a critique of illusion is one of the most familiar, and too often one of the most facile, means of interpreting the art of the 1960s. But Michelson's more sophisticated analysis does credit to Meyer Schapiro, with whom she studied art history in the 1950s. For Schapiro, the work of art always had political implications, but he never pointed them out in a simplistic or doctrinaire manner. For example, in his essay on the Abstract Expressionists (1957),

Schapiro argues that abstract art is capable of rendering a new and different range of human emotions. The Western tradition of representation had set "a particular standard of decorum or restraint in expression which had excluded certain domains and intensities of feeling." Though the Abstract Expressionists had not rejected past art because it was repressive, by turning away from this tradition "the notion of the humanity of art was immensely widened" (217). In Michelson's analysis of Snow (1971), Schapiro's lessons have been filtered through her interest in phenomenology and her experience of the French intellectual scene of the late 1950s and early 1960s. Nevertheless, Schapiro's confidence in the political relevance of abstract art remains evident in Michelson's work.

13. Rosenberg himself made the connection between his Action Painting theory and later "Process" Art. In both cases the object produced is interpreted as less important than the process that produced it. See Rosenberg (1972, 29, 59).

14. For an extended defense of Greenberg against the charges of essentialism and reductionism, see Kuspit (1979).

15. For more thorough analysis of Gidal's theory, see Rodowick (1983, 163–88).

16. The ideological roots of Renaissance perspective were pointed out by art historian Pierre Francastel. Marcelin Pleynet applied the notion to film in Gérard Leblanc's 1969 Cinéthique interview with Pleynet and Jean Thibaudeau. See also Jean-Louis Comolli's four-part "Technique and Ideology," especially part one, "Camera, Perspective and Depth of Field."

17. The anti-illusion schema plays a slightly more prominent role in Bershen's claim that sound cinema's twenty-four fps speed is the root cause of Frampton's twenty-four-unit structure. This notion is actually quite close to Greenbergian critic Michael Fried's notion of *deductive structure* (1964, 1966). According to Fried, the essential conditions of a medium do not dictate any particular sort of imagery. But the imagery may be *derived* from these conditions. In painting, for example, the composition may be based on the shape of the support, as in the work of Frank Stella (coincidentally, a long-time friend of Frampton's). The artist does not relinquish any control over the imagery, as the art-process schema suggests, but the features of the medium, and not some inner trauma, motivate his or her choices.

The anti-illusion schema has been more directly applied to *Zorn's Lemma*. A year later, writing in the British journal *Art and Artists*, Simon Field reiterated many of Bershen's points, but went further in the interpretation of the film's representation of space.

Of the film's last shot, he wrote: "this last shot is a neat summing up of the nature of the three dimensional illusion, and its use in cinema. . . . [after the figures] have disappeared into the woods the image without figures appears flatter, when the screen gradually goes white the direction towards flatness is extended. We are brought finally up against the screen as a two dimensional surface, cinema as a three dimensional illusion" (1972, 25).

18. The Latin alphabet had twenty-one letters until the first century B.C., after which it had twenty-three. "J" and "V" were added in the middle ages (bringing the total to twenty-five) and "W" was added some time later.

It is also an oversimplification to say that *Zorn's Lemma* uses the alphabet of *The Bay State Primer*, a section of which is recited at the beginning of the film. This section of the primer consists of twenty-four little pictures each with a rhymed couplet meant to teach a letter of the alphabet and, in some cases, a moral lesson. The first couplet, for example, is "In Adam's Fall, We sinned All." Because of the vagaries of spelling and typography in colonial America, there is no couplet for "I" or "V." Depending on the typeface, the year, the printer's style, and the letter's position in the word, "I" and "J" were sometimes interchanged, as were "V" and "U." Frampton exploits this feature of colonial orthography by making "I" and "J," and "V" and "U" interchangeable in the structure of *Zorn's Lemma*; this gives him a twenty-four-unit alphabetical structure that matches the conventional twenty-four fps shooting speed. But this is not to say that Frampton uses "the" alphabet from *The Bay State Primer*: in one section or another, the primer uses all twenty-six letters of the modern English alphabet, plus additional characters now obsolete.

Though Frampton adapted the primer's alphabet to suit his own needs, we ought not minimize the little book's influence on *Zorn's Lemma*. If anything, this influence has been underestimated. Like *Zorn's Lemma*, the primer includes the alphabetical couplets and a listing of the alphabet. But there is also a most striking parallel with the long central section of *Zorn's Lemma*, the 109 cycles of the alphabetical word lists. In the primer there is a shorter but similar series of alphabetical word lists, which children used to practice reading and pronunciation. The first list is of one-syllable words; the second has two-syllable words; and so on up to five- or six-syllable words. And following the alphabetical material in the primer was a catechism, which might be considered parallel to the mystical text read in the final section of the film.

Incidentally, *The Bay State Primer* is one of a number of obscure versions of *The New England Primer* first published by Benjamin Harris sometime between 1687 and 1690. Since Harris's primer was unprotected by copyright law, it was freely reprinted, occasionally under alternative titles, but usually with only minor changes. *The New England Primer*, in its various guises, was enormously popular. One historian estimates that between its first edition and the middle of the nineteenth century, three million copies were sold (Ford, 1962).

Chapter 6

1. See William Wees's analysis of the perception of Paul Sharits's flicker films (1992, 146–52).
2. According to Cobbing (1970), the term was invented in 1953 by the Swedish poet and artist Oyvind Fahlstrom.
3. For surveys of Concrete Poetry, see essays by de Campos (1956), de Vree (1970) and Waldrop (1976) and those collected in Kostelanetz (1982).
4. De Campos dismissed this type of poem as simplistic in 1956 (1982, 263).
5. From Williams (1967). The original begins: "les-bares in unlesbares übersetzen."
6. The names in the bottom half of the poem are the members of OuLiPo: FLL is François Le Lionnais; RQ is Raymond Queneau.
7. For a more complete discussion of *Alphabetical Africa* along these lines, see my "The Artful Mathematicians of the Avant-Garde" (1985).
8. The numerical/permutational distinction is also relevant to simple schematic works in other media. Mathews's "Liminal Poem" is numerical; LeWitt's *Serial Project No. 1* is permutational. Many of the claims I make about the spectator's response to types of simple schemata in film can be adapted to works in other media. Again, I direct your attention to my analysis of Abish's *Alphabetical Africa* in "The Artful Mathematicians of the Avant-garde."
9. The concept of spatial form in literature is reviewed in Spencer (1984).
10. Explaining the viewer's comprehension of the simple permutational schema film as the hypothesizing of the film's set of possible features is similar to David Bordwell's explanation of the viewer's comprehension of what he calls parametric film, a kind of narrative in which style is carefully patterned independent of the demands of the story (1985, 274–310). Both the parametric film and the permutational schema film ask viewers to "spatialize" their form in some way, but there are important differences in how this is accomplished. One of the most important differences involves the prominence of the features viewers are supposed to spatialize. Bordwell's parametric film is still narrative, however prominent style might be. Consequently, viewers must divide their effort between perceiving these stylistic patterns and constructing the story. On the other hand, in the simple schematic film, limited prototype matching frees the viewer to concentrate on the perception of the global template schemata. The major difference, however, is probably the function this spatialization serves in the viewer's efforts to comprehend the film. Bordwell emphasizes the spatialization of the film's conceptual space as a means of demonstrating the prominence of stylistic devices. My analysis appeals to the idea that spatialization is a common feature of mental representation that makes perception and memory more efficient. For me, the concept of spatialization helps distinguish between the comprehension of various types of simple schematic film.
11. *Zorn's Lemma*'s modified alphabet, derived from *The Bay State Primer,* is discussed in note 18 of chapter 5.
12. According to Charron (1990), Frampton's description of Webern's later work is generally accurate, but misses some details. Webern's row in which the last six notes are the retrograde inversion of the first six is called a *de*generative row.
13. This example was given in Charron (1990, 9).
14. Though the film is explicitly Webernian, Frampton's use of found material also suggests the film's debt to the aesthetics of John Cage.
15. The description of these permutations is from Frampton's description of the film in the interview with MacDonald (1980, 122–23).
16. Perhaps by "phrase," Frampton means something other than what I have been calling "cell," but it is unclear what else in the film "phrase" might refer to.
17. The film picks up an extra four seconds because the very first and the very last image of the film are held for seventy-two frames, not the twenty-four frames of every other image in the film. Also, one of the cells is ninety-five frames long, not ninety-six like the others. This does not affect the symmetry of the film, since each cell appears the same number of times in the first half of the film as in the second. There are, however, four unbalanced black frames scattered throughout the first half of the film.
18. Scott MacDonald (1988) told Frampton that he had been unable to discover the structure of *Palindrome* even though he had looked at it on an editing table. Frampton did not seem bothered by this and suggested that the film gives the viewer a sense of being carefully structured even if the structure itself is not evident.
19. This description is from Sitney (1978, 438).

Chapter 7

1. There are now some notable exceptions. David James includes a section on what he calls "Underground Intertextuality" in his *Allegories of Cinema* (1989, 140–65) that includes some examples of the assemblage strain (as well as some other kinds of films). In the fall of 1992, the VIPER film and video festival of Lucerne, Switzerland, mounted a major retrospective of assemblage filmmaking (see the exhibition catalog, *Found Footage Film* [Hausheer and Settele 1992]). And as of this writing, William Wees is working on an exhaustive study of the use of found footage in the avant-garde film.

2. Max Kozloff, Clement Greenberg, John Canaday, Dore Ashton, Irving Sandler, Hilton Kramer and Thomas Hess all criticized Pop in its early days.

3. Leo Steinberg's detailed analysis (1962) of the spatial construction of Jasper Johns's work provided an early exemplar for critics interested in the formal analysis of works with Pop iconography. Steinberg pointed out that Johns invariably chose flat subjects (see Fig. 6.7). This decision "placed him at a point outside the crowded room, whence one suddenly saw how Franz Kline bundles with Watteau and Giotto. For they were all artists who use paint and surface to suggest existences other than surface and paint" (1972, 42). Once again, we encounter the anti-illusion tactic, albeit with a twist that allowed Steinberg to distinguish himself from Greenberg. Johns has created a new kind of space, Steinberg concludes, but not one that is simply flatter than previous art, as an orthodox Greenbergian reading would suggest. Instead, Johns's space is the opposite of that of the early Modernist art. Cezanne had used loose, obvious brushwork to flatten his subjects, which viewers knew to be three-dimensional. Johns uses loose brushwork to suggest an atmospheric space in the rendering of subjects viewers know to be flat.

4. Ron Padgett (1964), Gerard Melanga (1964) and Ted Berrigan (1964).

5. Of course in the *Visionary Film* version of "Structural Film" the difference in psychologies is clear enough: Minimalism is concerned with the examination of the medium; Structural film is an attempt to represent human consciousness, the aspiration of the Romantic strain of the avant-garde cinema.

6. Koch's analysis of Warhol's impassive camerawork was clearly an innovative view of Warhol's early cinema. One way to understand Koch's innovation is to see his interpretation as an application of the poetic strain's "style-as-consciousness" heuristic (see pp. 37–40) to the minimal strain. Sitney happily accepts Koch's interpretation, since it helps Sitney relate the

minimal strain to the Romantic trajectory started in the Poetic avant-garde film.

Chapter 8

1. The term "assemblage" is sometimes distinguished from "collage." In this usage, assemblage refers to three-dimensional collections of found materials (in other words, sculpture) whereas collages are two-dimensional. Here I use assemblage as the umbrella term for any collection of found material, whether traditional flat collages or sculpture.

2. Victor Faccinto has produced an interesting body of work that is related to collage animation. In his "Video Vic" series (1970–74), Faccinto animates paper cutouts, but the cutouts are his own painted and drawn creations, not newspaper and magazine images. Of course, Faccinto uses many of the techniques I discuss here, but since he can paint or draw whatever he wants rather than making do with found material, he does not confront the assemblage aesthetic as the collage animator does.

3. Annette and her friend are discussed in Parsons's study of the development of aesthetic experience (1987).

4. Throughout this book I have tried to avoid gender-exclusive language. But I have yet to find an apt or elegant substitute for "craftsmanship," so I have stuck with this unfortunate term.

5. For interesting analyses of the Kuchars along these lines, see James's section entitled "The Critique of Authenticity" in his *Allegories of Cinema* (1989, 143–49), and MacDonald (1988, 297–302). For one of the few discussions of craft in the context of highly polished avant-garde films, see Paul Arthur's essay on Los Angeles filmmaking (1982).

6. These theories of metaphor are reviewed in Ortony, et. al. (1978).

7. See Tversky (1977). Tversky's research is reviewed in Glass and Holyoak (1986, 348).

8. Wees's ever-expanding catalog lists 148 filmmakers as of July 1992.

9. A preoccupation with death and sexuality also inflects the films of Christopher Maclaine, who, like Berman, associated with San Francisco's Beat poets. Maclaine's films appeal to the assemblage aesthetic, even though they do not use found footage. Since he was never securely employed, he lived hand-to-mouth and financed his films on a shoestring. As a result, *The End* (1953) and *The Man Who Invented Gold* (1957) look almost like compilation films because they were shot on a variety of film stocks under a variety of conditions. This look is enhanced by Maclaine's emphasis on and experimentation with

editing, making his episodic narrative films very disjointed. According to Conner, he saw Maclaine's work the year before he made *A Movie* (letter from Conner to the author, 25 May 1986). For an analysis of Maclaine's editing style, see J. J. Murphy (1983).

10. The flexibility of the conceptual space of the compilation narrative recalls Frampton's insightful observation about the narrative elements in Brakhage's work:

> "BRAKHAGE'S THEOREM: For any finite series of shots ["film"] whatsoever there exists in real time a rational narrative, such that every term in the series, together with its position, duration, partition and reference, shall be perfectly and entirely accounted for" (1972).

11. The San Francisco Mime Troupe's production is documented by R. G. Davis (1964, 36–39).

Afterword

1. James Hoberman (1984), Noël Carroll (1985) and Paul Arthur (1986–87) have written useful overviews of the avant-garde's New Narrative.

2. As Paul Arthur (1986–87) put it: "Pockets of narrative inventiveness have persisted in periods of the most adamant formalism and anti-industry rhetoric. . . . [T]here are enough possible progenitors for the current trend to form their own avant-garde counter-history" (82–83). As exemplary figures in this counter-history, Arthur cites Richard Myers, Paul Bartel, Jim McBride, James Broughton, Steve Dwoskin, Storm de Hirsch, and Walter Gutman.

3. I am not using "liberal" in its contemporary sense, in which it refers to the left side of the American political spectrum. The tradition of classical liberalism undergirds elements of both the right and the left of American politics. It supplies the rationale for both the contemporary liberal's broad interpretation of the First Amendment, as well as the more typically conservative view that the size of government should be severely restricted.

4. Among the central texts of communitarianism are Alasdair C. MacIntyre's *After Virtue: A Study in Moral Theory* (1981), Michael J. Sandel's *Liberalism and the Limits of Justice* (1982), and Michael Walzer's *Spheres of Justice: A Defense of Pluralism and Equality* (1983). For a more concise exposition of some basic communitarian arguments, see Charles Taylor's "Atomism" and "What's Wrong with Negative Liberty."

5. But for more intractable critics of liberalism, such as Alasdair MacIntyre, the notion of the good implicit in classical liberalism, even if it were spelled out, is meager and morally bankrupt.

REFERENCES

Alexander, Thomas Kent. "San Francisco's Hipster Cinema." *Film Culture* 44 (1967): 70–74.

Alloway, Lawrence. *American Pop Art*. Exhibition catalog. New York: Collier/Whitney Museum of American Art, 1974.

———. "Background to Systemic." *Art News* 65.6 (Oct. 1966): 30–33.

———. *Network: Art and the Complex Present*. Ann Arbor, MI: UMI Research Press, 1984.

———. "Sol LeWitt: Modules, Walls, Books." *Artforum* 13.8 (Apr. 1975): 38–44.

———. "Systemic Painting." Introductory essay in *Systemic Painting* (exhibition catalog). Solomon R. Guggenheim Museum. New York: Solomon R. Guggenheim Foundation, 1966. Rpt. in *Minimal Art*, ed. Gregory Battcock, 37–60. New York: Dutton, 1968.

Altman, Rick. "Dickens, Griffith, and Film Theory Today." *South Atlantic Quarterly* 88.2 (Spring 1989): 321–59.

American Federation of Arts. *A History of the American Avant-Garde Cinema*. New York: American Federation of Arts, 1976.

Anderson, John R. *Cognitive Psychology and Its Implications*. San Francisco: Freeman, 1980.

Anderson, Phil. "Four Films by Bruce Conner: A Review." *Afterimage* 6.1/2 (Summer 1978): 34–35.

Arnheim, Rudolf. "Perceiving and Portraying." *Times Literary Supplement*, no. 4152 (29 Oct. 1982): 1179–80.

Arthur, Paul. "The Last of the Machine?: Avant-garde Film Since 1966." *Millennium Film Journal* 16/17/18 (Fall/Winter 1986–87): 69–97.

———. "Structural Film: Revisions, New Versions, and the Artifact." *Millennium Film Journal* 1.2 (Spring/Summer 1978): 5–13; 1.4/5 (Summer/Fall 1979): 122–34.

———. "The Western Edge: Oil of L. A. and the Machined Image." *Millennium Film Journal* 12 (Fall/Winter 1982–83): 8–28.

Baker, Kenneth. "Keith Sonnier at the Modern." *Artforum* 10.2 (Oct. 1971): 77–81.

Baldwin, Carl R. "On the Nature of Pop." *Artforum* 12.10 (June 1974): 34–38.

Bannard, Darby. "Present-Day Art and Ready-Made Styles: In which the Formal Contribution of Pop Art Is Found to Be Negligible." *Artforum* 5.4 (Dec. 1966): 30–35.

Bannon, Anthony. "Albright-Knox Art Gallery Cinema Artist Adroitly Dabbles in Chemistry of Film Imagery." *Buffalo Evening News* 20 Oct. 1977.

Barthes, Roland. "Introduction to the Structural Analysis of Narratives." In *Image—Music—Text*, trans. Stephen Heath, 79–124. New York: Hill and Wang, 1977.

———. *Mythologies*. Trans. and selected by Annette Lavers, from 1957 and 1970 editions (Paris: Editions du Seuil). New York: Hill and Wang, 1972.

———. *S/Z*. Trans. Richard Miller. New York: Hill and Wang, 1974.

Bartlett, Frederic Charles. *Remembering: A Study in Experimental and Social Psychology*. Cambridge: Cambridge University Press, 1950.

Bartone, Richard. "The Forms of Repetition: Larry Gottheim's *Four Shadows*." *Millennium Film Journal* 4/5 (Summer/Fall 1979): 167–71.

Bass, Warren. "The Past Restructured: Bruce Conner and Others." *Journal of the University Film Association* 33.2 (Spring 1981): 15–22.

Battcock, Gregory. "Notes on *Blow Job*: A Film by Andy Warhol." *Film Culture* 37 (1965a): 20–21.

———. "Notes on *Empire*: A Film by Andy Warhol." *Film Culture* 40 (1966): 39.

———. "Notes on *Screen Test*: A Film by Andy Warhol." *Film Culture* 38 (1965b): 62–63.

———. "Superstar-Superset." *Film Culture* 45 (1967): 23–26.

———, ed. *Minimal Art: A Critical Anthology*. New York: Dutton, 1968.

———, ed. *The New American Cinema: A Critical Anthology*. New York: Dutton, 1967.

———, ed. *The New Art*. New York: Dutton, 1966.

Baudry, Jean Louis. "Ideological Effects of the Basic Apparatus." In *Movies and Methods*, Vol. 2, ed. Bill Nichols, 531–42. Los Angeles: University of California Press, 1985. (Originally "Cinéma: Effects Idéologiques Produit par l'Appareil de Base." *Cinéthique* 7/8 [1970]: 1–8.)

Beltz, Carl I. "Three Films by Bruce Conner." *Film Culture* 44 (1967): 56–59.

Benjamin, Jerry. "On Working at Andy Warhol's 'Factory.'" *Film Culture* 40 (1966): 40.

Bennett, Tony. "Text and Social Process: The Case of James Bond." *Screen Education* 41 (Winter/ Spring 1982): 3–14.

———. "Texts, Readers, Reading Formations." *PMLA* 16.1 (Spring 1983): 3–17.

Bennett, Tony, and Janet Woollacott. *Bond and Beyond: The Political Career of a Popular Hero*. New York: Methuen, 1987.

Berrigan, Ted. "The Upper Arm: For Andy Warhol." *Film Culture* 32 (1964): 14.

Bershen, Wanda. "*Zorn's Lemma*." *Artforum* 9.1 (Sept. 1971): 41–45.

Betsch, Carolyn. "A Catalogue Raisonné of Warhol's Gestures." *Art in America* 59.3 (May/June 1971): 47.

Billow, R. "Metaphor: A Review of the Psychological Literature." *Psychological Bulletin* 84 (1977): 81–92.

Black, John B., and Robert Wilensky. "An Evaluation of Story Grammars." *Cognitive Science* 3 (1979): 213–30.

Bloom, Harold. *The Visionary Company: A Reading of English Romantic Poetry*. Ithaca, NY: Cornell University Press, 1961.

Bochner, Mel. "Serial Art (Systems: Solipsism)." *Arts Magazine* 41.8 (Summer 1967): 39–43. Rpt. in *Minimal Art*, ed. Gregory Battcock, 92–102. New York: Dutton, 1968.

———. "The Serial Attitude." *Artforum* 6.4 (Dec. 1967): 28–33.

Bordwell, David. "The Art Cinema as a Mode of Film Practice." *Film Criticism* 4.1 (Fall 1979): 56–64.

———. "A Case for Cognitivism." *Iris* 9 (1989): 11–40.

———. *Making Meaning: Inference and Rhetoric in the Interpretation of Cinema*. Cambridge, MA: Harvard University Press, 1989.

———. *Narration in the Fiction Film*. Madison: University of Wisconsin Press, 1985.

Bordwell, David, Janet Staiger, and Kristin Thompson.

The Classical Hollywood Cinema: Film Style and Mode of Production to 1960. New York: Columbia University Press, 1985.

Bordwell, David, and Kristin Thompson. *Film Art: An Introduction*. 4th ed. New York: McGraw-Hill, 1993.

Boultenhouse, Charles. "Pioneer of the Abstract Expressionist Film." *Filmwise* 1 (1961): 26–27.

Bourdon, David. "Warhol as Filmmaker." *Art in America* 59.3 (May/June 1971): 48–53.

Brainard, Joe. "Andy Warhol's Sleep Movie." *Film Culture* 32 (1964): 12.

Brakhage, Stan. *The Brakhage Lectures*. Chicago: Good Lion, 1972.

———. "The Silent Sound Sense." *Film Culture* 21 (1960): 65–68.

———. *Brakhage Scrapbook: Collected Writings 1964–80*. New Paltz, NY: Documentext, 1982.

———. *Metaphors on Vision*. 2d ed. New York: Film Culture, 1976. Originally published as *Film Culture* 30 (1963).

Bremer, Claus. *Ideogramme*, Frauenfeld, Switzerland: Eugen Gomringer Press, 1964.

Brown, Robert K. "Interview with Bruce Conner." *Film Culture* 33 (1964): 15–16.

Bruner, Jerome. "On Perceptual Readiness." *Psychological Review* 64 (1957): 123–52.

Buchsbaum, Jonathan. "Canvassing the Midwest." *Millennium Film Journal* 7/8/9 (Fall/Winter 1980–81): 218–29.

———. "Composing for Film: The Work of Bill Brand." *Millennium Film Journal* 3 (Winter/ Spring 1979): 55–61.

Burnham, Jack. "Systems Esthetics." *Artforum* 7.1 (Sept. 1968): 30–35.

Butler, Christopher. *After the Wake: An Essay on the Contemporary Avant-Garde*. Oxford: Clarendon, 1980.

———. *Interpretation, Deconstruction, and Ideology: An Introduction to Some Current Issues in Literary Theory*. Oxford: Clarendon, 1984.

Butor, Michel. *A Change of Heart*. Trans. Jean Stewart. New York: Simon, 1959.

———. *Mobile: Etude pour une Représentation des Etats-Unis*. Paris: Gallimard, 1962.

Cage, John. *Silence*. Middletown, CT: Wesleyan University Press, 1961.

Camper, Fred. "The End of Avant-garde Film." *Millennium Film Journal* 16/17/18 (Fall/Winter 1986–87): 99–124.

———. "*Remedial Reading Comprehension* (Landow)." *Film Culture* 52 (1971): 73–77.

Carroll, Nöel. "Address to the Heathen." *October* 23 (Winter 1982): 89–163.

———. "Causation, the Ampliation of Movement and the Avant-garde Film." *Millennium Film Journal* 10/11 (Fall/Winter 1981–82): 61–82.

———. *Mystifying Movies: Fads and Fallacies in Contemporary Film Theory* (New York: Columbia University Press, 1988).

———. "Film." In *The Postmodern Moment: A Handbook of Contemporary Innovation in the Arts*, ed. Stanley Trachtenberg, 101–33. Westport, CT: Greenwood Press, 1985.

———. "The Power of Movies." *Daedalus* 114.4 (Fall 1985): 79–103.

———. "A Reply to Heath." *October* 27 (Winter 1983): 81–102.

———. "Toward a Theory of Film Editing." *Millennium Film Journal* 3 (Winter/Spring 1979): 79–99.

Carterette, Edward C., and Morton P. Friedman, eds. *Perceptual Processing.* Vol. 9 of *Handbook of Perception.* New York: Academic, 1978.

———. *Historical and Philosophical Roots of Perception.* Vol. 1 of *Handbook of Perception.* New York: Academic, 1974.

Cathcart, Linda. "An Interview with Paul Sharits." *Film Culture* 65/66 (1978): 103–8.

Chandler, John N. "Tony Smith and Sol LeWitt: Mutations and Permutations." *Art International* 12.7 (Sept. 1968): 16–19.

Charron, John. "Frampton's *Palindrome* and the Later Serial Music of Webern." University of Notre Dame, 1990.

Chipp, Herschel B. *Theories of Modern Art: A Sourcebook by Artists and Critics.* Berkeley: University of California Press, 1968.

Cobbing, Bob. "Concrete Sound Poetry." In *The Avant-Garde Tradition in Literature*, ed. Richard Kostelanetz, 385–91. Buffalo, NY: Prometheus, 1982.

Cockroft, Eva. "Abstract Expressionism: Weapon of the Cold War." *Artforum* 12.10 (June 1974): 39–41.

Cole, P. *Radical Pragmatics.* New York: Academic Press, 1981.

Collective for Living Cinema. *10 Years of Living Cinema.* New York: Collective for Living Cinema, 1982.

Collingwood, R. G. *The Principles of Art.* Oxford: Oxford University Press, 1938.

Comolli, Jean-Louis. "Technique and Ideology: Camera, Perspective, Depth of Field." *Film Reader* 2 (1977): 128–40. (Originally the first of six parts in *Cahiers du Cinéma* 229 [May 1971]: 4–21.)

Conner, Bruce. "Bruce Conner: A Discussion at the 1968 Flaherty Film Seminar." *Film Comment* 5.4 (1969): 16–25.

Conrad, Tony. "Inside the Dream Syndicate." *Film Culture* 41 (1966): 5–8.

———. "Tony Conrad on *The Flicker.*" *Film Culture* 41 (1966): 1–2.

Cook, Scott. "*Valse Triste* and *Mongoloid.*" *Millennium Film Journal* 7/8/9 (Fall/Winter 1980–81): 248–52.

Coplans, John. *Andy Warhol.* New York: New York Graphic Society, 1970.

———. "Art Is Love Is God." *Artforum* 2.9 (Mar. 1964): 26–27.

———. "An Interview with Roy Lichtenstein." *Artforum* 2.4 (Oct. 1963a): 31.

———. "The New Paintings of Common Objects." *Artforum* 1.6 (Dec. 1962): 26–29.

———. "Pop Art, USA." *Artforum* 2.4 (Oct. 1963b): 27–30.

———. "Sculpture in California." *Artforum* 2.2 (Aug. 1963c): 3–6.

———. *Serial Imagery.* Pasadena, CA: Pasadena Art Museum, 1968.

Cornwell, Regina. *Films by American Artists: One Medium Among Many: A Touring Collection of Films.* Exhibition catalog. London: Arts Council of Great Britain, 1981.

———. *Snow Seen: The Films and Photographs of Michael Snow.* Toronto: PMA Books, 1979a.

———. "Some Formalist Tendencies in the Current American Avant-Garde Film." *Studio International* 184.948 (Oct. 1972): 110–14.

———. "Structural Film: Ten Years Later." *Drama Review* 23 (Sept. 1979b): 77–92.

———. "Works of Ernie Gehr from 1968 to 1972." *Film Culture* 63/64 (1976): 29–38.

Cottringer, Anne. "On Peter Gidal's Theory and Definition of Structural/Materialist Film." *Afterimage* (London) 6 (Summer 1976): 86–95.

Cox, Annette. *Art-as-Politics: The Abstract Expressionist Avant-Garde and Society.* Ann Arbor, MI: UMI Research Press, 1982.

Croce, Benedetto. *Aesthetic as Science of Expression and General Linguistic.* 1922. Trans. Douglas Ainslie. New York: The Noonday Press, 1956.

Culler, Jonathan. *The Pursuit of Signs: Semiotics, Literature, Deconstruction.* Ithaca, NY: Cornell University Press, 1981.

———. *Structuralist Poetics: Structuralism, Linguistics, and the Study of Literature.* Ithaca, NY: Cornell University Press, 1975.

Currie, Hector, and Michael Porte, eds. *Cinema Now: Stan Brakhage, John Cage, Jonas Mekas, Stan Vanderbeek.* Cincinnati: University of Cincinnati, 1968.

Curtis, David. *Experimental Cinema: A Fifty-Year Evolution.* New York: Dell, 1971.

————, ed. *Film as Film: Formal Experiment in Film 1910–1975*. London: Arts Council of Great Britain, 1979.

Davies, John Booth. *The Psychology of Music*. Stanford: Stanford University Press, 1978.

Davis, R. G. "*Ubu Roi.*" *Artforum* 2.8 (Feb. 1964): 36–39.

de Beauregarde, R., and B. N. Colby. "Narrative Models of Action and Interaction." *Cognitive Science* 3 (1979): 43–66.

de Campos, Augusto, Decio Pignatari, and Haraldo de Campos. "Pilot Plan for Concrete Poetry." In *The Avant-Garde Tradition in Literature*, ed. Richard Kostelanetz, 259–66. Buffalo, NY: Prometheus, 1982.

De George, Richard, and Fernande De George. *The Structuralists from Marx to Levi-Strauss*. Garden City, NY: Doubleday, 1972.

Delahaye, Michel. "Andy: la mise à nu." *Cahiers du Cinema* 205 (Oct. 1968): 46.

de Vree, Paul. "Visual Poetry." In *The Avant-Garde Tradition in Literature*, ed. Richard Kostelanetz, 344–47. Buffalo, NY: Prometheus, 1982.

Dillon, George L. "Styles of Reading." *Poetics Today* 3.2 (Spring 1982): 77–88.

Dreyfus, Hubert L. *Husserl, Intentionality and Cognitive Science*. Cambridge, MA: MIT Press, 1982.

Drummond, Phillip. "Notions of Avant-garde." In *Film As Film: Formal Experiment in Film 1910–1975*, ed. David Curtis, 9–16. London: Arts Council of Great Britain, 1979.

Duberman, Martin. *Black Mountain: An Experiment in Community*. New York: Dutton, 1972.

Dunford, Mike. "Experimental Avant-Garde Revolutionary Film Practice." *Afterimage* (London) 6 (Summer 1976): 96–112.

Dusinberre, Deke. "St. George in the Forest: The English Avant-Garde." *Afterimage* (London) 6 (Summer 1976): 4–19.

Ehrenstein, David. *Film: The Frontline 1984*. Denver: Arden, 1984.

————. "An Interview with Andy Warhol." *Film Culture* 40 (1966): 41.

Elderfield, John. "Grids." *Artforum* 10.9 (May 1972): 52–59.

————. "Mondrian, Newman, Noland: Two Notes on Changes of Style." *Artforum* 10.4 (Dec. 1971): 48–53.

Eysenck, Michael W. *A Handbook of Cognitive Psychology*. London: Erlbaum, 1984.

Factor, Donald. "Assemblage." *Artforum* 2.12 (Summer 1964): 38–41.

Field, Simon. "Alphabet as Ideogram." *Art and Artists* 7.5 (Aug. 1972): 22–26.

————. "Interview with Frampton." *Afterimage* (London) 4 (Autumn 1972): 44–77.

"Filmography of Ernie Gehr." *Film Culture* 53/54/55 (Spring 1972): 38.

Finkelstein, Louis. "Seeing Stella." *Artforum* 11.10 (June 1973): 67–70.

Fish, Stanley. *Is There a Text in This Class? The Authority of Interpretive Communities*. Cambridge, MA: Havard University Press, 1980.

Flanagan, Owen J. *The Science of the Mind*. Cambridge, MA: MIT Press, 1984.

Fodor, Jerry. *The Modularity of Mind: An Essay on Faculty Psychology*. Cambridge, MA: MIT Press, 1983.

Ford, Paul Leicester, ed. *The New England Primer*. New York: Teachers College, Columbia University, 1962.

Foreman, Richard. "On Ernie Gehr's Film *Still*." *Film Culture* 63/64 (1976): 27–29.

Forge, Andrew. *Rauschenberg*. New York: Abrams, n.d.

Foster, Hal, ed. *The Anti-Aesthetic: Essays on Post-Modern Culture*. Port Townsend, WA: Bay Press, 1983.

Frampton, Hollis. *Circles of Confusion: Film/Photography/Video Texts 1968–1980*. Rochester, NY: Visual Studies Workshop Press, 1983.

————. Grant proposal. In the Hollis Frampton file at the Museum of Modern Art, New York.

————. "*(nostalgia)*: Voice-Over Narration for a Film of that Name." *Film Culture* 53/54/55 (Spring 1972): 105–11.

————. "Notes on *(nostalgia)*." *Film Culture* 53/54/55 (Spring 1972): 114.

————. "A Pentagram for Conjuring the Narrative." *Form and Structure in Recent Film*. Vancouver: Vancouver Art Gallery, 1972. Rpt. in Frampton, *Circles of Confusion*, 59–68.

Francastel, Pierre. *La Figure et le Lieu, l'Ordre Visuel du Quattrocento*. Paris: Gallimard, 1967.

Francis, Richard. *Jasper Johns*. New York: Abbeville, 1984.

Freedle, Roy O., ed. *Discourse Production and Comprehension*. Norwood, NJ: Ablex, 1977.

Fried, Michael. "Modernist Painting and the Formal Criticism." *American Scholar* 33.4 (Autumn 1964): 642–49.

————. "Shape as Form: Frank Stella's New Paintings." *Artforum* 5.3 (Nov. 1966): 18–27.

Frye, Northrop. *Anatomy of Criticism*. Princeton: Princeton University Press, 1971.

Gablik, Suzi. "Protagonists of Pop." *Studio International* 178.913 (July/Aug. 1969): 9–16.

Gardner, Howard. *The Mind's New Science*. New York: Basic, 1985.

Garver, Thomas H. "Bruce Conner Makes a Sandwich." *Artforum* 6.1 (Sept. 1967): 51–55.

Gehr, Ernie. "Program Notes by Ernie Gehr for a Film Showing at the Museum of Modern Art." *Film Culture* 53/54/55 (Spring 1972): 36–38.

Geldzahler, Henry. "Some Notes on *Sleep.*" *Film Culture* 32 (1964): 13.

Genette, Gérard. *Narrative Discourse: An Essay in Method.* Trans. Jane E. Lewin. Ithaca, NY: Cornell University Press, 1980.

Gernsbacher, M. A. "Surface Information Loss in Comprehension." *Cognitive Psychology* 17.3 (1985): 324–63.

Gerson, Barry. "*Doorway* by Larry Gottheim." *Film Culture* 68/69 (1979): 181–82.

Gibson, J. J. *The Ecological Approach to Visual Perception.* Boston: Houghton, Mifflin, 1979.

Gidal, Peter. *Andy Warhol: Films and Paintings.* London: Studio Vista, 1971.

———. "The Anti-Narrative." *Screen* 20.2 (1979): 93–99.

———. "Interview with Hollis Frampton." *October* 32 (Spring 1985): 93–117.

———. "Letter from Peter Gidal." *Afterimage* (London) 7 (Summer 1978): 120–23.

———. *Materialist Film.* New York: Routledge, 1989.

———. "Theory and Definition of Structural/Materialist Film." In *Structural Film Anthology*, ed. Peter Gidal, 1–21. London: BFI, 1976.

———, ed. *Structural Film Anthology.* London: BFI, 1976.

Glass, Arnold Lewis, and Keith James Holyoak. *Cognition.* 2d ed. New York: Random, 1986.

Gluck, Phyllis Gold. *Recent Art and Its Discourse: A Study of Selected Movements.* Diss. Columbia University, 1971. Ann Arbor, MI: UMI, 1976.

Gombrich, E. H. *Art and Illusion: A Study in the Psychology of Pictorial Representation.* Princeton, NJ: Princeton University Press, 1969.

———. *The Sense of Order: A Study in the Psychology of Decorative Art.* Ithaca, NY: Cornell University Press, 1979.

Gombrich, E. H., Julian Hochberg, and Max Black. *Art, Perception and Reality.* Baltimore: Johns Hopkins University Press, 1972.

Gotlieb, Carla. "Systemic Art: Reiteration, Multiplication, Permutation, Modularity." In *Beyond Modern Art*, ed. Carla Gotlieb, 170–95. New York: Dutton, 1976.

Grauer, Victor A. "A Theory of Pure Film, Parts 1 & 2." *Field of Vision* 1 (Fall 1976): 1–11; 3 (1978–79): 4–21.

Green, Samuel Adams. "Andy Warhol." In *The New Art: A Critical Anthology*, ed. Gregory Battcock, 229–34. New York: Dutton, 1966.

Greenberg, Clement. "American-Type Painting" (1955, revised 1958). In *Art and Culture: Critical Essays*, 208–29. Boston: Beacon, 1961.

———. *Art and Culture: Critical Essays.* Boston: Beacon, 1961.

———. "Byzantine Parallels." In *Art and Culture*, 167–70. Boston: Beacon, 1961.

———. "How Art Writing Earns Its Bad Name." *The Second Coming* 1.3 (Mar. 1962): 58–62.

———. "Modernist Painting." *Arts Yearbook* 4 (1961): 101–8. Rpt. in *Esthetics Contemporary*, ed. Richard Kostelanetz, 198–206. Buffalo, NY: Prometheus, 1978.

———. *Post-Painterly Abstraction.* Exhibition catalog. Los Angeles: Los Angeles County Museum of Art, 1964.

———. "Recentness of Sculpture." In *American Sculpture of the Sixties.* Exhibition catalog. Los Angeles: Los Angeles County Museum of Art, 1967. Rpt. in *Minimal Art*, ed. Gregory Battcock, 180–86. New York: Dutton, 1968.

Gregory, R. L. *Eye and Brain: The Psychology of Seeing.* New York: McGraw, 1966.

Guilbaut, Serge. *How New York Stole the Idea of Modern Art: Abstract Expressionism, Freedom, and the Cold War.* Trans. Arthur Goldhammer. Chicago: University of Chicago Press, 1983.

Gunning, Tom. "Doctor Jacobs' Dream Work." *Millennium Film Journal* 10/11 (Fall/Winter 1981–82): 210–18.

Haller, Robert A. "Excerpts from an Interview with Bruce Conner Conducted in July of 1971." *Film Culture* 67/68/69 (1979): 191–94.

Hanhardt, John G. "The Medium Viewed: The American Avant-Garde Film." In *A History of the American Avant-Garde Cinema*, American Federation of Arts, 19–47. New York: American Federation of Arts, 1976.

Harrison, Charles. "Abstract Expressionism." In *Concepts of Modern Art*, eds. Tony Richardson and Nikos Stangos, 168–210. Harmondsworth, UK: Penguin, 1974.

Harvey, Sylvia. *May '68 and Film Culture.* London: BFI, 1980.

Haskell, Barbara. *Blam! The Explosion of Pop, Minimalism, and Performance 1958–1964.* New York: Whitney Museum of American Art/Norton, 1984.

Hassan, Ihab. "Abstractions." *Diacritics* 5.2 (Summer 1975): 13–18.

Hastie, Reid. "Schematic Principles in Human Memory." *Social Cognition: The Ontario Symposium, Vol. 1*, eds. E. Tory Higgins, C. Peter Herman, and Mark P. Zanna, 39–88. Hillsdale, NJ: Erlbaum, 1981.

Hausheer, Cecilia, and Christophe Settele, eds. *Found Footage Film*. Lucerne: VIPER/Zyklop Verlag, 1992.

Hauptman, William. "The Suppression of Art in the McCarthy Decade." *Artforum* 12.2 (Oct. 1973): 48–52.

Hayum, Andree. "A Casing Shelved." *Film Culture* 56/57 (Spring 1973): 81–89.

Heath, Stephen. "Le Père Noël." *October* 26 (Fall 1983): 63–115.

Hoberman, James. "After Avant-garde Film." In *Art After Modernism: Rethinking Representation*, ed. Brian Wallis, 59–73. New York: New Museum of Contemporary Art, 1984.

———. "Ernie Gehr's *Geography*." *Millennium Film Journal* 3 (Winter/Spring 1979): 113–14.

Hoberman, James, and Jonathan Rosenbaum. *Midnight Movies*. New York: Harper, 1983.

Hochberg, Julian. *Perception*. 2d ed. Englewood Cliffs, NJ: Prentice, 1978.

———. "Visual Art and the Structures of the Mind." In *The Arts, Cognition, and Basic Skills*, ed. Stanley S. Madeja, 162–64. St. Louis: CEMREL, 1978.

Hochberg, Julian, and Virginia Brooks. "The Perception of Motion Pictures." In *Perceptual Ecology*. Vol. 10 of *Handbook of Perception*, eds. Edward. C. Carterette and Morton P. Friedman, 259–304. New York: Academic, 1978.

Hock, Louis. "Reconsidered Analysis by Louis Hock of *Remedial Reading Comprehension*, A Film by George Landow." *Film Culture* 63/64 (1976): 124–27.

Hoffman, R. R. "Recent Psycholinguistic Research on Figurative Language." *Annals of the New York Academy of Sciences* 433 (Dec. 1984): 137–66.

Holland, Norman N. *The Brain of Robert Frost: A Cognitive Approach to Literature*. New York: Routledge, 1988.

Horowitz, Leonard. "Art of Allowing." *Soho Weekly News* 27 Mar. 1975: 30+.

"In the Year of Our Ford." *Time* 3 Apr. 1964: 96+.

Iser, Wolfgang. *The Act of Reading: A Theory of Aesthetic Response*. Baltimore: Johns Hopkins University Press, 1978.

Jakobson, Roman. "Linguistics and Poetics." In *The Structuralists from Marx to Levi-Strauss*, eds. Richard and Fernande De George, 85–122. Garden City, NY: Doubleday, 1972.

———. "Two Types of Language and Two Types of Aphasic Disturbances." Part two of *Fundamentals of Language*, by Roman Jakobson and Morris Halle, 69–96. The Hague: Mouton, 1956.

James, David E. *Allegories of Cinema: American Film in the Sixties*. Princeton, NJ: Princeton University Press, 1989.

Jauss, Hans Robert. *Toward an Aesthetic of Reception*. Trans. Timothy Bahti. Minneapolis: University of Minnesota Press, 1982.

Jenkins, Bruce. "A Case Against 'Structural Film.'" *Journal of the University Film and Video Association* 33.2 (Spring 1981): 9–14.

———. "Frampton Unstructured: Notes for a Metacritical History." *Wide Angle* 2.3 (1978): 22–28.

———. "The Red and the Green." *October* 32 (Spring 1985): 77–92.

Johnson, Mark. *The Body in the Mind: The Bodily Basis of Meaning, Imagination, and Reason*. Chicago: University of Chicago Press, 1987.

Johnson-Laird, P. N. *Mental Models: Towards a Cognitive Science of Language, Inference, and Consciousness*. Cambridge, MA: Harvard University Press, 1983.

Josephson, Mary. "Warhol: The Medium as Cultural Artifact." *Art in America* 59.3 (May/June 1971): 41–46.

Kahneman, Daniel, Paul Slovic, and Amos Tversky, eds. *Judgment Under Uncertainty: Heuristics and Biases*. Cambridge and New York: Cambridge University Press, 1982.

Karp, Ivan C. "Anti-Sensibility Painting: An Early Exhibitor of the Controversial 'Pop Art' Presents His Case." *Artforum* 2.3 (Sept. 1963): 26–27.

Kelman, Ken. "Animal Cinema: Four Frames." *Film Culture* 63/64 (1976): 25–27.

———. "The Anti-Information Film (Conner's *Report*)." In *The Essential Cinema*, ed. P. Adams Sitney, 240–44. New York: Anthology Film Archives and New York University Press, 1975.

Kintsch, Walter. "On Comprehending Stories." In *Cognitive Processes in Comprehension*, eds. Marcel A. Just and Patricia A. Carpenter, 33–62. Hillsdale, NJ: Erlbaum, 1977.

Koch, Stephen. *Stargazer: Andy Warhol's World and His Films*. New York: Praeger, 1973.

Kostelanetz, Richard. *The Avant-Garde Tradition in Literature*. Buffalo, NY: Prometheus, 1982.

———. "Innovative Literature in America." In *The Avant-Garde Tradition in Literature*, ed. Richard Kostelanetz, 392–413. Buffalo, NY: Prometheus, 1982.

———, ed. *Esthetics Contemporary*. Buffalo, NY: Prometheus, 1978.

———, ed. *The New American Arts*. New York: Horizon, 1965.

Kozloff, Max. "American Painting During the Cold War." *Artforum* 11.9 (May 1973): 43–54.

———. "'Pop' Culture, Metaphysical Disgust, and the New Vulgarians." *Art International* 6.2 (Mar. 1962): 34–36.

———. "Post-Abstract Expressionism: Mask and Reality." In *The New American Arts*, ed. Richard Kostelanetz, 88–116. New York: Horizon, 1965.

Kramer, Hilton. "The New American Painting." *Partisan Review* 20.4 (July/Aug. 1953): 421–27.

Krauss, Rosalind E. "LeWitt in Progress." *October* 6 (Fall 1978): 47–60. Rpt. in Krauss, *The Originality of the Avant-Garde and Other Modernist Myths*, 244–58.

———. *The Originality of the Avant-Garde and Other Modernist Myths*. Cambridge, MA: MIT Press, 1985.

———. "Paul Sharits." *Film Culture* 65/66 (1978): 89–102.

———. "Paul Sharits' *Stop Time*." *Artforum* 11.8 (Apr. 1973): 60–61.

———. "Sculpture in the Expanded Field." *October* 8 (Spring 1979): 31–44. Rpt. in *The Anti-Aesthetic: Essays on Post-Modern Culture*, ed. Hal Foster, 31–42. Port Townsend, WA: Bay Press, 1983.

———. "Stella's New Work and the Problem of Series." *Artforum* 10.4 (Dec. 1971): 40–44.

Kubelka, Peter. "The Theory of Metrical Film." In *The Avant-Garde Film*, ed. P. Adams Sitney, 139–59. New York: New York University Press, 1978.

Kuspit, Donald B. *Clement Greenberg: Art Critic*. Madison: University of Wisconsin Press, 1979.

———. Letter to editor. *Art in America* 65.1 (Jan./Feb. 1977): 5–7.

———. "Pop Art: A Reactionary Realism." *Art Journal* 36.1 (Fall 1976): 31–38.

———. "Sol LeWitt: The Look of Thought." *Art in America* 63.5 (Sept./Oct. 1975): 42–49.

Lakoff, George. *Women, Fire, and Dangerous Things: What Categories Reveal About the Mind*. Chicago: University of Chicago Press, 1987.

Lakoff, George, and Mark Johnson. *Metaphors We Live By*. Chicago: University of Chicago Press, 1980.

Lakoff, George, and Mark Turner. *More than Cool Reason: A Field Guide to Poetic Metaphor*. Chicago: University of Chicago Press, 1989.

Lawder, Standish D. *The Cubist Cinema*. New York: New York University Press, 1975.

Lee, David. "Serial Rights." *Art News* 66.8 (Dec. 1967): 42–45, 68–69.

Leech, Geoffrey N. *Principles of Pragmatics*. London and New York: Longman, 1983.

Legg, Alicia, ed. *Sol LeWitt*. New York: Museum of Modern Art, 1978.

Le Grice, Malcolm. *Abstract Film and Beyond*. Cambridge, MA: MIT Press, 1977.

Leider, Philip. "Bruce Conner: A New Sensibility." *Artforum* 1.6 (Nov./Dec. 1962): 30–31.

———. "The Cool School." *Artforum* 2.12 (Summer 1964): 47–52.

———. "Saint Andy: Some Notes on an Artist Who, for a Large Section of a Younger Generation, Can Do No Wrong." *Artforum* 3.5 (Feb. 1965): 26–28.

Lerdahl, Fred, and Ray Jackendoff. *A Generative Theory of Tonal Music*. Cambridge, MA: MIT Press, 1983.

LeWitt, Sol. "Paragraphs on Conceptual Art." *Artforum* 5.10 (June 1967): 79–83. Rpt. in *Sol LeWitt*, ed. Alicia Legg, 166–67. New York: Museum of Modern Art, 1978.

Lichtenstein, Roy. "Interview with G. R. Swenson." In *Pop Art Redefined*, eds. John Russell and Suzi Gablik, 92–94. New York: Praeger, 1969. (Originally in "What Is Pop Art?" Part 1. *Art News* 62.7 (Nov. 1963): 24+.)

Lippard, Lucy. *Pop Art*. New York: Oxford University Press, 1966.

———. "The Silent Art." *Art in America* 55.1 (Jan./Feb. 1967): 58–63.

———. "Sol LeWitt: Non-Visual Structures." *Artforum* 5.8 (Apr. 1967): 46.

———. "The Structures, The Structures and the Wall Drawings, The Structures and the Wall Drawings and the Books." In *Sol LeWitt*, ed. Alicia Legg, 23–30. New York: Museum of Modern Art, 1978.

Mac Cormac, Earl R. *A Cognitive Theory of Metaphor*. Cambridge, MA: MIT Press, 1985.

MacDonald, Scott. "Acquired Tastes." *Facets Video Catalog*. Chicago: Facets Multimedia, 1989: 6–8.

———. "The Cinema Audience: Some New Perspectives." *Film Criticism* 3.3 (Spring 1979): 32–40.

———. *A Critical Cinema: Interviews with Independent Filmmakers*. Berkeley: University of California Press, 1988.

———. "Hollis Frampton's *Hapax Legomena*." *Afterimage* 5 (Jan. 1978): 8–13.

———. "I Don't Go to the Movies Anymore: An Interview with Bruce Conner." *Afterimage* 10.1/2 (Summer 1982): 20–23.

———. "I Never Understood Anything about Cowboys: An Interview with J. J. Murphy." *Afterimage* 9.7 (Feb. 1982): 12–18.

———. "Interview with Hollis Frampton: *Hapax Legomena*." *Film Culture* 67/68/69 (1979a): 174–76.

———. "Interview with Hollis Frampton: The Early Years." *October* 12 (Spring 1980): 103–26.

———. "Interview with Hollis Frampton: *Zorn's Lemma*." *Quarterly Review of Film Studies* 4.1 (Winter 1979b): 23–37.

———. "*Print Generation*." *Film Quarterly* (Fall 1978): 58–62.

———. "So Is This." *Film Quarterly* 39.1 (Fall 1985): 34–37.

———. "We Were Bent on Having a Good Time: An Interview with Robert Nelson." *Afterimage* 7.1/2 (Summer 1983): 39–43.

MacIntyre, Alasdair C. *After Virtue: A Study in Moral Theory.* Notre Dame, IN: University of Notre Dame Press, 1981.

Maciunas, George. "Some Comments on 'Structural Film' by P. Adams Sitney." In *Film Culture Reader*, ed. P. Adams Sitney, 349. New York: Praeger, 1970.

Mailloux, Steven. *Interpretive Conventions: The Reader in the Study of American Fiction.* Ithaca, NY: Cornell University Press, 1982.

Mancia, Adrienne, and Willard Van Dyke. "The Artist as Film-maker: Len Lye." *Art in America* 54.4 (July/Aug. 1966): 98–106.

———. "Four Artists as Filmmakers." *Art in America* 55.1 (Jan./Feb. 1967): 64–73.

Mandler, Jean. *Stories, Scripts, and Scenes: Aspects of Schema Theory.* Hillsdale, NJ: Erlbaum, 1984.

Mandler, Jean, and Nancy Johnson. "Remembrance of Things Parsed: Story Structure and Recall." *Cognitive Psychology* 9 (1977): 111–51.

Masheck, Joseph. "Kuspit's LeWitt: Has He Got Style?" *Art in America* 64.6 (Nov./Dec. 1976): 107–11.

———. "Warhol as Illustrator: Early Manipulations of the Mundane." *Art in America* 59.3 (May/June 1971): 54–59.

McCall, Anthony, and Andrew Tyndall. "Sixteen Working Statements." *Millennium Film Journal* 1.2 (Spring-Summer 1978): 29–37.

McClure, Michael. "*Dog Star Man*—The First 16mm Epic." *Artforum* 2.1 (July 1963): 54–55. Rpt. in *Film Culture* 29 (1963): 12–13.

Mekas, Jonas. "A Call for a New Generation of Filmmakers." *Film Culture* 19 (1959): 1.

———. "Editorial." *Film Culture* 32 (1964a): 1–2.

———. "Ernie Gehr Interviewed by Jonas Mekas." *Film Culture* 53/54/55 (1972): 25–36.

———. "The Experimental Film in America." *Film Culture* 1.3 (1955): 15–20.

———. "Movie Journal." *Village Voice* 7 Apr. 1975: 74.

———. *Movie Journal.* New York: Macmillan, 1972.

———. "Press Release." *Film Culture* 29 (1963): 7–8.

———. "Sixth Independent Film Award." *Film Culture* 33 (1964b): 1.

Melanga, Gerard. "From 'Sonnets on Eight Variations of Sleep: For Andy Warhol.'" *Film Culture* 32 (1964): 14–15.

Melanga, Gerard, and Jerry Katz. "Two Letters." *Film Culture* 40 (1966): 42.

Mellencamp, Patricia. *Indiscretions: Avant-garde Film, Video and Feminism.* Bloomington: Indiana University Press, 1990.

Mellow, James R. "New York Letter." *Art International* 12.2 (Feb. 1968): 73–74.

Mendelson, Lois. *Robert Breer: A Study of His Work in the Context of the Modernist Tradition.* Ann Arbor, MI: UMI Research Press, 1981.

Mendelson, Lois, and Bill Simon. "*Tom, Tom, the Piper's Son.*" *Artforum* 10.1 (Sept. 1971): 46+.

Metz, Christian. *The Imaginary Signifier: Psychoanalysis and the Cinema.* Celia Britton, Annwyl Williams, Ben Brewster, and Alfred Guzzetti, trans. Bloomington: Indiana University Press, 1982.

Meyer, Leonard B. *Emotion and Meaning in Music.* Chicago: University of Chicago Press, 1956.

———. *Music, the Arts, and Ideas: Patterns and Predictions in Twentieth-Century Culture.* Chicago: University of Chicago Press, 1967.

Michelson, Annette. "*Anemic Cinema*: Reflections on an Emblematic Work." *Artforum* 12.2 (Oct. 1973a): 64–69.

———. "Bodies in Space: Film as Carnal Knowledge." *Artforum* 7.6 (Feb. 1969): 54–63.

———. "Camera Lucida/Camera Obscura," *Artforum* 11.5 (Jan. 1973b): 30–37.

———. "Camera Obscura: The Cinema of Stan Brakhage." *New Forms in Film* (festival catalog), ed. Annette Michelson, 38–40. Montreux, Switzerland, 1974.

———. "Film and the Radical Aspiration." *Film Culture* 42 (Fall 1966): 34–42+. Rpt. in *Film Culture Reader*, ed. P. Adams Sitney, 404–21. New York: Praeger, 1970.

———. "*The Man with the Movie Camera*: From Magician to Epistemologist." *Artforum* 10.7 (Mar. 1972a): 60–72.

———. "Paul Sharits and the Critique of Illusionism: An Introduction." *Film Culture* 65/66 (1978): 83–89.

———. "Screen/Surface: The Politics of Illusionism." *Artforum* 11.1 (Sept. 1972b): 58–62.

———. "Toward Snow." *Artforum* 9.10 (June 1971): 30–37.

———. "What Is Cinema?" *Artforum* 6.10 (Summer 1968): 67–71.

Moritz, William, and Beverly O'Neill. "Fallout: Some Notes on the Films of Bruce Conner." *Film Quarterly* 31 (Summer 1978): 36–41.

Mosen, David. "*Report.*" *Film Quarterly* 19.3 (Spring 1966): 54–56.

Mossman, Toby. "A Comment on Literalness." *Arts Magazine* 42.4 (Feb. 1968): 14–17.

———. "An Interview with Tony Conrad." *Film Culture* 41 (1966): 3–5.

Motte, Warren F., Jr., ed. and trans. *Oulipo: A Primer of Potential Literature.* Lincoln: University of Nebraska Press, 1986.

Mukarovsky, Jan. *Aesthetic Function, Norm and Value as Social Facts.* Trans. Mark E. Suino. Michigan Slavic Contributions 3. Ann Arbor: University of Michigan Department of Slavic Languages and Literature, 1979.

Murphy, J. J. "Reaching for Oblivion." *Millennium Film Journal* 3 (Winter/Spring 1979): 122–25.

———. "Christopher Maclaine—Approaching *The End.*" *Film Culture* (Fall 1983): 88–100.

Murphy, G. L., and D. L. Medin. "The Role of Theories in Conceptual Coherence." *Psychological Review* 92.3 (1985): 289–316.

Neisser, Ulric. *Cognition and Reality: Principles and Implications of Cognitive Psychology.* San Francisco: Freeman, 1976.

Nisbett, Richard E., and Lee Ross. *Human Inference: Strategies and Shortcomings of Social Judgment.* Englewood Cliffs, NJ: Prentice-Hall, 1980.

Norman, Donald A. *Memory and Attention: An Introduction to Human Information Processing.* New York: Wiley, 1976.

Nosowitz, Harvey. *Chicago Reader* 4 May 1984, sec. 1: 18.

Nygren, Scott. *Mythic Vision: A Study of Bruce Baille's Film "Quick Billy."* Diss. State University of New York at Buffalo. Ann Arbor, MI: UMI, 1982.

Nyman, Michael. *Experimental Music: Cage and Beyond.* New York: Schirmer, 1981.

O'Doherty, Brian. "Bruce Conner and His Films." *New York Times* 26 Apr. 1964. Rpt. in *The New American Cinema,* ed. Gregory Battcock, 194–96. New York: Dutton, 1967.

Oldenberg, Claes. "I Am for an Art . . . ." In *Pop Art Redefined,* eds. John Russell and Suzi Gablik, 97–99. New York: Praeger, 1969.

Ono, Yoko. "Yoko Ono on Yoko Ono." *Film Culture* 48/49 (1970): 32–33.

Ortony, Andrew. "Beyond Literal Similarity." *Psychological Review* 86.3 (May 1979): 161–80.

———, ed. *Metaphor and Thought.* Cambridge and New York: Cambridge University Press, 1979.

Ortony, Andrew, Ralph E. Reynolds, and Judith A. Arter. "Metaphor: Theoretical and Empirical Research." *Psychological Bulletin* 85.5 (Sept. 1978): 919–43.

Ortony, Andrew, Diane L. Schallert, Ralph E. Reynolds, and Stephen J. Antos. "Interpreting Metaphors and Idioms: Some Effects of Context on Comprehension." *Journal of Verbal Learning and Verbal Behavior* 17 (1978): 465–77.

Ortony, Andrew, Richard J. Vondruksa, Mark A. Foss, and Lawrence E. Jones. "Salience, Similes and the Asymmetry of Similarity." *Journal of Memory and Language* 24.5 (1985): 569–94.

Osborn, Elodie. "The Young Filmmaker." *Art in America* 54.1 (Jan./Feb. 1966): 62–68.

Padgett, Ron. "Sonnet: Homage to Andy Warhol." *Film Culture* 32 (1964): 13.

Parsons, Michael J. *How We Understand Art: A Cognitive Developmental Account of Aesthetic Experience.* Cambridge: Cambridge University Press, 1987.

Penley, Constance, and Janet Bergstrom. "The Avant-Garde: Histories and Theories." *Screen* 19 (Autumn 1978): 113–27.

"Perverbs and Snowballs." *Time* 10 Jan. 1977: 55.

Peterson, James. "The Artful Mathematicians of the Avant-Garde." *Wide Angle* 7.3 (1985): 14–23.

———. "Bruce Conner and the Compilation Narrative." *Wide Angle* 8.3/4 (1986a): 53–62.

———. *In Warhol's Wake: Pop and Minimalism in the American Avant-garde Film.* Diss. University of Wisconsin-Madison. Ann Arbor, MI: UMI, 1986b.

Peterson, Richard. "Films by Linda Klosky." *Millennium Film Journal* 4/5 (Summer/Fall 1979): 179–83.

Pincus-Witten, Robert. "Anglo-American Standard Reference Works: Acute Conceptualism." *Artforum* 10.2 (Oct. 1971): 82–85.

———. "Bochner at MoMA: Three Ideas and Seven Procedures." *Artforum* 10.4 (Dec. 1971): 28–31.

Plagens, Peter. "Present-Day Styles and Ready-Made Criticism: In which the Formal Contribution of Pop Art Is Found to Be Minimal." *Artforum* 5.4 (Dec. 1966): 36–39.

Pleynet, Marcelin, and Jean Thibaudeau. Interviewed by Gérard Leblanc. "Economique, Ideologie, Formel." *Cinéthique* 3 (1969): 7–14. Rpt. as "Economic—Ideological—Formal." In *May '68 and Film Culture,* by Sylvia Harvey, 149–64. London: BFI, 1980.

Poggioli, Renato. *The Theory of the Avant-garde.* Trans. Gerald Fitzgerald. Cambridge, MA: Belknap Press of Harvard University Press, 1968.

Polan, Dana B. *The Political Language of Film and the Avant-garde.* Ann Arbor, MI: UMI Research Press, 1985.

Politoske, Daniel T. *Music.* Englewood Cliffs, NJ: Prentice, 1974.

Proweller, William. "American Painting of the 1960s: The Failure of Criticism and the Need for an Alternate Aesthetics." *Journal of Aesthetics and Art Criticism* 30.3 (Spring 1972): 319–26.

Putnam, Hilary. *Representation and Reality*. Cambridge, MA: MIT Press, 1988.

Quéréel, Patrice. *La Modification de Butor*. Paris: Classique Hachette, 1973.

The Reception of Films. *Wide Angle* 8, 1 (1986).

Renan, Sheldon. *An Introduction to the American Underground Film*. New York: E. P. Dutton, 1967.

Reveaux, Anthony. *Bruce Conner*. St. Paul, MN: Film in the Cities, 1981.

Reynolds, Mike. "Cinemanic: Column on Film." *Berkeley Barb* 11 Apr. 1975.

Rheuban, Joyce. "Films by John Knecht." *Millennium Film Journal*. 7/8/9 (Fall/Winter 1980–81): 242–47.

Richie, Donald. *Stan Brakhage—A Retrospective*. New York: Museum of Modern Art, 1970.

Rock, Irvin. *The Logic of Perception*. Cambridge, MA: MIT Press, 1983.

Rodowick, David N. *The Political Avant-Garde: Modernism and Epistemology in Post-'68 Film Theory*. Diss. University of Iowa. Ann Arbor, MI: UMI, 1983.

Rosch, Eleanor, and Barbara B. Lloyd, eds. *Cognition and Categorization*. Hillsdale, NJ: Erlbaum, 1978.

Rose, Barbara. "Problems of Art Criticism, V, The Politics of Art, Part II." *Artforum* 7.5 (Jan. 1969): 44–47.

———. "Quality and Louis." *Artforum* 10.2 (Oct. 1971): 62–65.

Rosenberg, Harold. "The American Action Painters." In Rosenberg, *The Tradition of the New*, 23–39. (Originally in *Art News* 51.10 [Dec. 1957].)

———. *Art on the Edge: Creators and Situations*. Chicago: University of Chicago Press, 1983a.

———. *The De-definition of Art: Action Art to Pop to Earthworks*. New York: Horizon, 1972.

———. "Hans Hofmann: Nature into Action." *Art News* 56.3 (May 1957): 34–36, 55–56.

———. *The Tradition of the New*. Chicago: University of Chicago Press, 1960.

Rosenblum, Robert. "Notes on Sol LeWitt." In *Sol LeWitt*, ed. Alicia Legg, 15–21. New York: Museum of Modern Art, 1978.

———. "Pop Art and Non-Pop Art." *Art and Literature* 5 (Summer 1964). Rpt. in *Pop Art Redefined*, by John Russell and Suzi Gablik, 53–56. New York: Praeger, 1969.

Rowe, Carel. *The Baudelairean Cinema: A Trend within the American Avant-Garde*. Ann Arbor, MI: UMI Research Press, 1982.

Rubin, William. "Younger American Painters." *Art International* 4.1 (Jan. 1960): 24–31.

Ruoff, Jeffrey K. "Home Movies of the Avant-garde: Jonas Mekas and the New York Art World." *Cinema Journal* 30.3 (1991): 6–28.

Russell, John, and Suzi Gablik. *Pop Art Redefined*. New York: Praeger, 1969.

Sandel, Michael J. *Liberalism and the Limits of Justice*. Cambridge, New York: Cambridge University Press, 1982.

Sayres, Sohnya, et al. *The 60s without Apology*. Minneapolis: University of Minnesota Press/Social Text, 1984.

Schapiro, Meyer. *Modern Art: 19th and 20th Centuries*. New York: Braziller, 1978.

———. "Recent Abstract Painting (1957)." *Modern Art: 19th and 20th Centuries*. New York: Braziller, 1978.

Schofer, Peter, and Donald Rice. "Metaphor, Metonymy, and Synechdoche Revis(it)ed." *Semiotica* 21.1/2 (1977): 121–49.

Searle, John R. *The Rediscovery of the Mind*. Cambridge, MA: MIT Press, 1992.

Segal, Mark. "Hollis Frampton/*Zorn's Lemma*." *Film Culture* 52 (Spring 1971): 88–95.

Selz, Peter. "Special Supplement: A Symposium on Pop Art." *Arts Magazine* 37.7 (Apr. 1963): 36–45.

Sharits, Paul. "Blank Deflections: Golden Cinema." *Film Culture* 48/49 (1970): 20–22.

———. "Notes on Films." *Film Culture* 47 (1969): 13–16.

Shedlin, Michael. "Marilyn." *Film Quarterly* 27.3 (Spring 1974): 47.

Simon, Bill. "New Forms in Film." *Artforum* 11.2 (Oct. 1972): 82.

———. "Reading *Zorn's Lemma*." *Millennium Film Journal* 1.2 (Spring/Summer 1978): 38–49.

Simon, Elena Pinto. "The Films of Peter Kubelka." *Artforum* 10.8 (Apr. 1972): 33–39.

Simon, H. A., and K. Kotovsky. "Human Acquisition of Concepts for Sequential Patterns." *Psychological Review* 70.6 (1963): 534–46.

Sinnott, Jan D. "A Model for Solution of Ill-Structured Problems: Implications for Everyday and Abstract Problem Solving." In *Everyday Problem Solving: Theory and Applications*, ed. Jan D. Sinnott, 72–99. New York: Praeger, 1989.

Sitney, P. Adams. "The Idea of Abstraction." *Film Culture* 63/64 (1976): 1–24.

———. "Interview with George Landow." *Film Culture* 47 (1969): 10–12.

———. "Michael Snow's Cinema." In *Michael Snow/A Survey*, ed. Michael Snow, 79–84. Toronto: Art Gallery of Toronto, 1970.

———. "Structural Film." *Film Culture* 47 (Summer 1969): 1–10.

———. "Structural Film" (second version). In *Film Culture Reader*, ed. P. Adams Sitney, 326–48. New York: Praeger, 1970.

———. *Visionary Film: The American Avant-Garde, 1943–1978.* 2d ed. New York: Oxford University Press, 1979.

———, ed. *The Avant-Garde Film: A Reader of Theory and Criticism.* New York: New York University Press, 1978.

———, ed. *The Essential Cinema: Essays on the Films in the Collection of Anthology Film Archives.* New York: Anthology Film Archives and New York University Press, 1975.

———, ed. *Film Culture Reader.* New York: Praeger, 1970.

Smithson, Robert. "A Cinematic Atopia." *Artforum* 10.1 (Sept. 1971): 53–55.

Snow, Michael. "Hollis Frampton Interviewed by Michael Snow." *Film Culture* 48/49 (1970a): 6–12.

———. "La Region Central." *Film Culture* 52 (1971): 58–73.

———, ed. *Michael Snow/A Survey.* Toronto: Art Gallery of Toronto, 1970b.

Soderquist, Claes. *"The Pleasure Dome," American Experimental Film 1939–1979.* Exhibition catalog. Stockholm: Moderna Museet, 1980.

Spencer, Michael. "Spatial Form and Post-Modernism." *Poetics Today* 5.1 (1984): 182–95.

Sperber, Dan, and Dierdre Wilson. *Relevance: Communication and Cognition.* Cambridge, MA: Harvard University Press, 1986.

Stein, Elliot. *"Valse Triste."* *Film Comment* 14.6 (Nov./Dec. 1978): 56+.

Steinberg, Leo. "Jasper Johns: The First Seven Years of His Art." [1962.] In *Other Criteria: Confrontations with Twentieth-Century Art*, 17–54. London: Oxford University Press, 1972.

———. "Other Criteria." *Other Criteria: Confrontations with Twentieth-Century Art.* London: Oxford University Press, 1972. 55–91.

———. *Other Criteria: Confrontations with Twentieth-Century Art.* London: Oxford University Press, 1972.

Stich, Stephen P. *From Folk Psychology to Cognitive Science: The Case Against Belief.* Cambridge, MA: MIT Press, 1983.

S[tiles], K[nute]. "Bruce Conner." *Artforum* 2.6 (Dec. 1963): 46.

Sukenick, Ronald. "Up from the Garret: Success Then and Now." *New York Times Book Review* 27 Jan. 1985: 1+.

Swenson, G. R. "What Is Pop Art?" 2 parts. *Art News* 62.7 (Nov. 1963): 24+; 62.10 (Feb. 1964): 40–43+. Rpt. in part in *Pop Art Redefined*, eds. John Russell and Suzi Gablik, 61–63, 79–83, 92–94, 110–12, 116–20. New York: Praeger, 1969.

Tannen, Deborah. "What's in a Frame? Surface Evidence for Underlying Expectations." In *New Directions in Discourse Processing*, ed. Roy O. Freedle, 137–81. Norwood, NJ: Ablex, 1979.

Tavel, Ronald. "The Banana Diary (*Harlot*)." *Film Culture* 40 (1966): 43–66.

Taylor, Charles. "Atomism." In *Powers, Possessions, and Freedom: Essays in Honour of C. B. Macpherson*, ed. Alkis Kontos, 39–61. Toronto, Buffalo: University of Toronto Press, 1979. Rpt. in Taylor, *Philosophy and the Human Sciences*, 187–210.

———. *Philosophy and the Human Sciences.* Cambridge, New York: Cambridge University Press, 1985.

———. "What's Wrong with Negative Liberty." In *The Idea of Freedom: Essays in Honour of Isaiah Berlin*, ed. Alan Ryan, 175–93. Oxford, New York: Oxford University Press, 1979. Rpt. in Taylor, *Philosophy and the Human Sciences*, 211–29.

Taylor, Gregory. "Beyond Interpretation: *The Lead Shoes* as an Abstract Film." *Millennium Film Journal* 25 (Summer 1991): 78–99.

———. " 'The Cognitive Instrument in the Service of Revolutionary Change': Sergei Eisenstein, Annette Michelson, and the Avant-Garde's Scholarly Aspiration." *Cinema Journal* 31.4 (Summer 1992): 42–59.

Thomas, Dan. "Towards Peter Kubelka." University of Wisconsin-Madison, 1981.

Thorndyke, Perry W. "Cognitive Structures in Comprehension and Memory of Narrative Discourse." *Cognitive Psychology* 9 (1977): 77–110.

Todorov, Tzvetan. *The Poetics of Prose.* Trans. Richard Howard. Ithaca, NY: Cornell University Press, 1977.

Tomkins, Calvin. *The Bride and the Bachelors: Five Masters of the Avant Garde.* 2d ed. New York: Viking, 1968.

———. *Off the Wall: Robert Rauschenberg and the Art World of Our Time.* New York: Penguin, 1980.

Tourangeau, Roger, and Robert J. Sternberg. "Aptness in Metaphor." *Cognitive Psychology* 13 (1981): 27–55.

Tucker, Marcia, and James Monte. *Anti-Illusion: Procedures and Materials.* New York: Whitney Museum of American Art, 1969.

Turim, Maureen. *Abstraction in Avant-Garde Films.* Ann Arbor, MI: UMI Research Press, 1985.

———. "Designs of Motion: A Correlation Between Early Serial Photography and the Recent Avant-garde." *Enclitic* 7.2 (Fall 1983): 44–54.

Turner, Mark. *Death Is the Mother of Beauty: Mind, Metaphor, Criticism*. Chicago: University of Chicago Press, 1987.

Tversky, A. "Features of Similarity." *Psychological Review* 84 (1977): 327–52.

Tyler, Parker. "Stan Brakhage." *Film Culture* 18 (1958): 23–24.

———. *The Three Faces of Film*. 2d ed. New York: Barnes, 1967.

Valle, Ronald S., and Rolf von Eckartsberg, eds. *The Metaphors of Consciousness*. New York: Plenum, 1981.

Vanderbeek, Stan. "The Cinema Delimina." *Film Quarterly* 14 (Summer 1961): 5–15.

van Dijk, Teun. "Cognitive Processing of Literary Discourse." *Poetics Today* 1.1/2 (1979): 143–59.

———. "Formal Semantics of Metaphorical Discourse." *Poetics* 4 (1975): 173–98.

van Dijk, Teun A., and Walter Kintsch. *Strategies of Discourse Comprehension*. New York: Academic Press, 1983.

Verbrugge, R. R. "The Role of Metaphor in Our Perception of Language." *Annals of the New York Academy of Sciences* 433 (Dec. 1984): 167–83.

Waldrop, Rosmarie. "A Basis of Concrete Poetry." In *The Avant-Garde Tradition in Literature*, ed. Richard Kostelanetz, 315–23. Buffalo, NY: Prometheus, 1982.

Walk, Richard D., and Herbert L. Pick, Jr., eds. *Perception and Experience*. Perception and Perceptual Development: A Critical Review Series 1. New York: Plenum, 1978.

Walzer, Michael. *Spheres of Justice: A Defense of Pluralism and Equality*. New York: Basic Books, 1983.

Warhol, Andy. "Rien a perdre." *Cahiers du Cinema* 205 (Oct. 1968): 40–46.

Warhol, Andy, and Pat Hackett. *POPism: The Warhol '60s*. New York: Harcourt, 1980.

Wasserman, Emily. "Yoko Ono at Syracuse: This Is Not Here." *Artforum* 10.5 (Jan. 1972): 69–73.

Wees, William C. *Light Moving in Time: Studies in the Visual Aesthetics of Avant-garde Film*. Berkeley: University of California Press, 1992.

Weinbren, Grahame. "Six Filmmakers and an Ideal of Composition." *Millennium Film Journal* 3 (Winter/Spring 1979): 39–54.

Weinbren, Grahame, and Arlene Zeichner. "A Selected Annotated Bibliography of Writings Connected with Avant-Garde Film." *Journal of the University Film Association* 33.2 (Spring 1981): 35–56.

White, Sheila J., and Virginia Teller, eds. *Discourses in Reading and Linguistics*. New York: New York Academy of Sciences, 1984.

Wieland, Joyce. "True Patriots Love." *Film Culture* 52 (1971): 64–73.

Williams, Alan. "Standard Gauge." *Film Quarterly* 39.1 (Fall 1985): 32–34.

Williams, Emmett, ed. *An Anthology of Concrete Poetry*. New York: Something Else Press, 1967.

Wilson, Simon. *Pop*. Woodbury, NY: Barrons, 1978.

Wolfe, Tom. *The Painted Word*. New York: Farrar, 1975.

Wollen, Peter. "The Two Avant-gardes." *Studio International* (Nov./Dec. 1975): 171–75.

Yates, J. "The Content of Awareness Is a Model of the World." *Psychological Review* 92.2 (1985): 249–84.

Youngblood, Gene. *Expanded Cinema*. New York: Dutton, 1970.

INDEX

BOOKS IN THE CONTEMPORARY FILM AND TELEVISION SERIES

Cinema and History, by Marc Ferro, translated by Naomi Greene, 1988

Germany on Film: Theme and Content in the Cinema of the Federal Republic of Germany, by Hans Gunther Pflaum, translated by Richard C. Helt and Roland Richter, 1990

Canadian Dreams and American Control: The Political Economy of the Canadian Film Industry, by Manjunath Pendakur, 1990

Imitations of Life: A Reader on Film and Television Melodrama, edited by Marcia Landy, 1991

Bertolucci's 1900: A Narrative and Historical Analysis, by Robert Burgoyne, 1991

Hitchcock's Rereleased Films: From Rope to Vertigo, edited by Walter Raubicheck and Walter Srebnick, 1991

Star Texts: Image and Performance in Film and Television, edited by Jeremy G. Butler, 1991

Sex in the Head: Visions of Femininity and Film in D.H. Lawrence, by Linda Ruth Williams, 1993

Dreams of Chaos, Visions of Order: Understanding the American Avant-garde Cinema, by James Peterson, 1994